A GENTLEMAN'S WORD

The **Institute of Southeast Asian Studies (ISEAS)** was established as an autonomous organization in 1968. It is a regional centre dedicated to the study of socio-political, security and economic trends and developments in Southeast Asia and its wider geostrategic and economic environment. The Institute's research programmes are the Regional Economic Studies (RES, including ASEAN and APEC), Regional Strategic and Political Studies (RSPS), and Regional Social and Cultural Studies (RSCS).

ISEAS Publishing, an established academic press, has issued more than 2,000 books and journals. It is the largest scholarly publisher of research about Southeast Asia from within the region. ISEAS Publishing works with many other academic and trade publishers and distributors to disseminate important research and analyses from and about Southeast Asia to the rest of the world.

A GENTLEMAN'S WORD

The Legacy of Subhas Chandra Bose in Southeast Asia

NILANJANA SENGUPTA

INSTITUTE OF SOUTHEAST ASIAN STUDIES
Singapore

First published in Singapore in 2012 by
ISEAS Publishing
Institute of Southeast Asian Studies
30 Heng Mui Keng Terrace
Pasir Panjang
Singapore 119614

E-mail: publish@iseas.edu.sg
Website: <http://bookshop.iseas.edu.sg>

All rights reserved. No part of this publication may be reproduced, stored in a retrieval system, or transmitted in any form or by any means, electronic, mechanical, photocopying, recording or otherwise, without the prior permission of the Institute of Southeast Asian Studies.

© 2012 Institute of Southeast Asian Studies, Singapore

The responsibility for facts and opinions in this publication rests exclusively with the author and her interpretations do not necessarily reflect the views or the policy of the publisher or its supporters.

ISEAS Library Cataloguing-in-Publication Data

Sengupta, Nilanjana.
A gentleman's word : the legacy of Subhas Chandra Bose in Southeast Asia.
1. Bose, Subhas Chandra, 1897–1945—Influence.
2. Indian National Army.
3. Indian National Army—History—World War, 1939–1945.
4. Burma Independence Army.
5. MIC (Organization)
6. Southeast Asia—Politics and government—1945–
I. Title.
DS442.6 S471 2012

ISBN 978-981-4379-75-5 (soft cover)
ISBN 978-981-4379-78-6 (hard cover)
ISBN 978-981-4379-79-3 (E-book PDF)

Photo credits
Front cover: Subhas Chandra Bose at a mass rally at Cathay Theatre, Singapore. *Source:* National Archives of Singapore.
Back cover (clock-wise): Members of the Rani of Jhansi Regiment, Bose at a Guard of Honour for General Aung San of Burma. *Source:* Datin Janaki Athi Nahappan. Reviewing the INA troops in Singapore, 1943. *Source*: Netaji Research Bureau.

Typeset by Superskill Graphics Pte Ltd
Printed in Singapore by Mainland Press Pte Ltd

To my dear mother,

Because of you I see the light in a Rembrandt

And the verdurous gloom of Pather Panchali.

CONTENTS

Foreword by S. R. Nathan	ix
Message by K. Kesavapany	xi
Message by Joyce C. Lebra	xiii
Preface	xv
Acknowledgements	xxiii
1. A Journey: A Dream	1
2. An Outsider in the Crescent and a Trial for Treason	38
3. End of a War, Beginning of Others	93
4. We are the Multitudes	166
5. "They Have Done Enough at Home": Escape from the Shadows	195
Bibliography	237
Index	245
About the Author	261

FOREWORD

Dozens of books, many recent, and scores of articles by scholarly researchers have been written about Subhas Chandra Bose and his role and exploits in the political struggle he waged towards gaining independence for India from the British Raj. His political and diplomatic efforts and military exploits in that struggle have been extensively researched in India and in Southeast Asia and published. With the passage of time, his sacrifices and determined efforts will become legendary to young Indians and eventually fade from their memory. What has not been distilled from his voluminous writings, speeches and exhortations about the social, economic and inter-racial and religious problems of India and Indian society, would be worth further researching.

Ms Nilanjana Sengupta has in her publication touched on some of the societal problems that concerned Bose and how he sought to address them from his early times, while he was engaged in leading the Municipal Corporation of Calcutta and while profiling himself actively as a budding freedom fighter. Ms Sengupta has drawn attention to his efforts to forge Hindu-Muslim unity; his interest in the emancipation of Indian women; and his attempts to prevent the exploitation of peasants and workers in India, among other issues. What comes to the fore from this research is his inexhaustible concern for the variety of social and economic problems that afflicted Indian society and cried out for redress.

Ms Sengupta has discovered in the course of her research how Bose took the opportunity, while establishing his Indian National Army and the Rani of Jhansi Regiment, to consider the possibility of translating some of his beliefs and ideas and trying them out, among the men and women in the two military organizations that he established in Southeast Asia.

This book by Ms Sengupta should help stir memories in India, if not in the state of West Bengal, to encourage further research and understanding from his writings and speeches, the views he expressed for addressing India's economic and societal problems, and consider which of them would be worthy of trying out in the context of today's India.

S. R. Nathan
Sixth President of Singapore
6 February 2012

MESSAGE

Most Indian families of my generation in Singapore and Malaysia would have had some connection with Subhas Chandra Bose and his struggle for India's independence through the Indian National Army. Even after World War II had ended, and for many years later, Bose's picture took pride of place in our homes.

Following my assumption of duty as Director of the Institute of Southeast Asian Studies in 2002, I had several conversations with then-President S.R. Nathan. He noted that, while there were many accounts of Bose's life and wartime exploits, his legacy had not been explored sufficiently and written about. Mr Nathan hoped that this would be done.

It was against this background that I decided to commission a book on Bose which would highlight his contributions to the emergence of nationalist movements in Southeast Asia. I also wanted the book to show how Bose had affected the lives of ordinary men and women living in Malaya.

About ten months ago, I came to know Nilanjana Sengupta. I discussed the idea of her writing the book. Coming from Calcutta, Bose's home town, she had a first-hand feel for the subject in the larger Indian context. What she needed was knowledge of developments in and around Southeast Asia. Reading voraciously, she came up to speed on the subject and completed writing the book in a record ten months. Although this book is very well researched, it is written engagingly for both the scholar and the layman. It brings to life an epic period of Singapore and Malayan history through the iconic figure of Bose and the legacy that he so richly left behind.

I would like to express my appreciation to Nilanjana for working so assiduously on a legendary personality who remains enshrined in the hearts and minds of many. I would also like to thank Rinkoo Bhowmik, another daughter of Calcutta, and the staff of ISEAS Publications Unit for all the hard work they have put into the production of this book.

K. Kesavapany
Director, Institute of Southeast Asian Studies

MESSAGE

Nilanjana Sengupta casts her net widely in this ambitious volume exploring the post-war impact of Subhas Chandra Bose on Southeast Asia. Because the study of Bose has been extensively explored by generations of scholars, Sengupta necessarily addresses some familiar ground.

Throughout the volume we hear echoes of his early spiritualism, secularism and egalitarianism. We hear also references to his mother's worship — extending to Bharat Mata [Mother India] — and his fostering of women's political and military roles, in for example his creation of the Rani of Jhansi Regiment. We encounter again his early political role in Calcutta and its extension to his relations with Gandhi and the Congress, preparing him for an even larger stage in Southeast Asia.

We shift to Burma and Malaya and the embryonic nationalism there in the 1920s under colonial rule and a discussion of the Japanese alliance. Subsequently, for a while the scene shifts to the Red Fort Trials in India and their impact on the British Indian army spread across Southeast Asia.

Sengupta discusses Bose's communication and propaganda techniques, his modern understanding of the mechanisms of mass communication, including his awareness of his personal impact. His emotional and absolute commitment to the goal of military liberation was a significant ingredient of his mesmerizing impact on audiences. The Rebellion of 1857 and the martyrdom of the Rani of Jhansi helped to foster his conviction that the military paradigm was imperative.

Sengupta forges new ground in her discussion of Bose's post-war impact on Southeast Asian leadership, the growth of nationalism, and the burgeoning labour union movement. Throughout Southeast Asia, political organizations such as the MPAJA and labour unions grew in each country, as Sengupta details. The consequence was that British and Dutch post-war attempts to reassert their colonial rule were thwarted by resurgent nationalism. The experience of INA veterans, the personal example of Bose's leadership, and the body of officers trained by the Japanese gave the colonial powers a rude awakening. Southeast Asian nationalism was now an established force in Southeast Asia.

Historians will welcome Sengupta's contribution to our understanding of Bose's continuing impact on the political landscape of Southeast Asia.

Joyce C. Lebra
Professor Emerita, University of Colorado

PREFACE

For me it all started with meeting three little old men at an *Udipi* restaurant on Serangoon Road, Singapore. Bala A. Chandran, Girish Kothari and Kishore Bhattacharya — all three in their eighties, with one of them having undergone an intestinal surgery in the recent past. I was chasing an article for a newspaper in Bombay for which I had already missed the deadline. As they filed in, refusing assistance from the young Tamil waitress and started speaking of their INA (Indian National Army) days, I noticed an unmistakable straightening of the shoulders and an *Ancient Mariner* like glitter in their eyes: it was that momentary transformation which sparked my interest in their story. Was it the easy camaraderie of old boys speaking of their alma mater? Around the same time I read another story of Laxmi Indira Panda of Orissa who had joined the Rani of Jhansi Regiment. After many frustrating trips down the corridors of power, she finally met the President of India when in her nineties. As she walked down the carpeted corridors of Rashtrapati Bhawan, she stopped to salute the pictures of national leaders. What was it about these men and women, I wondered, that made them less ordinary?

The 1940s was a decade of violence and trauma for Southeast Asian communities, as it was for the rest of the world. It began with the mass exodus of Burmese-Indian refugees in the face of Japanese invasion, witnessed the tragedy of Hiroshima and

Nagasaki — the only nuclear holocausts the world has known and the ruthless massacre of the Chinese communities as they faced the fury of Japan's wartime atrocities. The war, when it finally ended, had systematically torn apart indigenous ecosystems of culture and tradition, of old habits and communal practices.

The INA, as a movement, placed a motley group of individuals against this bleak terrain. Remarkably, it was a group that transcended barriers of caste, religion or race. Even the small cross-section at Singapore that I had the opportunity to meet consisted of expatriate Indians from the far-flung states of Kerala, Gujarat and undivided Bengal. Those who enlisted for the army were similarly widely diverse in their economic and educational backgrounds: just as there was a Ponnampalam who enlisted from a plantation at Seramban where he dried rubber sheets on a clothes line, there was also an S. A. Ayer, Reuter's Special Correspondent in Bangkok. These men and women's lives intersected for a brief while during the years 1943 to 1945 and at the end of the war the network unraveled again, even as life limped back to normalcy. Once the INA was disbanded, the former soldiers pursued divergent career paths: John A. Thivy founded the Malayan National Congress and worked as a diplomat in his later life, Janaki Davar travelled to London to work at the Indian High Commission and then returned to Malaysia and a career in politics and then there was also an L. Krishnan who joined Shaw Brothers and pioneered Malay film production. Yet the INA experience — the learning and memories, remained with them like an omnipotent alter ego. At times the past found manifestation in little physical gestures — like the *Jai Hind* with which the INA community greet each other even today and at times returned in haunting nightmares of near-fatal air-attacks (in his memoirs M. Z. Kiani wrote of the nightmares that plagued him for many months after his return from the front).

During the period of occupation, Japanese-trained voluntary and independent armies dotted almost every region of Southeast

Asia. Militant bands of men sporting uniforms and carrying weapons were ubiquitous in Burma, Java, Sumatra, Malaya, Indochina and the Philippines. The Japanese had raised these armies over a period of time — while the BIA (Burma Independence Army) of Burma had been raised before the outbreak of war in the Pacific, PETA (Sukarela Tentara Pembela Tanah Air) in Java was created only in October 1943. The range and quality of training offered to these armies had also differed — unlike the voluntary armies of Malaya or Indonesia, the INA and BIA had been trained by graduates of the Japanese Army Intelligence School, the Nakano Gakko. But here too the INA was remarkable in being the only army which enjoyed military status and fought alongside the Japanese as her ally.[1]

If the INA and its men were remarkable then it was a reflection of the leader, Subhas Chandra Bose, a major source of the veterans' perception of life. He was a man who had marched to the beat of a different drummer — at a time when the Indian political scene was dominated by Gandhi, he had distanced himself from the "authoritarianism" of the Gandhian movement and sought an alliance with the Axis Powers to press forward the independence struggle of his country.[2] He had escaped the confining political space of India and used Southeast Asia as a sounding board for his alternate viewpoint. He had united the contentious Indians and led them on a hitherto unknown path of armed struggle: Indians, forcibly disarmed by the British since the Sepoy Mutiny of 1857 (and the Singapore Mutiny of 1915), took to armed resistance against the British after the lapse of many decades. Bose is a leader who still arouses extreme emotions — to some he is a martyr and to others a quisling. His image too oscillates between fields of reality and the distortion thereof: even on my last visit to Netaji Research Bureau, Calcutta, in August 2011, I met a gentleman claiming Bose was alive and continued to reside in the high mountain passes of Russia!

For independent India, Subhas Chandra Bose had envisaged the political model of a secular, democratic, federal republic. During his presidential address at the Maharashtra Provincial Conference of May 1928, he had argued that though democracy was an occidental institution, it was not alien to the culture of India and cited examples of early models of democracy which had historically existed in the country:

> Speaking for myself, I stand for an independent Federal Republic ... India must fulfill her own destiny and cannot be content with colonial self-government.... While striving to attain liberty we have to note all its implications.... You cannot establish political democracy and endeavour at the same time to resist the democratization of the society.... Privileges based on birth, caste or creed should go, and equal opportunities should be thrown open to all ...[3]

The vision of an independent India with no state religion and based on equal opportunities for all was important to Bose and he was wary of any possible encroachments. In the early 1940s when the possibility of the INA marching into India at the head of the Japanese Imperial Army arose, he was careful in striking a deal with his allies. He insisted that the first drop of blood to be shed on Indian soil should be of a freedom-loving Indian and refused to walk on the proffered "stilts" of Japanese aid.[4] Bose was chary of the Japanese because of earlier Sino-Japan relations, on which he had commented that in attempting to satisfy her "imperial ambitions", Japan was wont to expand "at the expense of China". "The vastness", he wrote, "the potential richness, and the internal weakness of China, constitutes the greatest temptation for Japan": qualities, which he was aware, were equally true for the Indian subcontinent as well.[5]

In his search for an economic model that would institute complete, all-round undiluted freedom, a socio-economic structure and body-politic that would bring maximum happiness, Bose was convinced he had found the answer in Socialism. Socialism by providing every human being with the right to work, the right to a living wage and equal opportunities for all could ensure a fair, just and equitable distribution of wealth. And for this if necessary the State could take over control of the means of production and distribution of wealth.[6] As a political philosophy for free India he sought a synthesis of the "national unity and solidarity" of Fascism (he called it "National Socialism" and mentioned what he sought was distinct from what had been achieved in contemporary Germany) with the "planned economy of Communism".[7] In his later years he amended his views on democracy and felt for the immediate future of post-independent India, it was necessary to institute a State with some authoritative powers "... a State of an authoritarian character, which will work as an organ, or as the servant of the masses, and not of a clique or of a few rich individuals."[8] Once India had achieved a stable social, political and economic framework based on justice, equality, freedom, discipline and love, a government in accordance with the "will of the people" would be instituted.

In my explorations of this enigmatic leader, there are a few images, amongst others, of which I am particularly fond. One is from his early manhood when he was the favourite *Rangakakababu* [uncle] to his brood of young nephews and nieces: he listened to them with such serious intent that they felt they were adults speaking to a friend. This image reflects Bose's very genuine compassion for the people around him and his ability to relate to them — qualities which would win him the love of the multitudes in Southeast Asia. The other picture is of Bose in his mid-thirties, when he was exiled to Europe during 1933–34. His friends noticed him purchasing books on India in languages that he could not read: this almost obsessive passion for India would remain with him and drive him all his life. The last image is more poignant: Habibur Rahman, narrates the last few hours of Bose's life spent in a Japanese hospital at Taipei. The leader was convinced his end was near and told Habib that he had no regrets apart from not being able to witness his country attain freedom. Habib should go and tell his countrymen that he had fought for India's independence till his last breath.[9] Apart from the theme of sacrificial patriotism, these words reiterate a recurring motif of his speeches and writings — that of being true to one's pledge, of not breaching a promise.

A Gentleman's Word is about this promise that Subhas Chandra Bose made to the Indian people of Southeast Asia who had placed their love and trust in his hands. The book looks beyond the ubiquitous garlanded portrait of the leader and attempts an analysis and assessment of all that he left behind. At an individual level it looks at certain personalities like Aung San and Ahmad Boestamam who were influenced by his ideology as they continued their nation's struggle against colonialism. For the expatriate Indian community of Southeast Asia, the book traces the evolution of certain movements like those fostered by the emerging Indian trade unions and the Malayan Indian Congress which would help shape the community's socio-political future in the years to come. The book devotes considerable space to the issues of feminism that the Rani of Jhansi Regiment helped nurture. At a wider level, it captures some of the highlights of the Provisional Government of Azad Hind's [Free India] inter-communal relations with Burma, Malaya, Thailand and Japan.

Subhas Chandra Bose, in his first public appearance in Singapore on 4 July 1943, had mentioned:

> By participation in this common fight, we shall be qualifying for our freedom. By shedding our blood in a sacred cause, we shall be paying the price of liberty and, at the same time, we

shall be laying the only enduring foundation for our national unity. And last but not least, by winning freedom through our own efforts and sacrifice, we shall be acquiring the strength whereby we shall preserve our liberty for all time.[10]

A Gentleman's Word tells the tale of this journey of self-discovery of those who were inspired by him.

Notes

1. Professor Joyce Lebra mentions, it was the INA which, "… retained the strongest sense of its own national identity with the least actual Japanese training." Joyce Chapman Lebra, "The INA and Japanese Trained Armies in Southeast Asia", *The Oracle*, vol. 1, no. 1 (January 1979): 35.
2. Sisir Kumar Bose and Sugata Bose, eds., *The Essential Writings of Netaji Subhas Chandra Bose* (Calcutta/New Delhi: Netaji Research Bureau/Oxford University Press, 1997), p. 275.
3. Ibid., pp. 85–86.
4. Joyce Chapman Lebra, *The Indian National Army and Japan* (Singapore: Institute of Southeast Asian Studies, 2008), p. 143.
5. Sisir Kumar Bose and Sugata Bose, eds., *The Essential Writings of Netaji Subhas Chandra Bose*, p. 176. See the essay "Japan's Role in the Far East" for Bose's opinion on Sino-Japanese relationship, *The Essential Writings of Netaji Subhas Chandra Bose*, pp. 175–90.
6. Ibid., p. 113.
7. Ibid., p. 322.
8. Ibid., p. 320.
9. Government of Japan, "4th Section, Asian Bureau, Ministry of Foreign Affairs", August 1956, p. 416. Sugata Bose, *His Majesty's Opponent: Subhas Chandra Bose and India's Struggle Against Empire* (Cambridge MA: Harvard University Press, 2011), pp. 307–8.
10. Sisir Kumar Bose and Sugata Bose, eds., *Chalo Delhi, 1943–1945*, Netaji Collected Works, vol. XII (Calcutta/New Delhi: Netaji Research Bureau/Permanent Black, 2007), p. 44.

ACKNOWLEDGEMENTS

The last year has been one of the best years of my life. Since February 2011, which is when I started working on this book in all seriousness, I have met countless people, most of whom have become friends or at least close acquaintances. There was nobody I approached with details of the project, who did not reciprocate in all earnestness, and with each encounter my book was enriched with a new layer of understanding. On top of the list is K. Kesavapany, Director of ISEAS, who gave new meaning and direction to my life by offering me this project: it was he who set me off on this wonderful journey and encouraged me at every turn. I was overwhelmed when S. R. Nathan, former President of Singapore, agreed to actually read my manuscript. His critical marginal notes and the discussions he had with me gave me new insight. He even very kindly shared books from his personal collection with me. I met Krishna Bose, Chairperson, Netaji Research Bureau (NRB), Calcutta, twice over the course of the year and each time was an experience — Subhas Chandra Bose still resides over a large part of her consciousness and I could feel his palpable presence when I spoke to her. Her very illustrious son, Sugata Bose, Gardiner Professor of Oceanic History and Affairs, Harvard University, and author of some wonderful books, set aside time from his very busy schedule and spent two long afternoons at NRB with me. As I heard his measured tone and analysis of historical events and continuities, I could not resist anxiety pangs at my own temerity in deciding to research the same subject on which he had dwelled so knowledgeably and for so many years. During the year I shared a warm, albeit long-distance relationship with Joyce Chapman Lebra, Professor Emerita, University of Colorado, who was kind enough to read my initial project proposal and later clarified doubts and answered queries. Then there were the INA (Indian National Army) and Rani of Jhansi veterans. Despite their advanced years they were eager and energetic in sharing with me details of that period of their lives which they unanimously claim to be the most glorious. We rendezvoused at restaurants and residences and each time I came away fired by their enthusiasm for their leader. Today if Malaysia feels like a second home to me it is because of people like Rasammah Bhupalan, Dominic Puthucheary and Janaki Athi Nahappan who live there. The latter and her son, Ishwar Nahappan, welcomed me into their home and we spent a whole weekend ruminating and thumbing through her old albums. My *guruji*, Swami Muktirupanandaji and Swami Samachittanandaji of Ramakrishna Mission, Singapore, freely shared information and books from the RK Mission library. My friends at ISEAS — Tansen Sen, Head, Nalanda-Sriwijaya Centre, Geoffrey Wade, Senior Visiting Research Fellow, Asad-ul Iqbal Latif, Visiting Research Fellow — gave me a crucial sense of academic comradeship even as I spent many solitary hours at the ISEAS library. Rinkoo Bhowmik very kindly agreed to do the artwork for the cover and helped me in innumerable different ways in putting the finishing touches to the book while Madan Kunnavakkam added an interesting new dimension with his photographs. I had very perceptive editors in Triena Ong and Sheryl Sin who steered the project towards its logical conclusion. There were others — Johan Saravanamuttu, Norshahril Saat, Christina Goh, Desmond Yong of ISEAS and others — numerous staff members and librarians of Netaji Research Bureau, ISEAS and the National Library, Singapore who contributed to making this book what it is today. And of course there was my loving family — my husband, Arindam, who smilingly welcomed Subhas Chandra Bose as the fourth member of our household and our eight-year-old daughter Ananya. Once in a while she tiptoed into my study to express her concern about my long working hours and then, closing the door with infinite care, left to watch some more television — much to my consternation!

May the merits of this book be shared by all I have or have not mentioned above while the inadvertent flaws and follies come to my share.

Chapter 1

A JOURNEY: A DREAM

> "... Come my friends,
> 'Tis not too late to seek a newer world.
> ... To sail beyond the sunset, and the baths
> Of all the western stars, until I die."
> — Ulysses, Alfred Tennyson

PRELUDE

On 9 February 1943 Subhas Chandra Bose embarked on an undisclosed journey on a submarine, as a guest of the German navy. As he set off on this eastward journey he was unaware that he would not survive the war or that he was swiftly moving towards what would turn out to be the final phase of his life. His sole companion was an aide, Abid Hasan, a young nationalist who had joined Bose in his military mission in Berlin and would continue to work closely with him in Southeast Asia. Like other young, educated men who had thrown in their lot with Bose and the Indian nationalist cause in Europe, Hasan, a Hyderabadi Muslim, was part of a small, politically inclined Indian diaspora.[1] Their journey together would span the next three months, first in German and then Japanese submarines. Hasan writes that as he stepped aboard the German U-boat, the envisaged "romance" of travelling by a submarine fast dissipated: Bose was allotted a bunk in an unenclosed recess in the passage and the "stench of diesel" permeated the air.[2] They travelled through the North Sea, the strait south of Iceland, navigated around the Cape of Good Hope and after a hazardous submarine-to-submarine transfer off the coast of Madagascar, finally landed at an isolated islet near Sumatra on 6 May 1943. The trajectory would take Bose half way across the globe and he would arrive at Southeast Asia to spearhead the Indian nationalist struggle and lead the community to a new age of political consciousness.

This was not Bose's first expedition to Southeast Asia. In 1925 he had been detained at Mandalay, as a political prisoner of the British Raj — one of the many terms of captivity he served as an integral part of his tumultuous political career. The Mandalay prison, where Bal Gangadhar Tilak had spent six long years of captivity, was notorious in its reputation. Bose, confined in this wooden prison for over two years, was not only exposed to the dust and storms of Burma but also caught a first-hand glimpse of the Burmese people. With characteristic dry wit he observed to his brother Sarat Chandra Bose, "The wards in this jail are made of wooden bars or palisades and are not brick built. I am sure when we are locked in at night, to an outsider we look like so many human beasts prowling about in a lighted cage ... God only knows where our metamorphosis is going to end."[3] It was during this period of incarceration, with typhoid and sand-fly fever raging among the inmates that Bose had picked up the rudiments of the Burmese language and decided that "... Burma is a marvellous country". He admired the considerably advanced social system of Burma where "women were more powerful than in any European country", their indigenous education system and folk art and wondered when the Burmese people, like the Indians, would be free once again.[4]

When setting off for Southeast Asia, his wife Emilie Schenkl came to Berlin to bid him goodbye. They had had a long and committed relationship for the previous nearly ten years and their daughter, Anita, was barely a few months old.[5] For a person like Bose, wont to form enduring bonds with family and friends alike, this parting must have been quite a wrench. But then, he was used to making emotional sacrifices for his cause. He had already lost his father while exiled in Europe in 1934 and shortly afterwards was to lose his mother while leading the nationalist campaign in Southeast Asia.[6]

The journey to the Southeast was kept under wraps till the very last minute. Clandestine arrangements had been underway for several months with even Hasan being unaware of the developments. When told that he was to leave with Bose for an unknown destination, he had surmised that he was being sent to Mecca for a haj pilgrimage to form contacts with the Indians there. It was only when they arrived at Kiel that he realized that there were other plans afoot. This would again ring a familiar bell. Bose's previous secret getaway to Europe via Kabul and the Soviet Union had been similarly shrouded in mystery. In 1941 when he eluded the British police and escaped from Calcutta, while interned at his residence, nobody apart from a select few of his family coterie knew of his whereabouts.[7] The next day's *Hindustan Standard* had carried a double column headline: "What has happened to Shri Subhas Chandra Bose? Unexpected exit from home", even as international press and the British police got into a major furore for the next few days over his unexpected disappearance.[8]

In fact in a life intercepted by many journeys, the one to Southeast Asia was not an exceptional one at all. One of the first journeys of his life had been from his native town of Cuttack in Orissa to Calcutta to study at the Presidency College. By then he was an assiduous reader of Swami Vivekananda and as he moved to the seething metropolis, he promised himself, "I was not going to follow a beaten track, come what may; I was going to lead a life conducive to my spiritual welfare and uplift of humanity."[9] Even as he was moving from the easy familiarity of his hometown to the anonymity of city life, he was undertaking a parallel journey in his mind towards a better understanding of the self and a firmer hold of his convictions. The same convictions and a need for a higher purpose in life would drive him to study Sri Aurobindo and Swami Vivekananda while still in his teens and set him apart from the crowd of the city. In his unfinished autobiography, *The Indian Pilgrim*, he himself acknowledges this with self-deprecatory humour: he writes of a reception for Acharya Jagadish Chandra Bose where much to his repugnance young participants put up an English play and even sang "God save the King" in honour of the famous scientist, "Amongst a gathering of boisterous young men, I sat with my eyes closed like a stern puritan."[10]

Chronologically reviewed, the next vital journey of his life would be the one he made to Europe to continue his studies at Cambridge and to sit for the qualifying exam of the Indian Civil Service. It was in England, even as his severely anti-British mind was full of misgivings about the imminent career choice, Subhas for the first time breathed the air of a free country. It dawned on him what it meant to be free citizens of a free republic, to live outside the police regime of India where every student was a "revolutionary suspect".[11] But in terms of moving closer to his dream of assimilating himself in the freedom struggle raging in India, perhaps his return journey from Cambridge was of more significance. It was by the time of this journey that he had shaken off all indecision and emerged as a man of destiny. He had already tossed aside the career option in a foreign bureaucracy and decided to commit himself wholeheartedly to his cause. Albeit the decision had not come easy: he had spent months grappling guilt, "I know how many hearts I have grieved — how many superiors of mine I have disobeyed. But on the eve of this hazardous undertaking my only prayer is — may it be for the good of our dear country."[12] He had already written to his would-be political guru, Chittaranjan Das, from Cambridge and on the homeward-bound ship he mulled over the possible strategies for the Indian National Congress, "In my view the Congress-League scheme is entirely out-of-date. We must now frame the Constitution of India on the basis of *Swaraj* [self-rule] ... I am of the view that right from now when the work of destruction is going on, we must begin to create."[13] Even as his young, enthusiastic mind bubbled over with ideas, many of which he would eventually implement in India and thereafter in the Southeast, the die had been cast — from here onwards with each journey he would move further away from all that was familiar and yet each step would bring him closer to self-actualization.

From this return journey home from Cambridge in 1921 to his final exodus to first Kabul, Moscow and onward to Europe under the guise of Orlando Mazzotta with an Italian passport was a long gap of twenty years. In the meantime he had risen to become a political leader of national repute in India, his career as the young radical in the Congress had gone through many twists and turns even as he realized co-functioning with the more conservative Gandhi conformists was virtually impossible. When all else failed Bose had tried to build up a clandestine nexus with the various factions of the Axis Powers. From late 1938 he tried to reach out to Germany, Italy, Japan and the Soviet-directed Comintern. Between the years 1933 and 1938, he had met German and Italian officials during his visits to Europe, though he had been denied a visa to the Soviet Union. On 22 December 1938 he met the Nazi officer, Dr O. Urchs in Bombay. He was aware of the evils of Nazism; however in his *realpolitik* view, Germany was the only power which could confront the British. The Japanese as the war allies of the Germans were another potential ally to whom Bose sent out feelers.

As he set off on his long trek to Germany in 1941, Bose by now in his fourth decade was already half way to becoming a legend. He had set aside an eminent career in the ICS and pressed himself to the service of his country. Added to this was his flawless academic record, his humanitarian work at the time of floods and famines in India, his popular appeal with the youth and minorities of his country and the unprecedented second victory as the Congress President. All these factors had figured in giving him an almost super-human aura, a reputation akin to that of a mythological hero. His secret and perilous escape to Europe amidst the greatest war known to humankind in an attempt to carry the nationalist struggle outside the borders of India would further reinforce this reputation. In Germany he would raise the Azad Hind Fauj [Free India Army]: an army formed of British Indian prisoners-of-war captured during Rommel's *blitzkrieg* in North Africa who would be trained by the Germans and wear the German uniform and yet swear an oath of allegiance to their leader, Subhas Chandra Bose. They would march to the tunes of a Hindustani adaptation of Tagore's *"Jana gana mana"* and would fly the Congress tricolour with a springing tiger evocative of a certain Indian pride and aggression as their emblem.[14] And perhaps more importantly, hereafter Bose would be addressed as "Netaji", the Indian equivalent of a respected leader. The epithet coined by his own men would give him a specific Indian term of reference. As Alexander Werth from the German Foreign Office correctly

Cambridge days: with friends K.P. Chattopadhyay, Dilip K. Roy and C.C. Desai. Subhas Chadra Bose standing on the right, England, 1920.
Source: Courtesy of the Netaji Research Bureau.

Early sojourn to Burma: imprisoned at Mandalay, 1926.
Source: Courtesy of the Netaji Research Bureau.

Commanding first army of Congress Volunteers: in military uniform with Motilal Nehru and J.M. Sengupta at the Calcutta session of the Indian National Congress, 1928.
Source: Courtesy of the Netaji Research Bureau.

With young team from the Volunteer Corps in Calcutta, 1929.
Source: Courtesy of the Netaji Research Bureau.

Bose being carried out on an ambulance at the Bombay pier on his way to being exiled to Europe, 1933.
Source: Courtesy of the Netaji Research Bureau.

With Gandhi and Vallabhbhai Patel at the Haripura Congress, 1938.
Source: Courtesy of the Netaji Research Bureau.

Travelling with an Italian passport: disguised as Orlando Mazzotta, 1941.
Source: Courtesy of the Netaji Research Bureau.

With the first officers of the Indian Legion, Europe, 1942.
Source: Courtesy of the Netaji Research Bureau.

commented, the term combined a "sense of both affection and honour" and would become inextricably linked to his persona, like Bapu for Gandhi or Panditji for Nehru.

Bose's close-to-mythical reputation, the legends and symbols surrounding his every act of patriotic sacrifice would reach their climax in Southeast Asia. The foundation of the political and military model that had already been laid at the Indian Legion in Germany would be played out to its logical conclusion on the other side of the globe. But as Bose, accompanied by Hasan, headed to Southeast Asia with the news of Hitler waging war against Soviet Russia and the Axis disintegration hanging heavy in the air, there were certain things which set this journey apart from all the others he had undertaken in the past. For one, right from the time they switched to the more spacious Japanese submarine commanded by Captain Izu, there was a feeling of elation and home-coming: "... we did feel that we had come back to an Asian nation ... it was something akin to a home-coming. We could be less formal ... the food was entirely to our liking."[15] After their landing as well, Bose achieved quite a few early successes. On the submarine Bose had allowed himself little rest as he clocked in his usual long hours of work, rigorously preparing himself for his role in the Southeast Asian theatre and his first encounter with the Japanese Premier. Hasan reminiscences of the elaborate sessions of role-play Bose conducted, with him taking the part of the Japanese Prime Minister Tojo. Bose would leave for Tokyo almost as soon as he reached the island of Sabang in Indonesia and eventually meet General Tojo on 10 June 1943 at the Japanese capital. The latter was impressed with Bose and on 16 June at a session of the Imperial Diet pledged "everything possible" to help India wrest her freedom.[16] Unlike Berlin where Bose was increasingly getting the feeling that he was being used as a bait to create pressure on the British and had to wait till the very end for a meeting with Hitler, a meeting which did not yield any concrete results apart from a promise of transport to Asia, in Asia it did not take Bose too long to garner the unreserved backing of the Japanese Prime Minister.[17] Whereas in Europe, Mussolini's Foreign Minister, Count Ciano noted in his diary with obvious scepticism: "I received Bose, head of the Indian insurgent movement. He would like the Axis to make a declaration on the independence of India, but in Berlin his proposals have been received with a great deal of reserve."[18] Despite Bose's repeated proposals, a firm German declaration supporting Indian independence had eluded him. Bose had managed to achieve the establishment of a propaganda centre called the Free India Centre where radio scripts had been prepared in more than half a dozen Indian languages which were then broadcast by a powerful German transmitter. But in a turn of events, in the eastern theatre of his nationalist campaign, Bose would first take over the formal leadership of the Indian Independence League (IIL) and the Indian National Army (INA) from the ageing Indian revolutionary, Rashbehari Bose and then on 21 October 1943 would officially proclaim the Provisional Government of Free India at the Cathay Theatre in Singapore. In the space of those first few months he would also initiate the Rani of Jhansi Regiment, the first all-women army for the national cause.

The sense of home-coming in Asia was perhaps reaffirmed by the presence of a large Indian diaspora in the Southeast. The Indian community of Burma, Malaya, Thailand, Indonesia, Vietnam, milled around Bose in tumultuous ovation as thousands came forward in response to his call of "Total Mobilisation for Total War". There was another factor, which contributed to a sense of familiarity — the Ramakrishna Mission at Norris Road, Singapore. Here Bose would spend long hours in meditation away from the war raging outside.[19] As he once again faced his childhood idols, Sri Ramakrishna and Swami Vivekananda, it was almost as if Bose had completed a full circle and putting his past behind him was poised at an imperative juncture of his life.

But even as he prepared to pitch himself into the Asian theatre of the war, which would eventually stretch on for many years to come and prove to be longer and perhaps even more complex than the one in Europe, providence would surely have smiled at the irony of it all. For Bose, despite his best efforts, was already running late. 1942 was a year when the course of the Second World War shifted. Hitler's troops were held up in the USSR, facing their first Russian winter, while the U.S. had swung into action in aid of the Allies. In fact just as Bose was setting off on his eastward journey, the Germans suffered their greatest defeat at Stalingrad. The Japanese Imperial Army after their amazing conquests at the beginning of their offensive had been badly beaten in naval engagements in the Coral Sea and at Midway. Had the long cherished attack on India happened in the first flush of Japanese victories, maybe then Bose would have emerged a winner. But history took other turns and the British intercepted the messages sent by Rashbehari Bose to him. In the meantime the British had formed the South East Asia Command (SEAC) and in October 1943 Churchill appointed Lord Louis Mountbatten as the Supreme Allied Commander, South East Asia. Major interventions were afoot to revive the greatly depleted and demoralized British Army. The momentum of the war was already moving against the Axis Powers. In the meantime most of the year 1942 was wasted while the Japanese first overcame their internal dilemma about importing Bose to Asia and replacing the leadership of Rashbehari Bose and then worked out his complicated transportation logistics with the Germans. In fact even before Bose and the INA started the military campaign, the shadow of failure loomed large.

It would not be correct to assume that Bose was unaware of these developments of the war. He had always maintained his own sources of military intelligence, which were independent of the Japanese war propaganda. In one of his early letters to a close friend, Dilip Kumar Roy, he had argued for the Bengal revolutionaries, citing an Irish parallel: "You might just as well say that the Sinn Fein movement is a failure also since it hasn't delivered the goods yet ... A revolutionary movement for national liberation is not like a chance detonation which makes the age-long prison-walls topple once and for all. It is a slow laborious work of building up brick by brick a citadel of strength without which you can't possibly challenge the powers that be."[20] He had looked beyond the apparent failure of these movements and been aware of the symbolical value of waging war against British imperialism. In reconfirmation of the same rationale, Bose and the INA would meet with failure in the campaigns of 1945 and yet manage to leave a legacy for India and Southeast Asia. As the emerging Asian nations struggled to shed their colonial skins, from the INA's defeat would emerge a myriad legacies of Bose, which would remain a part of collective popular memory for the years to come.

SUBHAS CHANDRA BOSE: SOME FACETS OF HIS PHILOSOPHY AND BELIEF

By the time Subhas Chandra Bose arrived at Singapore on 2 July 1943 to spearhead the Indian freedom movement in Southeast Asia, he had already spent over two decades closely involved with the nationalist cause in India. His political career was marked by certain strong convictions: his belief in an armed struggle and military discipline as an alternate path for wresting freedom, his faith in an all-encompassing secularity and a firm belief that no country could be completely free when the women and minority groups were not involved as equal partisans of the struggle. These beliefs had evolved with the years and would characterize the INA movement in Southeast Asia.

Repudiation of Passive Resistance

The Jallianwala Bagh Massacre in 1919 was a human tragedy of the dimension Indians had not witnessed in the recent past. It occurred on 13 April — a day that happened to be *Baisakhi*, one of the largest festivals of north India. Fifty soldiers of the British Indian Army, under the orders of Brigadier General Dyer, opened fire on an unarmed, motley gathering of men, women and children. The shooting continued till ammunition ran out and the number of fatalities rose steadily. The bloodshed of thousands of innocents had a symbolic value that history could not ignore. Anti-British sentiments in India surged to an all-time high and more importantly it catapulted to the forefront of the political arena three leaders who would shape the future of nationalist India — Mohandas Karamchand Gandhi, Jawaharlal Nehru and Subhas Chandra Bose.[21] As noted historian, Gerard H. Corr mentions in *The War of the Springing Tiger*, for both Bose and Gandhi the *road to destiny* began in 1919, the year of Jallianwala Bagh.

In Bose's work *The Indian Struggle*, large parts of which were written during his first exile in Europe and the second part completed just before his departure to Southeast Asia, there is a comment on Gandhi amongst the other more polemical writings, which sums up his attitude towards the senior leader rather succinctly: "He [Gandhi] has failed because while he has understood the character of his own people — he has not understood the character of his opponents ..."[22] The comparatively innocuous sentence captures well the dichotomy of Bose's opinion which did not alter much over the years: while he admired the senior leader for propelling the Congress from an elitist debating body to a national organization with mass appeal and his instant connect with the teeming millions of India, he did not subscribe to his philosophy of Civil Disobedience. Bose, fed on the activism of Sri Aurobindo and Swami Vivekananda, embodied an alternate philosophy of leadership based on a commitment to an uncompromising armed resistance to the British. Freedom would not come with across-the-table negotiations with the British; it had to be wrested. In one of his early speeches delivered at Kuala Lumpur he declared: "From my experience, I am convinced that so long as the Indian people remain unarmed, so long as the British Government has a modern army under its control and so long as we do not take up arms for our struggle of freedom, we shall not be able to achieve independence for India. I do not know of one instance ... where a nation has been able to achieve full independence without resorting to arms."[23] It was this philosophy and commitment to an armed resistance against the British opposition that he would be imparting to the multi-ethnic communities of Southeast Asia.

It is true that the easy camaraderie and emotional bonding which Bose had shared with his political guru, Chittaranjan Das, on whose death he had grieved like at the death of a father and about whom he would openly admit: "As for myself I can say that I fought with him on innumerable questions. But I knew that however much I might fight, my devotion and loyalty would remain unshaken. And that I would never be deprived of his love" were never replicated in his relationship with Gandhi.[24] Bose came away disillusioned from his first meeting with Gandhi at Bombay: "... there was a deplorable lack of clarity in the plan which the Mahatma had formulated ... did not have a clear idea of the successive stages of the campaign which would bring India to her cherished goal of freedom."[25] And this feeling remained over the years: Gandhi would always be the *Mahatma* and never became the *Bapu* he was for Nehru.

But his lack of faith in the passive resistance of Civil Disobedience did not stem from this emotional divide. As a ringside observer of the Civil Disobedience movement in his own country, Bose had watched it unfold and was not too happy with the outcome. Non-cooperation as a Civil Disobedience movement emerged under the stewardship of Gandhi as India's defence mechanism to the Jallianwala Bagh bloodbath. It did not take the movement long to spread its wings as spinning the *charkha* [spinning wheel for making cotton yarn], wearing *khadi* [indigenously manufactured cotton fabric], enrolment in the volunteer corps, boycott of all things British, including government institutions and government functions became ubiquitous. As in the past the British reacted with hostility and by the end of 1921 most of the nationalist leaders, apart from Gandhi, were imprisoned and Congress volunteer organizations declared unlawful. But despite British reprisals, the popularity of the movement did not wane, with the average Indian assuming spontaneous leadership. In 1922 when non-cooperation was at its height, Gandhi decided to abruptly call it to a halt after the violent attack on a police outpost at Chauri Chaura. In a response that was ironical as it was expected, the British arrested Gandhi, jailed him for six years and effectively put an end to the first phase of Civil Disobedience. Political stalwarts like C. R. Das (Chittaranjan Das) and Motilal Nehru were taken by surprise and decided to branch off from Gandhi and form their own Swarajist Party in 1923. Bose, then a political initiate, would later observe in *Indian Struggle*: "No one could understand why the Mahatma should have used the isolated incident at Chauri Chaura for strangling the movement all over the country ... situation in the country as a whole was exceedingly favourable for the success of the Civil Disobedience campaign."[26] He would also recall Das' deep frustration: "The Mahatma opens a campaign in a brilliant fashion; he works it up with unerring skill; he moves from success to success till he reaches the zenith of his campaign — but after that he loses his nerve and begins to falter."[27]

The same sense of futility and missed opportunity would assail Bose time and again as would the ineptitude of the strategy of passive resistance adopted by the Congress. In 1927 with the political support for the Conservatives in Britain being considerably grim and with the Labour Party already emerging as a credible alternative, the Simon Commission was sent to India to review constitutional reforms somewhat earlier than scheduled. The people of the subcontinent viewed the Commission right from its inception, comprising as it did of seven British MPs including Chairman Sir John Simon, with suspicion. The Commission was met by outraged crowds, with *hartals* [closure of shops etc. as protest] and black flag demonstrations wherever it travelled. Even as the country went up in flames, Congress decided to boycott the Commission and challenged Lord Birkenhead, the Secretary of State for India, to draft a constitution that was acceptable to the people. Bose would work throughout the summer of 1928 on the all-party "Nehru Report", a memorandum on the new Dominion Constitution for India that eventually the British ignored and refused to implement.

But the "Nehru Report" also created its own share of controversies within the Congress. At the Madras session of the Congress in December 1927, Nehru with the support of Bose and other young leaders passed a resolution to change the goal of Congress from dominion status for India to one of complete independence.[28] But Gandhi, though not present at the Working Committee meetings, was of the opinion that the resolution had been passed a year too early and described it in *Young India* as

"Hastily conceived and thoughtlessly passed".[29] With the senior leader's opposition, the resolution stood rejected. Subsequently in 1928, during the Calcutta Congress when Gandhi proposed a resolution that called for the British to grant dominion status to India within two years, it was the turn of the younger nationalists to oppose the move. By the time Congress's call for *Purna Swaraj* [complete independence] finally came in 1930, the situation according to Bose, had deteriorated: "There is absolutely no doubt that if the Congress Working Committee had taken courage in both hands, they could have anticipated the movement of 1930 by two years and the appointment of the Simon Commission could have been made the starting point of such a movement."[30] As the Congress remained entangled in its own controversies and vacillated between resolutions, manifestos and counter-manifestos, for Bose this was again loss of precious time when the country was ready, but the leaders were found wanting and in this dilemma, the only party which gained any advance was the British.[31]

Gandhi's *Dandi* March, the second of his pan-India movements, began in March 1930 immediately following the declaration of *Purna Swaraj*. This non-violent protest against the British salt laws proved to be a political masterstroke. It was beyond any socially divisive possibilities and provided a crucial link between *Swaraj* and rural grievances of India — sweeping up the country on a tidal wave of Civil Disobedience. On 2 March Gandhi wrote to the Viceroy, Lord Irwin, offering to stop the march if his demands of reduction of land revenue, cutting down of military spending, waver of the salt tax were met. However, Irwin chose to ignore his letter and Gandhi remarked, "On bended knees I asked for bread and I have received stone instead."[32] Though the salt *satyagraha* [Gandhi's policy of civil resistance] proved to be an unprecedented success in India and made non-violence the cynosure in the eyes of the world press, it failed to yield any major concessions from the British for dominion status and what was even more damaging, it failed to attract Muslim support — in fact many Muslims actively boycotted the *satyagraha*. Gandhi was arrested under an 1827 regulation calling for the jailing of people engaged in unlawful activities, and held without trial near Poona.

Civil Disobedience continued through the Gandhi-Irwin Pact and the subsequent Roundtable Conferences of 1930–32. Again, the Roundtable Conferences that were organized by the British as damage control after the debacle of the Simon Commission, did not yield anything concrete for Indians or the Indian Constitution. On the other hand they only succeeded in further accentuating the inter-communal divisions already prevalent in the country. The First Roundtable was held without any participation from the Congress, while in the Second, Gandhi was the sole official Congress representative and understandably it ended in failure. Bose, disturbed by this prospect would observe: "… leaders arrayed against him in a solid phalanx, he would be at a great disadvantage."[33]

In 1939 Viceroy Linlithgow declared India's participation in World War II without consulting the provincial government. As Bose went in and out of prisons and continued his bitter wrangling with the more conservative Gandhi conformists, he was slowly driven to the realization that a parting of ways with Gandhi and non-violence was necessary. Not only was the shared political space becoming too stifling for the coexistence of two viewpoints which were so radically opposed to each other, *Purna Swaraj* would not be achieved through Civil Disobedience. The endless cycle of resistance followed by ruthless reprisal would continue without any compromise forthcoming from the British. Another factor that convinced him was the war. As the war took shape and gradually enveloped all the continents, Bose realized that a nation that did not possess military strength could not hope to preserve its independence.

On 3 September 1939, Subhas Bose was addressing a Forward Bloc mass rally on the Marina Beach at Madras when he received the information that Britain had declared war on Germany and that the Viceroy, Lord Linlithgow, without consulting the Congress or any other representative body had announced India's participation in the war.[34] For Bose this was an opportune moment to strike against the British, weakened as they were at the prospect of war and their dependence on the British Indian Army, but the majority of the Congress leaders thought otherwise. According to Gandhi it was not the way of non-violence to "seek India's independence out of British ruin". The final parting of ways happened with Bose's departure to Europe while under house arrest to seek collaboration with the Axis military alliance, leaving the country open to Gandhi's third and most powerful national movement — Quit India and the consequent August Revolution. Both men with a burning sense of mission continued to forge their own paths of destiny: Gandhi even as he rode the crest of the popular Quit India movement was increasingly disheartened by the communal tensions under which India was disintegrating while Bose started on an uncharted journey which would end at the battlefields of Burma.

Subhas Chandra Bose: The Evolving Soldier

A variety of images do the rounds among the wide circle of Bose aficionados. Just as Bose himself at one point in his life had been in a quandary about whether he should join Gurudev Rabindranath Tagore at Santiniketan or join the Ramakrishna Mission for humanitarian work or teach at the National College, the different images convey the evolution taking place within as life's experiences taught him diverse lessons at different times. In some he wears an elegantly draped Kashmiri shawl with the Bengali *dhoti* and *kurta* [Bengali attire], in some he is the *pucca* colonial in western attire while in others he wears the Congressman's Gandhi cap. But the image which has retained its hold over popular imagination is where he is the soldier: in khaki tunic, forage cap and knee-high boots, preferably astride a stallion, looking on with an expression of unwavering self-belief. This is the image he consciously adopted once in Southeast Asia and today *Netaji* has become synonymous with his military greens. This is the image one is accustomed to seeing at busy crossroads of Bombay or Calcutta or in lovingly preserved portraits at Malaysia. This is the last picture that is available of him in the words of his sole companion, Colonel Habibur Rahman, on that final fateful flight to Tokyo, "So he stood with his clothes burning and himself making desperate efforts to unbuckle the belts of his bush coat ... As I was fumbling with his belts I looked up and my heart nearly stopped when I saw his face, battered by iron and burnt by fire."[35] The symbols evocative of valour and a martial code of life that he had initiated with the Azad Hind Fauj, first in Europe and then in Asia, found their final fructification through being embodied by the man himself.

Interest in the military and everything martial was one of the enduring passions of Bose's life. This active bias towards the military was the source from which sprang his later-day faith in armed resistance as an alternate strategy against the British. The military interested him partly because he saw it as a way to gain physical strength and confidence; a disciplined solution for making Indians physically competitive with the British. The idol of his growing up years was Swami Vivekananda, who advocated salvation through sweating it out at a football field rather than a philosophical understanding of the *Gita*. It also came from his adolescent years in Bengal when the nationalist youth was under the influence of Sri Aurobindo and his radical, hard-line leadership. Physical fitness was considered a pertinent trait for being a nationalist and was actively promoted at community fairs such as the Hindu *mela*. Indigenous martial sports like lathi [a martial sport played with long wooden sticks] and wrestling were encouraged by revolutionary organizations like the Anushilan or Jugantar Samities.[36] Perhaps all of this was a reaction to the Martial Race theory propagated by British army officials: an order of classification of the Indian ethnic groups into neat little racial boxes.[37] Men like Lieutenant-General Sir George MacMunn saw Indians as the "great bearded *Sikh* with his uncut Nazarite hair" or the "square-shouldered *Musalman*" or the "squat, pug-faced little Mongolian *Gurkha*" for the ease of army recruitments.[38] The theory postulated the genetic qualities that make a useful soldier which apart for a few exceptional cases, were considered to be lacking in most Indians. Bengalis unfortunately fell under the non-martial category and were considered physically weak, effeminate and not battle worthy. Bose, like other Bengalis of the time, rose to the challenge and in adapting a militant lifestyle, endeavoured to prove the British assumption wrong.

Bose's first brush with the military was soon after his arrival to Calcutta from Cuttack where he volunteered for service in the newly formed 49th Bengalees but failed the eye test and was refused admission. He was more successful in his second attempt. While he was studying at the Scottish Church College, the Government of India started a university unit of the Indian Defence Force. Bose was one of their zealous recruits and took a spontaneous liking to camp life. He felt the military training added to his "strength and self-confidence". In the *Indian Pilgrim* he describes an incident when they entered Fort William which was normally out of bounds for Indians: "... we experienced a queer feeling of satisfaction, as if we were taking possession of something to which we had an inherent right." At Cambridge too he attempted to gain admission to the University Officers' Training Corps but was not allowed to do so by the War Office.

Later in his political life he tried to import some of this military discipline to the Congress. It was customary at Congress sessions to have the volunteers organized into something akin to army units or Volunteer Corps, who, though unarmed, would provide the guard of honour and maintain law and order. In 1928, the responsibility of managing the Volunteer Corps as a part of the Calcutta Congress fell to Bose. He took the project with seriousness and starting with a recruitment drive, going on to give the volunteers military training and uniforms. Once the Calcutta Congress was over, it was Bose's plan that the skills and training of the volunteers should reach the villages of Bengal and beyond.[39] Eventually, with the successful completion of the war of independence, the regiment could be absorbed into the national army of independent India. However, Gandhi as a "sincere pacifist" was not comfortable with this show of military muscle and later sardonically described it as the "Bertram Mills circus". However, what is of import, the nucleus of the idea to form a battle-hardy Indian army had already taken hold and waited to find tangible form in the Azad Hind Fauj of Europe and then Asia.

Secularity and Ethnic Unity

Bose sought to create a spirit of justice, equality and discipline in the INA. These were the values from which emerged the INA watchword — *Ittefaq*, meaning unity which would be the cornerstone of its philosophy. Both in Europe and Asia, while working with the rich panoply of Indian castes, religions and races, his emphasis, right from the outset, was on secularism. At every step of the way he reinforced secular practices to forge a close bond within the multi-ethnic community of the INA

— be it by introducing communal living, joint celebration of religious festivals, merit-based promotions or strict penalties for discriminatory behaviour.

Yet, Bose's understanding of secularity was a little different from that of Nehru. Unlike *Nehruvian* secularism that relegated religion to a completely private realm, away from the mainstream of a nation's life, for Bose secularism meant a harmonious and informed coexistence. Unlike Nehru, his secularism did not exclude but included — he believed in integration based on a robust understanding and acceptance of differences. This philosophy of composite nationalism came naturally to Bose, part of a subliminal understanding of the world around him from his childhood days. In Cuttack he had grown up in a colony that was predominantly Muslim, where his Hindu father was a respected patriarch and it was customary for the family to participate in Muslim festivals: "In fact, I cannot remember ever to have looked upon Muslims as different from ourselves in any way, except that they go to pray in a mosque."[40] For him the Hindu-Muslim rift was an "artificial creation" by the British for their own advantage, a sort of Catholic-Protestant divide found in Ireland.[41] In fact, Bose was sensitized to discrimination early in life. When at the age of seventeen he went on a precocious hunt for a guru, he had faced the caste divide of India: "At Buddha Gaya we had a similar experience ... when we went for a bath we were told by some men there not to draw the water from the well because we were not *Brahmans*."[42] Apart from the sense of personal rejection, this must have been quite a blow for a young, vociferous reader of Hindu philosophy.

During his growing up years in Calcutta there was a rising political consciousness among the Muslims of Bengal. The Bengal partition from 1905–12 had heightened this consciousness. The Muslim League had already been formed in 1906 in Dacca and voiced the need to accept communal electorates. Bose started his political career under the tutelage of C. R. Das who recognized the need to involve all factions and minority groups of the Bengali society — Muslims, peasants, workers, the youth and women. At an early presidential address to the Bengal Provincial Congress, Das reached out to all religious communities: "We can frankly tell the Anglo-Indian community that there are no Extremists among us, no Moderates. The Hindus and *Mahomedans* of Bengal are all Nationalists ... We want Home Rule, broad based on the will of the people of India."[43] Das was instrumental in forging the Bengal Pact in 1923 with the Muslim leaders of Bengal. The resulting Hindu-Muslim alliance lasted for the next couple of years and was one of the high watermarks in the relationship between the two communities.

Just as Das had spoken as a Bengali populist reaching across class, ethnic and caste lines, so would Bose in his political career. As the CEO of the Calcutta Municipal Corporation and in the spirit of the Bengal Pact, Bose was of the view that a percentage of new and replacement positions should be assigned to Muslims where qualified candidates from the community were available. He faced stiff opposition from a range of nationalist newspapers; though Gandhi wrote in his defence in *Young India*: "I note that the chief executive officer of the Calcutta Corporation has come in for a good deal of hostile criticism because of his having given 25 out of 33 appointments to *Mussalmans* ... it is a creditable performance."[44] Later too, he would repeatedly earn the ire of the Hindu nationalist camp for his attempts at inter-communal rapprochement, but as he said himself, he could put his own popularity at stake rather than "forsake truth".[45]

In Bengal, Bose endeavoured to bring together the Hindus and Muslims — two communities sharing the same history, speaking the same language, in most cases following the same customs;

with religion as the only, though seemingly insurmountable, dividing line. In Southeast Asia his canvas would be much wider — the INA would encompass Gujarati merchants, Tamil plantation labourers, Bengali clerks, Sikhs from the British Indian Army — men and women from all castes and all religious beliefs ... yet his overarching strategy would remain the same: communal harmony at all cost. All his life, Bose himself would be a practising Hindu and yet religion would never be a part of his public persona, it would remain restricted to a corner of his room or a secluded monastery in Singapore.

Women as Equal Partisans in National Politics

From the start of his political career in Bengal, Bose was careful in encouraging and aligning the nationalist struggle led by the women with the mainstream independence movement of the country. As early as in 1920 he had written from Cambridge to his dear friend Hemanta, conveying his enthusiasm for the women's role in national politics: "Really, when will Indian women once again assume their role as educators of society? So long as India's women will not wake up, India will never wake up. When I heard Mrs Sarojini Naidu speak here the other day, I could hardly contain the happiness that was surging within my breast."[46] Later, after beginning his active political career, while touring the districts of Bengal he was consistent in addressing the women of the towns. He would urge them to boycott foreign cloth, carry on propaganda among women and organize *Mahila Samities* [women's societies] for concerted effort. As he kept reminding them, more than their responsibility to their homes, the women had an even "greater duty" to their country.[47] He would create a separate cadre of women in the Bengal Volunteers at the time of the Calcutta Congress in 1928. The women formed a 300-strong contingent of volunteers, dressed in the national colours of green saris with red borders and paraded on the streets of Calcutta.[48] Latika Ghosh, niece of Sri Aurobindo, was their commander and was referred to as "Colonel Latika". Despite naysayers, the sight of these uniform-attired women parading on the streets of old-fashioned Calcutta created quite a stir. The newspapers of the time mention: "As the ladies clad in their spectacular saris marched past to the sound of the bugle and the beating of the drum, there could be traced not a touch of all the frailties that are so commonly attributed ... with the womanhood of Bengal."[49]

Besides, bringing women volunteers to the forefront in the political arena, the women's wing of the Bengal Volunteers served another purpose: it formed the nucleus which tied the other groups of women revolutionaries at work in Bengal at that time, into a loose network. Thus while there was active interface with Lila Nag's Deepali Sangha in Dacca, women for the Bengal Volunteers were recruited from Kalyani Das's Chhattri Sangha in Calcutta. Educated in the foremost women's academic institutions, Victoria and Bethune of Bengal, this was a new breed of young avant-garde women who led and volunteered for these groups. The organizations encouraged education, gave training in physical fitness and encouraged political awareness among women.[50] Geraldine Forbes, who had interviewed many of these women, has written: "If there were a living figure who encouraged their activities, it was Subhas Chandra Bose, considered by many of the women revolutionaries Bengal's champion of women's rights."[51]

The Bengal Volunteers and the ensuing women's movement that evolved with the Bengal revolutionary groups acting as feeders to the movement was a crucial link to the Rani of Jhansi Regiment that was to take shape later. This experience of networking and recruiting women from various women's groups and women's colleges and initiating them into self-defence training would prove to be of great value for Bose in Southeast Asia. Though Bose's primary objective was nationalism, he worked with a much larger canvas while dealing with women, both in India and in Asia. The comprehensiveness of his vision can be gauged from a speech he delivered at Vienna in 1935. In it he delineated the work on women being done in India in three broadly outlined categories:

a. Social and educational programmes which covered women's education, vocational training, mother and child welfare programmes, health and sanitation.
b. The organizations which focused on specific women's movements for the furthering of their basic rights like equal voting rights or right to property.
c. Those organizations such as the women's wing of the Congress which formed the political voice of women.[52]

In the same spirit in 1938, Bose, along with Nehru, insisted that a separate Planning Commission for women should be formed. One of the most comprehensive reports prepared under the aegis of the National Planning Commission would be on women and their future role in independent India. The Women's Commission, chaired by Rani Lakshmi Bai Rajawade, had a predominantly female membership and the report recognized economic inequality as one of the key reasons for the subordination of women. It also dealt with the absence of fundamental rights for property, lack of mobility and the existence of gender discrimination in professional fields. The report proceeded along the lines suggested by the Fundamental Rights Resolution adopted at the Karachi Congress in 1931 and advocated equal opportunities in education for both men and women. What was remarkable about the Women's Commission was that it was controlled and driven by women themselves. In a perpetuation of the same vision, under the Provincial Government in Southeast Asia, Bose would appoint a separate planning commission for women for conducting research in areas on nation-building where women could particularly contribute.[53]

SOUTHEAST ASIAN RESPONSES AND LEGACIES

Bose arrived at the island of Sabang near Sumatra on 6 May 1943 and on 16 August 1945 he left on his final journey to Bangkok and thereafter to Saigon. The period of his intense involvement in Southeast Asia was packed into a compressed time-frame lasting only a couple of years and yet elicited a powerful reaction from the resident Indian community. As INA propaganda took Bose on countless journeys crisscrossing Malaya, Burma, Thailand, Indonesia and French Indochina, the immigrant community of civilian Indians was swept up on a tidal wave of nationalist sentiments. Everywhere the reaction was noticeably uniform: he spoke in stirring Hindustani or English, rapidly translated into Tamil for the large Tamil-speaking diaspora and the audience responded with equal fervour, committing their services and material possessions to the Indian nationalist cause. He was the nationalist who had brought Indian political consciousness and freedom struggle to Southeast Asian soil and could with ease reach across barriers of caste, race, age or sex. It was a rare opportunity for the immigrant community to integrate with the sacrifice of past martyrs and prove themselves to be worthy sons and daughters of India. Colonel Prem Kumar Sahgal, Bose's military secretary, later to be tried for treason at the Red Fort, records the first reactions of the Southeast Asian Indians in that they: "... felt that almost a God had come there ... here was the man who had come in answer to their prayers ... he would be able to lead them on the right path, the path to Indian independence."[54] This was one of the most common responses to Bose in Asia — one of blind, almost hypnotic adulation. He was nothing less than a messiah who had come to deliver salvation to the masses and his mass rallies were like a personal epiphany to some. It was a time when Indian households took pride in hoisting the tricoloured flag and in a fascinating story, the *Syonan Sinbun* on 29 October 1943 reports that some Indians looked upon Bose as the "Lord Krishna of the moment" who had appeared to scourge the evils of colonialism. This kind of reaction contributed to the making of the legend that is inextricably linked to the persona of Netaji Subhas Chandra Bose of today. It deifies him as a heroic figure for whom no sacrifice is impossible. The legend is fed by rumours and actual incidents of his life. It remains palpable over the years as it draws from the well of frustrated reaction to post-independence reality. The legatees of the myth remove him from the ordinary, place him on a pedestal and take him to be an idol fit for worship, albeit from a distance.

In a poem penned by James J. Puthucheary, a Malayan of Indian origin and a lieutenant from the Azad Guerrilla Regiment, who fought at the Burma front, there is yet another kind of response to the nationalist struggle and so in effect to Bose. In emotional content it is as powerful as the first but there is no psychological distancing from the idol. The poem titled, "Death Curse", reads:

>Blood from my wounds drip
>Drop by drop
>Into an uncongealing pool
>Wounds do not pain
>There's even a joy in them

> ... For my blood would have choked
> Your throat and sealed your lips
> And only then my blood congeal.[55]

The poem is remarkable because it is so close in expression and rhetoric to some of Bose's own writings. The concept of selfless sacrifice, of the merging of pain and pleasure, the sense of urgent need for a kind of self-immolation for the cause — these are all recurring motifs in Bose's writing. From the prison in Mandalay he had written: "I am not sure that there is no happiness in the pain you get by banging against the iron bars of this cage. The realisation that my love for my country — the love that has brought me here — is real comes through this pain. This is why, I think, even if the heart bleeds, one finds in this some happiness, peace and a sense of fulfilment."[56] What Puthucheary's poem implies is a more evolved internalization of the ethos that Bose stood for than what is evident in the first response recorded by Sahgal. It is this kind of subliminal identification with the man that would lead to the more informed choices and a more definitive perpetuation of Bose's legacy. Some of the Indians who had experienced his presence and leadership would lead lives of dedication like him — for a cause, men and women who would keep his memory alive with their action — be it in the field of nationalist struggle, women's movements or in their attempt at improving the economic and political lot of their nations. Like the first, in this reaction too there is an element of seeking the unattainable, but it is the unattainable which makes the fight all the more dearer, more worthwhile.

Rasammah Bhupalan was a girl of sixteen when she witnessed Netaji's oration at a mass rally at the Ipoh Club Padang. She would soon join the Rani of Jhansi Regiment, much against the wishes of her family and move to the Singapore camp at Waterloo

Street and later travel to the Burma battle front. She writes in her autobiography: "For all the Indians in SEA, this was a great event ... My sister ... and I were deeply moved. We regarded our sacrifices to be far more important for India than our sheltered lives."[57] This is yet another facet of the reaction that Bose elicited. Layered in its implication, it expresses the impulse of a young girl to go beyond the call of everyday life and identify herself with a cause that would eventually take her closer to self-discovery and fulfilment. This kind of response would create an enduring legacy of import among the women of Southeast Asia.

Participation in the nationalist struggle invested the migrant Indians, living as a minority community across Southeast Asia, with a rare sense of dignity and pride. The INA was a conduit which helped them connect back to their roots and make a meaningful contribution to the freedom struggle of their country. The military training and the attendant handling of arms bestowed on them a new found self-confidence and honed their leadership skills. Simultaneously, exposure to Subhas Chandra Bose's speeches and INA propaganda meant an immersion training in national and world history. At the INA camps the Indian society came together in a powerful alchemy of new ideas and political views as the partisans were exposed to not only nationalism but also to diverse radical schools of political thought. Many INA veterans recall being initiated to the writings of Bernard Shaw, Marx, Lenin, and the works published by the Fabian Society during their INA days and emerging at the end of the war with a more politicized understanding of the world around them.[58] As the war drew to a close and the INA was disbanded, the same sense of pride and political awareness in the Indian community would diversely express itself: in the Indian workers' widespread and often militant labour movements, in drawing the Asian Indian women out of their more traditional roles and expectations and inspiring some of them to take up mainstream roles for causes of equality and emancipation and in a more prominent participation by Indians in Southeast Asian politics.

The INA experience left in its wake a large and maybe still not completely mapped terrain of legacy. The Indian community of Southeast Asia was the foremost to be impacted. But the seismic waves of socio-political change would spill over to the Asian nations as well. Anti-British exhortations by the INA and the subsequent Red Fort trials of November 1945, which triggered powerful public resentment in India, were instrumental in subverting Indian loyalty to the armed forces of the British Empire. This meant the British Indian Army, the supreme tool for perpetuating British hegemony in Asia, could not be used for suppressing local nationalist movements as effectively as it had been done before. Bose's arrival in East Asia also heralded an era of better understanding between the Indian and some of the other indigenous communities. Bose was formally introduced to the Asian leaders of the time at the Greater East Asia Conference, held in Tokyo in November 1943. Right from the initial days Bose attempted to forge close diplomatic ties with them. This translated into better inter-communal relations during the war, particularly with Burma and the evolution of a more cohesive anti-colonial movement. Subhas Chandra Bose himself emerged as a role model in speech and military strategy towards whom some from the new generation of Asian leadership would gravitate. On 5 July 1943 he made one of his first public appearances at the Singapore Padang, opposite the Municipal Building (now City Hall) to address the INA. The 5 July speech set an important precedent and the subsequent larger-than-life INA rallies left a trail of memories in the oral history recordings of the time.[59] S. R. Nathan, former President, Singapore, writes: "In retrospect, Bose's great Padang speech marked the dawn of mass politics in Malaya among Indians ... Malays and Chinese were not parties to the Indian struggle but, nevertheless, Bose's presence created a certain atmosphere which led many to take an active part ..."[60] Indeed the period immediately following the war saw Southeast Asia awakening in a connected crescent of protest: the anti-colonial voice was determined to be heard and a new generation of leadership emerged which was aggressive, more militaristic and less inclined to procrastinate over across-the-table negotiations.

In his last note addressed to the Indians of East Asia, Bose held out a promise: "The roads to Delhi are many and Delhi still remains our goal ... India shall be free and before long."[61] The words have come to personify an indomitable human spirit in the face of impossible odds. And in the ultimate analysis, it is this spirit of human courage and determined action that is perhaps his greatest legacy. Whether in his alliance with the Japanese or in his dealings with the British, Bose refused to acknowledge a subordinate position for himself or his countrymen. In the subsequent years his anti-British resistance might have lost its relevance but Bose, as an embodiment of sheer human will, can never cease to impress and inspire.

Notes

1. Recruiting Indian students and residents to his cause was a major focus for Bose in Europe. Abid Hasan, N. G. Swami, and Habibur Rahman were prominent members of the INA who joined him in Europe and later followed him to Southeast Asia.
2. Abid Hasan, "A Soldier Remembers", *The Oracle*, vol. VI, no. 1 (January 1984): 2.
3. Sisir K. Bose, ed., *In Burmese Prisons, Correspondence May 1923–July 1926*, Netaji Collected Works, vol. III (Calcutta/New Delhi: Netaji Research Bureau/Permanent Black, 2009), p. 51.

4. Correspondence with Dilip Kumar Roy, Ibid., pp. 86–87, 131.
5. Anita Bose, Subhas Chandra Bose's only child was born in November 1942. Bose left for Asia in first quarter of 1943. He saw his daughter for the first (and possibly last time) in Vienna in December 1942.
6. Lieutenant General Isoda, who replaced Colonel Yamamoto as head of the Hikari Kikan in 1944 quoted in Leonard A. Gordon, *Brothers Against the Raj: A Biography of Indian Nationalists* (New Delhi: Rupa & Co., 2008), p. 507. "I went to give my condolences to Bose. Bose said that he was his mother's favourite, with tears in his eyes. It was the first and last time that I ever saw Bose being kind of a sissy."
7. In the summer of 1940, Bose started a movement for the removal of the Holwell Monument in Calcutta. He was arrested under the Defence of India Act on 2 July and detained in the Presidency Jail. Even as war broke out in Europe, the thought of an alliance with the Axis Powers to free India gripped his mind. In December 1940 he was moved to his home for medical reasons following a hunger strike while under detention. It was during this phase of house arrest at his father's residence at Elgin Road, Calcutta that he managed to escape under cover to Europe with the help of a few family members. He reached Berlin in April 1941 via Kabul and Moscow, two-and-a-half months after leaving Calcutta.
8. The double column headline in *Hindustan Standard* mentioned in S. N. Bhattacharya, *Netaji Subhas Bose in Self Exile: His Finest Hour* (New Delhi: Metropolitan Book Company Pvt. Ltd., 1975), p. 22.
9. Sisir K. Bose and Sugata Bose, ed., *The Indian Pilgrim: An Unfinished Biography*, Subhas Chandra Bose, Netaji Collected Works, vol. I (Calcutta/New Delhi: Netaji Research Bureau/Oxford University Press, 1997), p. 51.
10. Ibid., p. 180.
11. Ibid., p. 99.
12. Ibid., letter to brother, Sarat Chandra Bose, from Cambridge, 1921, p. 229.
13. Letter to C. R. Das from Cambridge, 2 March 1921, ibid., p. 215.

14. The emblem of the Springing Tiger which Bose adopted for the INA is reminiscent of Tipu Sultan (The Tiger of Mysore) and his valour in the Fourth Anglo-Mysore War, 1799 against the British. In Southeast Asia, Bose would revert to the original Congress emblem of a *charkha*.
15. Abid Hasan, "A Soldier Remembers" (2nd instalment), *The Oracle*, vol. VII, no. 1 (January 1985): 22.
16. Bose met the Japanese Prime Minister on 10 June 1943 and Gordon mentions in *Brothers Against the Raj*, p. 493: "The passionate nature, confidence and very presence of the Indian made a surprisingly positive impact on Tojo. He became a firm supporter of Bose." His impact on Tojo was also mentioned in Joyce Lebra Chapman, *Jungle Alliance: Japan and the Indian National Army* (Singapore: Asia Pacific Press, 1971), p. 116.
17. A detailed account of the meeting with Hitler is available in Sugata Bose's *His Majesty's Opponent: Subhas Chandra Bose and India's Struggle Against Empire* (Cambridge MA: Harvard University Press, 2011), p. 219 and in Gordon, p. 484. Bose could not make much progress in Germany and the time he spent in Europe eventually turned out to be largely an unnecessary detour primarily because of Hitler's ambivalent stance towards India and the British. While for him Indians were way down the racial ladder, the British were the only other Anglo-Saxon race at par with the Germans. Despite the Germans waging war against the British, Hitler still harboured dreams of a future alliance with them: "England was still Hitler's love. His picture of the future was that some time Germany would join with England against the USA", *Memoirs of Ernst von Weizsacker* (state secretary of the German Foreign Office) (London: Victor Gollancz, 1951), p. 258.
18. Count Ciano was Mussolini's foreign minister and son-in-law. The quotation is from Malcolm Muggeridge, ed., *Ciano's Diary, 1939–1943* (London: William Heinemann, 1947), pp. 354–55.
19. The Ramakrishna Mission has since shifted to Bartley Road though the old building still stands.

20. Dilip Kumar Roy, *Netaji: The Man, Reminiscences* (Bombay: Bharatiya Vidya Bhavan, 1966), p. 161.
21. Gandhi became an eminent national leader with the Civil Disobedience movement following the passing of the Rowlatt Act in 1919. The Jallianwala Bagh massacre was a part of the British repressive measure.
22. Sisir Kumar Bose and Sugata Bose, eds., *The Indian Struggle: 1920–1942*, Subhas Chandra Bose, Netaji Collected Works, vol. II (Calcutta/New Delhi: Netaji Research Bureau/Oxford University Press, 1997), p. 329.
23. "An Amphibious Monster", speech delivered in Kuala Lumpur on 5 September 1943. Sisir K. Bose and Sugata Bose, eds., *Chalo Delhi, 1943–1945*, Netaji Collected Works, vol. XII (Calcutta/New Delhi: Netaji Research Bureau/Permanent Black, 2007), p. 92.
24. Letter to the Bengali author Sarat Chandra Chattopadhaya, 12 August 1925. *In Burmese Prisons, Correspondence May 1923 – July 1926*, p. 108.
25. *Indian Struggle: 1920–1942*, p. 59.
26. Ibid., p. 81.
27. Ibid., p. 77.
28. From Nehru to Gandhi on 11 January 1928. *Selected Works of Nehru*, vol. III (New Delhi: Orient Longman, 1972), p. 12. Reference by Bose in *Indian Struggle: 1920–1942*, p. 161.
29. The National Congress, Young India, 5 January 1928. *The Collected Works of Mahatma Gandhi*, vol. XXXV (New Delhi: Government of India, Publications Divisions, 1958–1982), p. 438.
30. *Indian Struggle: 1920–1942*, p. 175.
31. "There was tremendous enthusiasm all over the country at the time and everyone had expected the Congress to act boldly, but while the country was ready, the leaders were not." *The Indian Struggle: 1920–1942*, p. 175.
32. Despite the rather clichéd comparison, attention should be drawn to Bose's speech at the Assembly: "... We refuse to beg with bated breath and whispering humbleness to subsist in our own land. Self-government is our right — a right not to be granted to us by

a foreign power. Self-government is our birth right — the right to feel the Indian sun, the right to smell the Indian flowers, the right to think our own thoughts, to sing our own songs and to love our own kind." Gordon, p. 408. The difference of approach between the two leaders cannot be overemphasized.
33. *Indian Struggle: 1920–1942*, p. 237.
34. According to Mihir Bose in *The Last Hero*; also in Sugata Bose's *His Majesty's Opponent*, p. 170.
35. As narrated by Colonel Habibur Rahman, Bose's last companion, S. A. Ayer, *Unto Him A Witness: The Story of Netaji Subhas Chandra Bose in Southeast Asia* (Bombay: Thacker, 1951), pp. 110–13.
36. The *Anushilan Samiti, with Jugantar* as its offshoot, were secret revolutionary organizations which functioned under the guise of fitness clubs in British-ruled Bengal. One of the most eminent mentors was Aurobindo Ghosh, a proponent of militant nationalism.
37. The Martial Race theory formed the basis for army recruitments in British India. Ironically enough, those races were found to be "martial" that proved to be loyal and fought on the side of the British during the Sepoy Mutiny of 1857. The British wielded this weapon well and used it for further heightening the class divides and ethnic tensions already prevalent in India. A series of insightful articles by Nirad C. Chaudhury on the subject was published in 1930 in the "Modern Review".
38. George MacMunn, *The Martial Races of India* (London: Sampson Low, Marston and Co., 1933), p. 1.
39. Gordon, *Brothers Agianst the Raj*, p. 195.
40. *The Indian Pilgrim: An Unfinished Biography*, p. 15; View on Muslims also expressed in Sisir Kumar Bose and Sugata Bose, eds., *The Essential Writings of Netaji Subhas Chandra Bose* (Calcutta/New Delhi: Netaji Research Bureau/Oxford University Press, 1997), pp. 321–22.
41. Ibid., p. 15.
42. Ibid., p. 69.
43. C. R. Das, *India for Indians*, 3rd ed. (Madras: S. Ganesh, 1921), pp. 13–14.
44. *Young India*, 31 July 1924. *The Collected Works of Mahatma Gandhi*,

vol. XXIV (New Delhi: Government of India, Publications Divisions, 1958–1982), p. 479.
45. "I know that by asking you to make a compromise I run the risk of losing the popularity which perhaps I possess. But believe me, I do not give so much value to popularity that I will forsake truth for it." Bose's speech at Shraddhananda Park, *Amrita Bazar Patrika*, India, 13 November 1927, p. 5.
46. Letter written on 2 March 1920. *An Indian Pilgrim: An Unfinished Biography*, p. 201.
47. Reference to his speech in the Nadia district, quoted in *Gordon*, p. 238.
48. Chitra Ghosh, "Subhas Chandra Bose: His Contribution to Women's Movement in India", in *Netaji Subhas Chandra Bose: Relevance to Contemporary World*, edited by S. R. Chakravarty and Madan C. Paul (New Delhi: Har-Anand Publication, 2000), p. 112.
49. *The Forward*, India, 18 December 1928.
50. Geraldine H. Forbes, "The Women Revolutionaries of Bengal", *The Oracle*, vol. II, no. 2 (April 1980): 4.
51. Ibid., p. 7.
52. Speech at Vienna Ball Club on 22 April 1935, quoted in Chitra Ghosh, "Subhas Chandra Bose: His Contribution to Women's Movement in India", p. 115.
53. *Netaji Subhas Chandra Bose: A Malaysian Perspective* (Kuala Lumpur: Netaji Centre, 1992), p. 106.
54. Interview of Colonel Prem Sahgal, Oral History Interview, Nehru Memorial Museum and Library, New Delhi, cited in Gordon, *Brothers Against the Raj*, p. 495.
55. The poem Death Curse is taken from *No Cowardly Past: James J. Puthucheary — Writings, Poems, Commentaries*, 2nd ed., edited by Dominic Puthucheary and Jomo K. S. (Petaling Jaya: Strategic Information and Research Development Center, 2010), p. 236.
56. Letter written to Sarat Chandra Bose on 12 August 1925 from Mandalay prison: *In Burmese Prisons, Correspondence May 1923–July 1926*, pp. 110–11.

57. Aruna Gopinath, *Footprints on the Sands of Time: Rasammah Bhupalan, A Life of Purpose* (Malaysia: Arkib Negara, 2007), p. 62.
58. James Puthucheary's exposure to Marxism began in his INA days. Other veterans too like Girish Kothari (interview with the author on 12 September 2011, Singapore) and Bala A Chandran (interview with the author on 15 September 2011, Singapore) recall discussions on radical political schools of thought.
59. National Archives of Singapore, Oral History Centre, Ascension no. 000050, Reel 1; Ascension no. 000025, Reel 6; Ascension no. 000365, Reel 9.
60. S. R. Nathan, *An Unexpected Journey: Path to the Presidency* (Singapore: EDM, 2011), p. 108.
61. *Chalo Delhi,* pp. 407–10.

Chapter 2

AN OUTSIDER IN THE CRESCENT AND A TRIAL FOR TREASON

> "The air broke into a mist with bells,
> The old walls rocked with the crowd and cries.
> Had I said, "Good folk, mere noise repels —
> But give me your sun from yonder skies!"
> They had answered, "And afterward, what else?"
> — The Patriot, Robert Browning

SUBHAS CHANDRA BOSE IN SOUTHEAST ASIA AND THE CONTEMPORARY SCENARIO

Introduction: The Southeast Asian Crescent

As Subhas Chandra Bose made his way through treacherous oceans towards the Southeast Asian crescent, large tracts of this great connected landmass were under the imperial regime of Japan. From Bengal at the Western tip, down through Burma, Thailand and stretching to Malaya (Malaysia and Singapore) on the East, the crescent at one point had formed the commercial heart of the British Asian Empire and would soon be the heartland

The journey to Southeast Asia: a submarine to submarine transfer in a rubber raft, April 1943.
Source: Courtesy of the Netaji Research Bureau.

With the crew of the Japanese submarine, Bose and Abid Hasan in the front row, on the left, May 1943.
Source: Courtesy of the Netaji Research Bureau.

The Indian National Army (INA) gathered at the Padang, Singapore, opposite Municipal Building (now City Hall), 5 July 1943.
Source: Courtesy of the Netaji Research Bureau.

Taking the salute with Mohammad Zaman Kiani, Padang, Singapore, 5 July 1943.
Source: Courtesy of the Netaji Research Bureau.

Reviewing the INA troops in Singapore, 1943.
Source: Courtesy of the Netaji Research Bureau.

Preparation for the onward march to Delhi: reviewing the mechanized unit in Singapore, 1943.
Source: Courtesy of the Netaji Research Bureau.

Reviewing the Rani of Jhansi Regiment with Captain Lakshmi, Singapore camp, 1943.
Source: Courtesy of the Netaji Research Bureau.

Members of the Rani of Jhansi Regiment, Singapore camp, 1943. A picture of the Rani of Jhansi is propped on an easel.
Source: Courtesy of Datin Janaki Athi Nahappan.

Oath of Allegiance: proclaimation of the Provisional Government of Azad Hind [Free India] at Cathay Theatre, Singapore, 21 October 1943.
Source: Courtesy of the Netaji Research Bureau.

Cabinet members of the Provisional Government of Azad Hind, 21 October 1943.
Source: Reproduced with permission from the National Archives of Singapore.

At a mass rally at Cathay Theatre, Singapore.
Source: Reproduced with permission from the National Archives of Singapore.

Raising the INA flag before Cathay Theatre, Singapore.
Source: Reproduced with permission from the National Archives of Singapore.

Leaders of the Greater East Asia Conference, November 1943.
Source: In public domain.

At the Greater East Asia Conference: with Ba Maw of Burma and Jose Laurel of the Philippines, Tokyo, November 1943.
Source: Courtesy of the Netaji Research Bureau.

The onward march to Delhi: INA soldiers march, holding aloft Bose's portrait, 1944.
Source: Courtesy of the Netaji Research Bureau.

At the Burma Front, 1944.
Source: Courtesy of the Netaji Research Bureau.

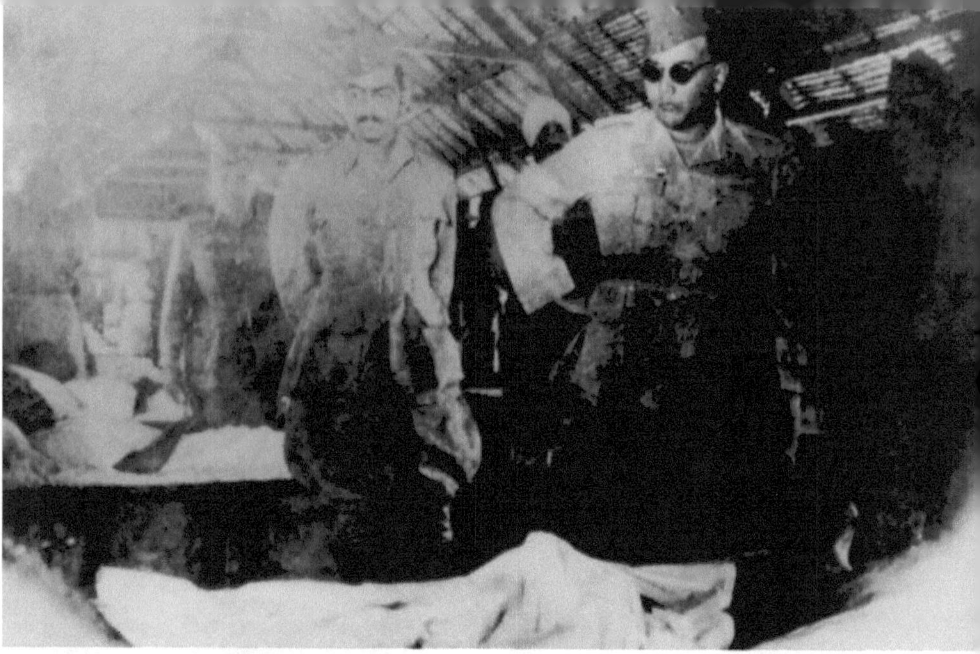

Visiting the war wounded at the Burma front, 1944.
Source: Reproduced with permission from the National Archives of Singapore.

With the INA top team: from left to right, A.C. Chatterjee, M.Z. Kiani, Habibur Rahman, 1944.
Source: Courtesy of the Netaji Research Bureau.

The last autographed photo available with Janaki Athi Nahappan, given to her by Bose on 17 August 1945, in Bangkok. The photograph is from the battlefront in Burma.
Source: Courtesy of the Netaji Research Bureau.

The final goodbye at Saigon Airport, 17 August 1945.
Source: Courtesy of the Netaji Research Bureau.

of INA (Indian National Army) operations. To the common Indian labourer working at the plantations of Malaya or the dockyards of Burma, Subhas Chandra Bose was a comparatively unknown name. Though hailed as something akin to a legend in the nationalist circles of Rashbehari Bose and Mohan Singh, he would have to start afresh and reach out as a populist leader to the large community of Indians present here.

Unlike other parts of Asia, the Southeast had always lacked a single, dominant ethnic group and been diversified in terms of language, culture, religion and even colonial regimes. So while Laos, Cambodia and Vietnam were clubbed together to form French Indo-China, Indonesia had been rechristened the Dutch East Indies and the Philippines formed an isolated little pocket of first Spanish and then American dominion. Thailand, never under Western colonial rule, had however for centuries been economically ruled by British financiers. Earlier, in many senses, this area of Asia had been a "spillover" from the two, more coherent neighbouring regions of India and China.[1] Whereas portions of the West and central, maritime Southeast Asia came under "Indian-Sanskritic-Hindu-Buddhist" influences; the cultural base of Vietnam was Chinese with the Chinese form of Buddhism practised here. But the organic unity of this region in terms of spiritual beliefs and cultural practices was torn apart by the early twentieth century as rival European powers began to carve out their own colonial empires. The teak forests of Burma and her ruby mines, the possibility of huge commercial advances from rubber, coffee, palm plantations, the Malayan tin mines and Indonesian oil wells made sure that by the twentieth century, France, Britain, Netherlands and the U.S. held more or less complete dominance over this part of Asia.

The shadow lines of the imposed boundaries laid down by colonial rule fostered continuous and often bloody conflicts between the ethnic minorities of this region, as they came to be ruled by people mostly indifferent to their welfare. However, the "Pan-Asian nationalism" of Japan promised to change all that. Since the 1870s, when the Japanese began to catch up with the West, other Asian nations watched her progress with admiration, and with Japan's victory over Russia in the Russo-Japanese War of 1905, the admiration changed to active acceptance of their pan-Asian ideology. The pro-Japanese winds of change that blew across Asia, rode on the waves of "Greater Asianism", which implied a political and cultural solidarity among Asian people to counter Western influences. So, before the Japanese *blitzkrieg* actually occurred in the 1930s and 1940s, the Japanese influence was emerging as an omnipotent force in Southeast Asia — Sun Yat-sen spent several years in Japan and students from Vietnam travelled to Tokyo in preparation of their nationalist struggle against the French. The Japanese in turn actively sought out the subterranean bodies of anti-colonial movements which had burgeoned all over Asia.

Subsequently in 1943, when Subhas Chandra Bose made his way towards Asia, a unity of sorts had been forged across Southeast Asia, albeit a "bloodstained" one, under the Japanese regime.[2] While, Bose would travel to Indonesia and Vietnam on INA propaganda trips and the Indian Independence League set up its centres there as well, the central crescent, stretching from the Eastern borders of India on one end to Singapore on the other, would remain the crucible of the INA's military operations. The IIL (Indian Independence League) headquarters would shift from Thailand in the pre-Bose years, to Singapore in Bose's time; while before the Kohima-Imphal campaigns in January 1944 the advance headquarters would move to Rangoon. Towards the end of the war, Bose would once again reassemble his civilian administration at Singapore and Bangkok. He would be the pivotal figure surrounded by a milieu of the large Indian expatriate community of the crescent, estimated at an approximately two million. With Bose, the Indians would ride a tidal wave of emotions — first euphoria at marching under the Indian tricolour with a noble mission which changed to despondency as, by 1945, the Greater East Asian Co-prosperity Sphere dissolved and the nationalist movements it had fostered, faltered.

As Bose reached Southeast Asia and began the frenetic pace of his nationalist campaign, the political scene in India was experiencing a temporary lull. The Cripps Mission had failed, Calcutta had felt the impact of the first Japanese bombs earlier on; while the supporters of Bose's Forward Bloc continued their harangue against the British, Congress members pledged loyalty to the Allies in the World War, though continuing to demand self-rule from the British government. Gandhi's Quit India movement of 1942 had been the last nationalist intervention and had been suppressed by the British with a heavy hand. Almost all frontline Congress leaders, including Gandhi and Nehru, as well as rank-and-file activists, were imprisoned. But in this political vacuum, a human tragedy of inconceivable dimension was taking shape, unnoticed by all, in the rural outskirts of undivided Bengal.

The great Bengal famine of 1943 was apparently triggered by a cyclone that hit coastal Bengal and Orissa in late 1942. Huge tracts of paddy fields were flooded resulting in a complete failure of the autumn crop. Poor farmers were forced to eat their surplus and even the seeds that had been kept aside for planting in the winter of 1942. Opinion is divided on whether there was actual food shortage at that point in British-administered Bengal. Nobel laureate Amartya Sen argues that rather than running short on supply, the root cause was the rumours of shortage which in turn led to hoarding and a resulting price inflation.[3] But the fact remains that over the years Bengal peasants had switched to cultivating jute and other cash crops, abandoning the cultivation of low-value rice. By 1940 as much as 15 per cent of India's rice was coming from Burma and a majority share of this import was finding its way to Bengal.[4] With the fall of Burma to the Japanese, this huge source of rice was turned off at one stroke. Traders began hoarding in earnest and with little or no intervention from the government to control the free market process, prices soared and the famine situation soon spiralled out of control, killing a devastating three-and-a-half million Bengalis.[5] The poor from rural Bengal thronged to the city, dying by the thousands on the way or simply collapsing at the bus or train terminals. In Mrs Vijay Lakshmi Pandit's writings there are heart-rending descriptions of the times.[6] She writes of the "hollow-eyed" children and nursing mothers with "wrinkled faces", she witnessed at the relief centres of Bengal.[7] As the starving and the destitute roamed the streets of Calcutta and decaying corpses piled up on the wayside, news reached Bose across the borders. He offered to supply a 100,000 tons of Burmese rice to the starving millions and declared at the time of the creation of the Provisional Government in October, "There can be no doubt that these famine conditions have been largely due to the policy of ruthless exploitation of India's food and other resources for Britain's war purposes over a period of nearly four years."[8] The Bengal famine would be repeatedly referred to in the INA propaganda speeches. The INA's newspaper, *Azad Hind* [Free India], would mention this disaster on 17 December 1943: "... while the famine is still raging in Bengal, malaria is also taking a heavy toll of lives ... there is no quinine for the poor people." There would be references to precious shipping space being allotted to carrying whiskey cases for the British troops instead of badly needed medicines.

The famine of 1943 had two rather important effects on the INA operations in Southeast Asia. On the one hand, while the stories of human suffering of this "man-made" tragedy motivated the

Indian community to join the nationalist movement and spurred them on to the battlefield, it also ensured that India remained completely entangled in her own administrative issues and in handling the slow fight to normalcy which followed the debacle. Added to this was the tight wartime censorship of the British information bureau which ensured that all INA-related news was completely blacked out in India.[9] So as 1943 passed to 1944, the Japanese were pushed back in Burma and there were no longer any air raids on Calcutta or the coasts of Orissa, concerns in India about the Japanese and the war taking place across the border of Burma, dropped out of sight. Southeast Asia was left to its own resources as it forged forward on its chosen nationalist path.

Subhas Chandra Bose in Southeast Asia: A Brief Timeline

Subhas Chandra Bose arrived at the island of Sabang, off the coast of Indonesia, on 6 May 1943 and almost immediately on arrival left for Tokyo to meet Hideki Tojo, the Japanese prime minister. His first radio messages, after a lapse of several months while he had undertaken the long submarine journey from Germany, were transmitted from the Japanese capital. These messages contributed to the sense of anticipation that preceded his eventual landing at Singapore on 2 July 1943. The drum-roll of his impending arrival was heard in the newspapers of the time. *Syonan Times* hailed him as the "Idol of Indian Youth".[10] The newspaper carried double column headlines announcing his participation in the Indian Freedom Movement:

> Subhas Chandra Bose coming ... to take active part in Indian Independence move ... announcement of arrival in Tokyo signal of victory ... The Indian Independence Movement in Toa [East Asia] has the powerful support of Nippon ... But it is a movement

organised and carried on by the sons and daughters of India who are free citizens of Toa.[11]

News of his radio broadcasts in English and Hindustani, to be aired on "225 metres" also received publicity.

On 4 July 1943 Bose made his first public appearance at the Cathay Theatre in Singapore as he formally accepted the leadership of the IIL from the veteran leader, Rashbehari Bose. He spoke in Hindustani and drew an evocative picture of the INA's victory march to Delhi. Bose also announced his intention of establishing the Provisional Government of Azad Hind [Free India]. The following day, on 5 July he appeared at the Singapore Padang, opposite the Municipal Building (now City Hall) to address the INA. The first INA had been previously formed under the active leadership of the Japanese major, Fujiwara Iwaichi, Captain Mohan Singh from the Punjab Regiment of the British Indian Army and an anti-colonial activist, Giani Pritam Singh. On 17 February 1942, soon after the fall of Singapore to the Japanese, almost 40,000 Indian troops who surrendered at Singapore had volunteered to join the INA. But subsequently, in December 1942, following his rift with the Japanese, Mohan Singh had disbanded the INA. The complete dissolution of the INA was prevented only with assurances offered by Rashbehari Bose and the Japanese of Subhas Chandra Bose's imminent arrival to assume leadership of the movement.

By 5 July 1943 therefore, the strength of the INA had greatly dwindled and some 12,000 soldiers of the INA as well as a rapturous crowd of civilians gathered to hear Bose's historic speech at the Padang. The audience responded with a tumultuous ovation as he spoke: "Let your battle-cry be 'To Delhi! To Delhi' How many of us will individually survive this war of freedom,

I do not know. But I do know this ... our task will not end until our surviving heroes hold the victory parade on another graveyard of the British Empire — Lal Kila ... of ancient Delhi."[12] S. R. Nathan, former President of Singapore, who was present on the day, recalls the slight drizzle that started mid-way through the speech. Bose was not too pleased when some from the audience got restive and looked for shelter.[13] Soon after, on 12 July, Bose fulfilled a long cherished dream and addressed the first recruits of the all-women Rani of Jhansi regiment.

In the subsequent months, Bose's journeys criss-crossed Southeast Asia. He had already visited Saigon, Vietnam en route from Tokyo to Singapore and now travelled to Malaya, Burma, Thailand and Indonesia. The Indian community at Vietnam was small while Malaya had approximately a million resident Indians. As his powerful publicity campaigns continued, the number of volunteers to the cause soared. Some 18,000 civilians enlisted for the INA while thousands joined the IIL's branch offices in support functions.[14] The Indian POWs who had not committed their allegiance to the INA in 1942, under the leadership of Mohan Singh, were now "swept off their feet" and took the combined strength of the INA to more than 40,000.[15]

On 21 October 1943, Bose proclaimed the formation of the Provisional Government of Azad Hind. Yet again the Cathay Theatre of Singapore was filled to capacity as Bose and his Cabinet of ministers took the oath of allegiance. In a voice choked with emotions the leader declared, "In the name of God, I take this sacred oath — that to liberate India and the 38 crores of my countrymen, I, Subhas Chandra Bose, will continue this sacred war of freedom till the last breath of my life."[16] The Provisional Government soon received diplomatic recognition from nine states of the Axis powers — this would bequeath a constitutional legitimacy to the new government and help strengthen the INA's case at the subsequent Red Fort Trials held by the British in India.

In November 1943 Subhas Chandra Bose travelled to Tokyo to attend the Greater East Asia Conference. During the visit he met Tojo and now as the head of the Provisional Government of Azad Hind, asked Japan to hand over the Andaman and Nicober Islands and also for the Provincial Government's jurisdiction over abandoned Indian property in Southeast Asia. At the Greater East Asia Conference held between 5–6 November and attended by Presidents and Heads of States from Manchuko, Reformed Government of the Republic of China, Burma, Thailand and the Second Philippine Republic, Bose, despite his status as an observer, cut an impressive figure. At the end of Bose's address, Tojo reiterated Japan's support for India's liberation war and also declared the intention to transfer the Andaman and Nicober Islands to the Provisional Government. The promise was kept by the Japanese and the formal transfer of the islands happened in December 1943.

Bose returned to Singapore on 25 November 1943, after brief stopovers in Nanjing, Shanghai and Manila. On 7 January 1944 the advance headquarters of the Provisional Government was moved from Singapore to Rangoon in readiness for the offensive into India. The first division of the INA, consisting of around 10,000 soldiers and divided into three regiments or brigades (Azad, Gandhi and Nehru) had already been raised and placed under the command of Mohammad Zaman Kiani. From these three regiments the best soldiers were handpicked to form the No. 1 Guerrilla Regiment and in November 1943 the Regiment was sent to Burma under Shah Nawaz Khan. The soldiers themselves named it the Subhas Brigade, much against the wishes of Bose. Bose himself, after moving to Rangoon, spent much of his time raising resources and recruiting civilian volunteers to his cause. On 4 February 1944 the entire Subhas Brigade moved from Rangoon to Mandalay and Prome. The soldiers were stationed at the Arakan sector where they experienced some early successes against the British Division and could take up position at Mowdok, on the Indian side of the Indo-Burmese border.

The Imphal offensive was initiated on 8 March 1944 and by 18 March the INA moved into north-eastern India towards Imphal and Kohima, much to the jubilation of the troops. The morale of the army was at its peak and on 5 April 1944, Bose announced the formation of the National Bank of Azad Hind and the Provincial Government issued postage stamps as well as sample currency notes. The Japanese expected Imphal to fall by end-April and indeed Shaukat Ali Malik, commander of the Bahadur Group, hoisted the Indian tricolour at Moirang, 45 km away from Imphal, Manipur on 14 April 1944. The siege of Imphal lasted three-and-a-half months and by then the INA troops had started feeling the shortage of essential supplies. Whereas the British were supported by continuous airlift of supplies organized by the Americans, the INA was at a distinct disadvantage. Despite the fierce fight put up by the Azad Brigade under Gulzara Singh and the Gandhi Brigade under the command of Inayat Jan Kiani, during the entire month of May, the INA could not seize control of Imphal. Unfortunately, an early monsoon towards the end of June wrought havoc with the terrain and the supply situation worsened as the INA troops decided to wait and watch. On 10 July 1944, the Japanese informed Bose of the unsustainable situation and asked him to issue orders for the withdrawal of the INA troops from Imphal. With their food and medicine supply lines cut-off, this was one of the worst periods for the INA and witnessed some desertions to the British side. The INA's retreat through, "some of the world's worst country, breeding the world's worst diseases" commenced on 18 July 1944.[17] Lack of food and monsoon ailments took a heavy toll as the troops trudged back through rivers of green mud. Bose was to later compare the war at Imphal to a "fight between the human spirit on the one side and steel and armour on the other".[18]

But despite the reverses, Bose returned to Burma on 10 January 1945 to obstruct the advancement of British troops along the banks of the River Irrawady and perhaps, it was this second coming of the INA without much hope of victory, which is more poignant and has become axiomatic of Bose's unrelenting spirit. While Prem Kumar Sahgal was stationed at Mount Popa, Gurbaksh Singh Dhillon took up his position on the eastern banks of the Irrawady. But it was not to be and the Japanese and INA defences crumbled at the face of William Slim's strategic assault. On 29 April Prem Kumar Sahgal was captured near Allanmyo, while on 18 May Shah Nawaz Khan and Gurbaksh Singh Dhillon were imprisoned near Pegu — the Hindu-Muslim-Sikh trio to appear at the Red Fort Trials later.

On 24 April 1945, Subhas Chandra Bose started on yet another harrowing retreat through the enemy-infested jungles of Burma to reach the safe sanctuary of Thailand. Besides the soldiers of the INA and the women of the Rani of Jhansi Regiment, some senior ministers of the League and the military commanders, M. Z. Kiani and J. K. Bhonsle, accompanied him. After a torturous twenty-six-day long trek, they reached Thailand on 21 May 1945. Bose's faith in his cause was yet undaunted and at a public address in Thailand he declared: "But the roads to Delhi are many, like the roads to Rome. And along one of these many roads we shall travel and ultimately reach our destination, the metropolis of India."[19] In a desperate bid to lift flagging morale, "Netaji Week" was celebrated across Southeast Asia between 4 and 10 July 1945. The *Syonan Shinbun* reports of the programme that was flagged off with singing of the Indian national anthem and patriotic songs on the radio at 8.30 a.m. and included military parades by the Balak Sena [Youth Wing] from the Indian National School and Azad School. The parade was headed by the brass band of the Rani of Jhansi Regiment: "... the long column of women soldiers, cadets and schoolchildren created quite a stir among the populace of areas it marched through." The programme also included stirring speeches by Bose and other leaders of the League as well as the laying of the foundation stone in Singapore of the memorial dedicated to the "Unknown Soldier of the Azad Hind Fauj".[20]

But with the bombing of Hiroshima and Nagasaki, the war came to a grinding and conclusive end and, on 16 August 1945, Subhas Chandra Bose left Singapore on a final journey-of-no-return with three of his close compatriots. They travelled first to Bangkok and then to Saigon. On 17 August he left Saigon aboard a Japanese Air Force bomber, accompanied by his deputy chief-of-staff, Habibur Rahman. They transited at the Taipei airport and soon afterwards the fateful aircraft met with a fatal accident. Bose, who suffered serious burn injuries while struggling out of the aircraft, breathed his last on 18 August, at a hospital in Taipei. He was yet to turn forty-nine.

Bose and Contemporary Burma

Burma and India had always shared a curious love-hate relationship. In matters of commerce, the Burmese were ever-skeptical of the Indians: they felt a majority of their land's wealth was siphoned off to India as large numbers of Indians thronged to Burma under the aegis of the British, to do business. But in terms of spiritual exchange, Buddhism had tied the two countries in a close bond. Another factor was their shared political history — Burma, like India, was a British subject and in fact was administered as an Indian province until the separation in 1937. The Burmese nationalist movement had often looked towards the Indian National Congress for direction. The contact between the two movements was facilitated by the presence of a large Indian community in Burma and by the fact that several prominent Indian freedom fighters had served their prison terms in Burmese prisons between the two World Wars.[21] Bose himself had been interned in the Mandalay prison in 1925. His letters from this period were full of rather evocative descriptions of Burma: he had described the darkness that enveloped the prison inmates after a dust storm as "Cimmerian darkness" and mentioned, "I am again using a Miltonic expression for is not saintly Milton as effective in his descriptions of darkness as Shakespeare is sweet in his description of fairy moonlight?"[22] He had taken pains to find out about Burmese heritage: "You probably know that the percentage of literate people in Burma, both among males and females, is more than in any part of India. This is due to the indigenous and wonderfully cheap system of primary education through the agency of priests. In Burma, even today every boy is supposed to don the yellow robe ..."[23] During his two-year prison term Bose met some Burmese political leaders, including radical Buddhist monks. He would retain this interest in the political issues of Burma and her freedom movement even while in India.

The nationalist struggle in Burma began as a subterranean revolutionary movement. The Burmese radicals with members of Ba Maw's group founded the clandestine National Revolutionary Party which began to plan for the Burmese army of independence on the model of the Irish Republican Army. In the 1930s, Ba Maw, later to become the Burmese Premier, was the most vehement advocate of Burmese self-rule, while Aung San was a fiery young nationalist. Aung San had been in touch with the Japanese and with help from his Japanese collaborators, smuggled out a hand-picked group of thirty young radicals and under cover sent them to Japan for military training. This small group of *Thakins* was the nucleus of the Burma Independence Army (BIA) when it was formed in 1941 on Thai territory. The BIA would gain popularity among the native Burmese, despite the fact that it failed to achieve much of a military record. In the BIA the indigenous people saw the resurgence of the Burmese military tradition which had been subverted by the British as they had formed the Burmese army from resident Indians, Gurkhas and Anglo-Burmans.[24]

The BIA, which had been gathering strength south of the Thai border, would get the chance to move back to their native country in the wake of the Japanese invasion of Burma. The Japanese attack which started with the blitzing of Rangoon in December 1941, would soon turn into a full-scale land invasion from neutral Thailand, thrusting up the river valleys and quickly seizing first Moulmein and then Rangoon.[25] The *Thakins*, now commanding the BIA, moved into Burma in the vanguard of the Japanese advance. In the towns of South Burma, the BIA received a hero's welcome. By the time they reached Rangoon, they were about 12,000 members strong and by the end of the year their numbers would swell to about 18,000.[26] The BIA took this opportunity to vent their patriotic rage on some old enemies of Burma — the Indian moneylenders and bankers primary among them.

Indians were not a popular class of people in Burma. Indian migrations to Burma had begun as early as the 1850s following the British annexation of the Burma Delta in 1852. The British brought in thousands of Indians to develop the rice cultivation of Burma and to relieve the problem of over population in the famine-stricken areas of India.[27] Rangoon was the focal point of this seaborne migration and steadily absorbed the regular tide of incoming Indians. The percentage of Indian population in Rangoon rose from a 16 per cent in 1872 to a staggering 56 per cent by 1941.[28] The numbers went up so quickly that in the pre-war years, Rangoon was virtually an Indian city and it was impossible to get by without knowing Hindustani, the accepted lingua franca of the trading class.[29] The group was predominantly made up of Telegus and Tamils, with a substantial number of Muslims from Chittagong and Bengalis. Whereas the majority of this migratory population worked as manual labourers — dock labourers, the ubiquitous Indian rickshaw-pullers, dhobis, municipal workers, a small but significant percentage were also skilled professionals — tradesmen, merchants and the dreaded Chettyar moneylenders.

Relations between the Indian and the native Burmese community soured over the years and the resentment was heightened by the *Saya San*-led peasant rebellion of 1930–32 and the violent Buddhist-Muslim riots of 1938: "Many Burmese regarded the Indians who had settled among them as unscrupulous opportunists looting their country on the coat tails of the British."[30] In fact, during the years 1940 and 1941, the major issue in Burmese politics was Indian immigration as the large number of Indian employers present in Burma gave very few jobs to the unemployed in Burma: a political pamphlet doing the rounds after the Indo-Bamar riots read, "Indians are everywhere: shoe-makers to physician, prison guard to prison warden, all positions are monopolized by Indians."[31] The Burmese retaliated by saying, "You must be either Indians or Burmans, you cannot be both."[32]

Inter-communal antagonism came to a head with the Japanese invasion and in an ironical reversal of the earlier immigration pattern, with the fall of the British, there began a mass exodus of the resident Indians. By the autumn of 1942, somewhere in the region of

600,000 Indians fled by land and by sea, making this the largest mass migration of the time. Of this number as many as 80,000 perished on the way of disease, malnutrition or sheer exhaustion.[33] Some tried to escape by sea from the docks in Rangoon, while others went over land through the high mountain passes of Manipur and Assam. As this great column of humanity pressed on towards India and refugee camps on the wayside functioned without basic sanitation, the British population along with the British Commissioner fled on the first available boats. With the arrival of the monsoon, the situation deteriorated even further: the routes through the valleys of Assam became virtual "green hells" of mud, starving people died by the thousand and as the dead were left to decompose in the mud, cholera broke out to claim its own share of the devastation.

The flight of the civilian population, after the Japanese bombings and the triumphant entrance of the BIA in March 1942, left Rangoon a virtual ghost town. The Indian labour force which had made up nearly 74 per cent of Rangoon's Indian population fell to a drastic 24 per cent.[34] By the time of Subhas Chandra Bose's arrival in Burma, the remaining Indians, numbering around 800,000, had regrouped and remained together in pockets of areas as a substantial minority. Bose's arrival had an electrifying effect on this group: "… a large proportion of the city's remaining Indian residents had been glowing with pride."[35] On 1 August 1943, Bose came to Burma as Ba Maw's guest to participate in the Burmese independence celebrations. In the speech delivered on 1 August and broadcast over Rangoon Radio he declared: "The independence of Burma … has a twofold significance for us. It shows in the first place what a nation can achieve if it knows how to seize an opportunity … Secondly, just as the conquest of India supplied the British with a jumping-off ground for their attack on Burma in the nineteenth century, similarly the emancipation of Burma has supplied the Indian independence movement in East Asia with a springboard for its attack on Britain's army of occupation in India during the twentieth century."[36] On behalf of the Indian community, he offered a *nazar* or gift of 250,000 rupees to the Burmese government in appreciation of their hospitality. The resident Indians responded with patriotic fervour to Bose's call and despite wartime hardships, out of the total sum of 215 million rupees which the Azad Hind Government raised, 150 million came from Burma.[37]

Bose, right from the time of his arrival, worked on building diplomatic relations with the Burmese leadership and exhorted the local Indians to forget their past differences. The sensitivity inherent in the Indo-Burmese relation was enhanced when the *Thakins* decided to march against the Japanese and support the returning British instead. And yet, the INA and Burmese leaders would continue to consider themselves comrades-in-arms. As Colonel G. S. Dhillon remarks: "... one is amazed as to how on earth could it be possible for the Indian National Army to operate and wage a war of liberation from the land erstwhile so hostile? ... we did not suffer the loss of a single life at Burmese hands during the days of our defeat and hundreds of miles of retreat."[38] In fact, the meeting between Bose and the Burmese Head of State, Ba Maw, in August 1943, was especially significant since it led to improvement in the status of the resident Indians in Burma. The *Syonan Shimbun* of 23 August 1943 reported that immediately following Bose's departure from Rangoon after attending the Independence Day celebrations, the Government of Burma issued a declaration that the Indian-British subjects resident in Burma or passing through Burma would be treated not as "enemy subjects" but as subjects of a "friendly third power".

Ba Maw first met Bose at Singapore in July 1943 and then at the Greater East Asia Conference held in Tokyo the same year.

The Burmese Premier remarked: even before he actually met Bose he had heard about him in a "vague and rather romantic sort of a way" and the fact that he had been confined in Mandalay somehow seemed to bring him "closer to us and our struggle".[39] Thus, as "stars or something" prepared the way for the two leaders' wartime comradeship, the Indian community in Burma embarked on a new voyage of improved relations with the local Burmese.[40]

Bose and Contemporary Thailand

Rabindranath Tagore while leaving Thailand had dedicated a poem to Siam:

> ... in thy fragrant altars with candles lighted
> And incense breathing peace.
> Today at this hour of parting I stand in thy courtyard,
> Gaze in thy eyes
> And leave thee crowned with a garland
> Whose ever-fresh flowers blossomed ages ago.

During his brief journey to Siam in 1927, Tagore had been deeply touched by her ancient culture, and on his return to Santiniketan, sent one of the professors of Visva Bharati University, Prafulla Kumar Sen, to Thailand. In so doing, the poet unwittingly contributed to the churning waters of the Indian freedom movement in Southeast Asia. Sen, a revolutionary and a nationalist, arrived in Thailand in 1932, was appointed at the Chulalongkorn University and later came to play a significant role in the Indian nationalist movement in Thailand.

Thailand was the only Southeast Asian country, which had managed to evade colonial rule, and instead continued under an absolute monarchy till the 1930s. It was also one country that had taken an early pro-Japanese stance. By the 1930s, a significant element of the Thai military elite embraced the pan-Asian dream peddled by the Japanese and envisaged a Japanese alliance would help them fulfill their aspiration of forming a "greater-Thailand" by recapturing the territories that had been lost to the French in Indo-China and to the British in Malaya. Thus, in 1941, the invading Japanese army could negotiate a free passage through Siam with the Thai prime minister, Field Marshal Phibul Songkhram.

Today, Phibul Songkhram's regime in Thailand has become synonymous with the rise of a certain kind of ultra-nationalism in Thailand. The Siamese coup d'état of 1932 transformed the government of Thailand from an absolute to a constitutional monarchy. Although nominally a constitutional monarchy, Thailand was ruled by a series of military governments. Phibul Songkhram, one of the most prominent Thai military leaders, worked on building a leadership cult in Thailand. Throughout the year 1939, photographs of Phibul Songkhram were to be found everywhere; his slogans appeared in newspapers, were plastered on billboards and were broadcast over the radio.[41] For this new leadership to survive and for Thailand to finally achieve the status of an Asian "superpower", Phibul Songkhram together with his lieutenant Wichitwathakan, worked on the *Thaification* of Siam. A series of cultural mandates were issued by the government which required Thais to salute the national flag, know the new national anthem penned by Wichitwathakan, and use the national Thai language as opposed to the prevalent local dialects. The businesses of non-Thai minorities, like the traditionally merchant Thai-Chinese or the Thai-Indian, were aggressively bought over by the state, as the Government started doling out preferential contracts to ethnic Thais.[42] Around the same time, with the growing prospect of war in Southeast Asia, the Japanese made Thailand their military base.

Indians were never present in Thailand in overwhelming numbers, unlike Burma or Malaya.[43] This comparatively small community was predominantly made up of urban commercial traders who had migrated to Thailand in search of economic advancement. The immigration pattern was voluntary and did not follow that of the indentured Indian labour force in Malaya. Again, Tamils seem to have been the earliest group of migrants, arriving from Penang and the Malayan Peninsula. Dawoodi Bohra Muslims from Surat and Ahmadabad and Punjabis from Northern India soon followed. Most of this migrant community settled in Bangkok, trading in textiles, precious stones and minerals while the tailoring shops, run by the Sindhis in Sukhumvit, gained increasing popularity.

During the reign of Phibul Songkhram, as the Indians faced the nationalist mandates and restrictions were placed on their movement, the community turned to one Swami Satyananda Puri for advice. Prafulla Kumar Sen, who had taken up the alias Satyananda Puri, was a scholarly figure held in veneration by the Thai-Indians. An Oriental philosopher, he had learnt the Thai language in six months' time, and in October 1940 he established the Thai Bharat Cultural Lodge (TBCL) to facilitate a deeper bonding with the native Thai. In his discussions with Phibul Songkhram's government, the TBCL was given the right to issue permits for the domestic travel of Indians and soon emerged as a venue where the Indian community would converge. By 1941, TBCL had assumed a political colour and moved closer to the Japanese who had been sending out military intelligence agents to identify potential allies. At this time in Thailand, there were present two other remarkable men affiliated to the Indian Independence League — the young Sikh, Gyani Pritam Singh, who had been involved with the failed *Ghadr* Conspiracy of 1915, and the older Baba Amar Singh — again a nationalist who had spent twenty-two long years in the dreaded Andaman jail.[44] Pritam

Singh, who had already worked behind the enemy lines of the British Indian troops in Malaya, would soon find an ally in a young Japanese Intelligence Officer, Fujiwara Iwaichi. Together they would press a propaganda offensive on the captured Indian troops of the defeated British Army. One of the earliest to respond would be Captain Mohan Singh. By December 1941 they would persuade Mohan Singh to help the Japanese in winning over soldiers to their side and the first INA would be born: "From the conversations among these three men [Fujiwara, Pritam Singh and Mohan Singh] the first Indian National Army was born."[45]

The Bangkok Conference of 1942, chaired by Rashbehari Bose and widely attended by the IIL members from all over Southeast Asia, was held on Thai soil.[46] Bose, once he arrived in Asia, visited Thailand repeatedly in transit from Malaya to Burma. He reached out to the Indian community and built diplomatic ties with the Prime Minister, Phibul Songkhram, donating generously to Thai hospitals and the Chulalongkorn University. On 8 August 1943 he addressed a large audience at the Chulalongkorn University Hall. In response, Phibul Songkhram extended all possible cooperation to the INA, including allowing the building of army barracks near the Thai-Burma border. As in other parts of Southeast Asia, the Indians rallied round Bose: one Darshan Singh Bajaj alone donated 95,000 *tael* to the nationalist cause.[47] Bose tried to build bridges between the spurring IIL and Puri's TBCL (renamed the Indian National Council), bringing the Indian community, which had split apart along the lines of their allegiance to these two pioneering bodies, together. Later as the INA operations moved to Singapore, and then to Rangoon, he nominated Isher Singh Narula the representative of the Provisional Government of Azad Hind in Thailand. At the end of the war Bose would reassemble his civilian forces yet again at Bangkok for a brief period. In June 1945, Prince Wan Waithayakon of Thailand, in the presence of the Chief Justice of the Thai Supreme Court and Anuman Rachodhon, the President of TBCL, offered to grant Bose asylum in the eventuality of Japan's defeat.[48] Some senior members of the Provisional Government also urged him to remain underground in the friendly Thai nation. But as things would come to pass, history would propel him forward towards a more violent destiny and on 17 August 1945, Bose would board the last fateful flight from Bangkok to Saigon on his final "adventure into the unknown".

Bose and Contemporary Malaya (Malaysia and Singapore)

A certain Mr Ridley earned quite the reputation of a maverick in Malaya during the last decades of the nineteenth century. The botanist and Director of the Gardens, Strait Settlements, 1888–1911, was nicknamed "Mad Ridley" for his efforts to develop the cultivation of rubber in the Malayan Peninsula — perhaps slightly irreverent for a man on whose efforts would rest so large a share of the wealth that Malaya would come to earn from her plantations![49]

Coffee was first introduced as a commercial crop in Malaya but soon abandoned because of its vulnerability to disease. On the other hand, the British were getting increasingly frustrated with the American dominance on the Brazilian rubber supply, even more so after the growth of motor cars and other rubber-using industries in the West: "Young rubber plants were brought, sometimes smuggled, to London from Brazil and sent to the tropical colonies ..."[50] World over, the demand for rubber was on the rise and gradually the emphasis of the British shifted entirely to large-scale production of rubber in Malaya. Consequently as thousands of hectares of cultivable land was set aside for rubber, rubber exports soared: from 104 tons in 1905 to a staggering 56,782 tons in 1915. Interpreted in dollar terms, this meant a rise from $529,000 to $93,660,000 or from a conservative 0.7 per cent of total export value to a whopping 57.7 per cent.[51] This entire "Rubber Boom" was dependent on the backbreaking efforts of a migrant population of largely Indian labourers brought in by the British.

While the tin mining industry of Malaya was more or less monopolized by another immigrant community — the Strait Chinese, rubber estate hands were almost all Indians: during the decade of World War I an average of 50,000–80,000 Indian labourers were immigrating to Malaya per year and the number rose to a fantastic 102,155 *kangani* recruits in 1926.[52] Plantation work, be it rubber, spices, oil palm or tea, required simple, repetitive, unskilled work for which the British deemed the Indians, particularly the South Indian Tamils to be adequately subservient and suitable. According to K. S. Sandhu, up to 1941, of the total Indian immigration to Malaysia, labour comprised 72.5 per cent, of which South Indians occupied a huge 92.3 per cent bracket, with the balance made up of diverse other Indian communities.[53] Of the South Indians, an overwhelming number, nearly 87 per cent, were Tamils.[54] To quote a planter's observation around 1911: "The Tamil struck me as being a poor specimen, both in physique and morale and of being abject, cowardly and generally lacking in vitality ... The blind admiration for the white man by these Tamils is really rather pathetic."[55] The entire, close-knit world of the rubber estates came to be built on two founding tenets — imperial power on one hand and the systemic exploitation of plantation hands on the other. Be it in the form of bonded labour or under the supposedly "free labour" system run by the *kanganies*, their endemic condition remained the same.

As years passed, certain characteristic features emerged. Firstly, life on the plantation was highly regimented with the European planter at the top of the pyramid, followed by the clerk or the *kirani*, from Asian stock but from Ceylon or Malayalam speakers from Kerala. Separated from the labourers by the communal barrier, they ensured the "General Instructions of the Company" were followed, conducted the early morning parade and roll-call, made sure the labourer dismounted from his bicycle every time he passed the planter's bungalow or parted his hair in the traditional way with a tuft.[56] After this came the *kangani*, or the overseer, the actual leader of the tappers, while the South Indian labourers were at the bottom of the pile. Most numerous, they led the lifestyle planned and standardized by the management in miserable "line houses" — amidst squalor and hopelessness.

The stiff regimentation brought with itself a wage system that was even more stifling for the labourer. The Indian Immigration Committee which, since its inception in 1907, had effectively controlled labour immigration to the planters' advantage, went to great pains to calculate monthly cost of individual subsistence and then settle wage rates.[57] As the Great Depression set in and the rubber prices plummeted, the wages were reduced in a commensurate way and the payrolls went down by almost 80 per cent as labour was cut down and wages revised. But though by 1934, the rubber industry had revived, the wages remained at the same post-Depression level.[58] This trend of subsistence wages meant the labourers were left with very little margin after meeting their basic expenses. This margin they could either use for remitting to India, or to buy a return passage home or, as it happened in most cases, spend it on toddy — the only means of easy entertainment available on the plantations.

Another characteristic feature of plantation life was the lack of educational facilities. Even with the Labor Code of 1923, which stipulated the provision of a school on every estate having ten children or more of school-going age, the estate schools were single-teacher/multi-class affairs, often housed in dilapidated sheds. Besides, since the medium of instruction was Tamil or Malayalam, even the rudimentary schooling that was available did not help in securing any future gains for the tappers' families.

This large mass of humanity lived on in comparative isolation in the insular worlds of their estates. With the unbending plantation discipline, which made it difficult even for relatives to visit their families living on the estates, they were virtually cut-off from the external world. Though conditions improved marginally with buses and roads in the 1930s opening up channels of communication, Malaya continued to exist with her three widely divided ethnic groups — the Malays, the Chinese and the Indians.

The South Indian plantation workers also remained fragmented from the mainstream Indian immigrants of Malaysia. The relatively smaller group of educated Indians, who had moved to Malaya on their own volition in search of better economic prospects, remained largely aloof to the sub-culture of oppression prevalent on the distant estates. The urban population of Indians consisted of North Indians, particularly the Sikhs who joined the military or the police force, the traders from the Coromandel and Malabar coasts, textile merchants from Sind, Chettyar moneylenders — a diverse group of people who came to represent the Indian petty bourgeoisie in Malaya.

The Indian community in the other part of the Strait Settlements, the area that forms the state-republic of Singapore today, was characterized by the same class-divide. Indians, who had been present in Singapore from the first days of her foundation as a British trading post by Raffles, were largely made up of convict labour. Again dominated by a large percentage of Tamils, they were the ones who built the city-state. They filled the swamps, worked on land reclamation projects, constructed roads like Serangoon Road and North Bridge Road that form the connecting conduits of city life today. The educated Indians filled the subordinate posts of the administrative machinery and also came to represent the trading community. Later, with the establishment of Singapore as a British military base, large contingents of the British Indian naval and air forces also came to be located here. Yet the community was characterized by little or no inter-class mingling — the British as the rulers, forming the only point of common reference, to whom each of these individual classes separately affiliated themselves.

Formation of CIAM (Central Indian Association of Malaya)

The 1920s saw the formation of a number of Indian associations in this region. However, these bodies remained isolated pockets of intermittent activity, with no obvious "coordination among them".[59] One expression of this tentative unity was the CIAM. Formed in 1936, it was a federation of a number of existing Indian Associations and Chambers of Commerce. Under it, the educated Indian intelligentsia came together to highlight the plight of the plantation labourers, appealing to the Indian Government to stop assisted labour migration to Malaya in 1938. Soon CIAM was converted to an extension of the Indian National Congress. There were efforts to organize the Indian labour and the 1930s saw sporadic strikes and agitations for better wages and working conditions. 1941 saw one of the bloodiest strikes in the Klang district of the Selangor State: among other things the rubber plantation workers agitated for parity of pay between Chinese and Indian labour, provision of proper educational facilities for the children and putting an end to the molesting of the women folk by the European planters and their Indian assistants. The British, for obvious reasons, came down with a heavy hand on the strikers — over 300 were arrested, police troops killed some of the strikers and scores of others were deported. By pulverizing the strikers and ruthlessly dispersing them, the British sought to underline the weakness of the Indians: "For large sections of the Indian population, the violent suppression of the Selangor estate laborers was a traumatic experience. It underlined their impotence in the face of a ruthless colonial power in a colony where they comprised only a small percentage of the total population."[60] As an aftermath, in the 1940s the British banned all strikes and government employees, the majority of whom were Indians, were denied unionization.

Malay Nationalism

While the British effectively silenced the Indian voice of dissent, there was yet another force at work in the Malayan Peninsula which was in essence counter-Indian — that of a rival Malay nationalism. Triggered as a reaction to the economic hardships of the post-Depression days, Malay nationalism soon gathered strength and like in Burma or Thailand, there was evidence of a growing hostility between the Indian and the ethnic Malay communities. Malay newspapers began to devote more and more space to discussions on the political threat posed by the Chinese and the Indian. In 1937, when Sir Shenton Thomas, the High Commissioner, announced that non-Malays would be admitted to responsible posts of the technical services, one Abdul Zainuddin wrote in criticism: "I am not hot-headedly advocating that every Malay should and must be given employment in the Government service, but appointments which are the Malays' should, and must, remain the Malays'."[61]

In 1938 the radicals of the Malay nationalist movement formed the Kesatuan Melayu Muda (KMM) under the leadership of Ibrahim Yaacob. This body had been growing close to the Japanese during the pre-war years and with outbreak of war, Japanese sponsorship was further accentuated. With the assistance of the Japanese chief-of-staff, several Malay leaders of the KMM got together to form the Kesatuan Rakyat Indonesia Semenanjung (KRIS). Reminiscent of the Malay dagger, KRIS was headed by Ibrahim Yaacob with Mustapha Hussain as his deputy and sought to form a coveted Malay dominant "Greater Indonesia".

Formation of INA

It was in this situation that the Japanese *blitzkrieg* took place, and Singapore fell on 15 February 1942. The Nippon Army steamrolled through fragile British defense as the Japanese withoutmuch-ado cycled into the Malayan Peninsula, from where they had landed at Kota Bahru. On 17 February 1942, soldiers from the British Indian Army gathered at Farrer Park, Singapore. The Japanese major, Fujiwara Iwaichi, addressed them and at the end of the address around 40,000, an overwhelming majority of the Indian troops, volunteered to join the INA.

Singapore was the INA headquarters during the initial months of Subhas Chandra Bose's arrival in Southeast Asia and remained the rear headquarters after the INA advance headquarters were moved to Rangoon in preparation of the offensive into India. The Indian Independence League's central headquarter office was located at Chancery Lane while Bose himself took up residence at a two-storied, seaside bungalow on Meyer Road. The rooms and balconies of this house were witness to much of the INA's wartime strategizing and here Bose wrote the Proclamation for the Provisional Government till late into the night of 19 October 1943. At the end of the war, the IIL Cabinet gathered at Meyer Road again to discuss the plans of their final surrender and from here, on 16 August 1945, Subhas Chandra Bose left Singapore on his final journey. Later the INA veteran, John A. Thivy, recommended that the Indian Embassy be located at the Meyer Road bungalow but his plans came to naught and the house passed into the hands of a Chinese family and eventually was pulled down.

In Malaya, the greatest contribution of Bose was in his success at drawing out scores of Indian men and women, particularly Tamil plantation workers to join the nationalist movement. And this was a harbinger of the change that was about to take place. As Stenson mentions, the "younger generation" who were either born in Malaya or educated in India or China, in the midst of "intense nationalist feeling", came to represent the beginning of a "true industrial proletariat" to whom their "elders' subservience to authority, their passive acceptance of their condition, and, in particular, their addiction to toddy drinking represented an apathy and degeneracy of which they were ashamed and which they were determined to remove."[62]

The conflicting Malay and Indian nationalisms would go through twists and turns of history and take on different avatars in the future — the Malayan Indian Congress (MIC) and the United Malay National Organisation (UMNO). The relationship between these two bodies would be marred by many uneasy moments that would confound and exacerbate the inter-race relations in Malaysia, but the Indian community would have been given a platform and a voice since the INA.

SUBHAS CHANDRA BOSE AND THE JAPANESE ALLIANCE

Background: A Time of Shifting Alliances and New Bonds

World War II saw the world divided into two warring factions: the Allies and the Axis Powers. While the United Kingdom, the British

Commonwealth Nations, Australia, New Zealand, Canada, France, Poland and Union of South Africa, formed the anti-German coalition, the tripartite agreement between Germany, Italy and Japan with their recognized hegemony over Continental Europe, the Mediterranean Sea, East Asia and the Pacific respectively, dominated the Axis Powers. Ellery C. Stowell calls the tripartite agreement a "momentous political union" of the "have-not powers" against the pre-emption of the "have powers"; a union born of a common fear of the intervention of the U.S. in Asia and the aid extended to Great Britain which could, in the long run, prove to be a menace to Japan's ambitions of expansion and Germany's dreams of a European domination.[63] The U.S. formally entered the European theatre with the attack on Pearl Harbour by the Japanese and subsequently led the Allied forces in the Pacific theatre from 1941 to 1945.

Subhas Chandra Bose, who had been attempting a coalition with the anti-British factions since 1938, found himself in a world of rapidly changing dynamics. The period of German-Soviet diplomatic ties was disrupted with the Soviet invasion of German-occupied Poland and eventually came to a decisive end with Germany's surprise attack on the USSR in June 1941. Japan's non-aggression treaty with Soviet Russia too unravelled and, on 23 June 1941, Japan declared war on Russia, with Italy quickly following suit. Great Britain countered this move by declaring her support for Russia. This last development upset Bose greatly: "Besides his own sympathies for the Soviets, he knew that the German invasion had moved many of his former colleagues on the Indian left closer to their rulers' view that Nazi Germany was *the* enemy."[64] While continuing to exert pressure on the Axis Powers to endorse Indian independence, he watched with dismay as Hitler's army faced their first winter at Stalingrad.

On the other hand, Japan's power was on the rise in the East. During the First World War, Japan had joined the Allied powers, though it had played only a minor role in fighting German colonial forces in East Asia. But Anglo-Japanese relations which had been gradually deteriorating since the Washington Conference of 1921, were positively strained by the 1930s. In 1940, Japan formally joined the Axis powers and occupied French Indo-China after Germany had conquered France. This further intensified Japan's conflict with the United States and Great Britain which reacted with an oil boycott. The resulting oil shortage and failures to solve the conflict diplomatically, made Japan decide to capture the oil-rich Dutch East Indies and to declare war on USA, Great Britain and Australia on 8 December 1941.

Bose had been sending feelers to Japan since 1938. He had met Japanese officials in Calcutta, including one Mr Ohasi of the Foreign Ministry, and in 1940, sent one of his trusted men from the Forward Bloc, Lal Shankar Lal, to Japan to seek help. The mission had come to naught with Lal's plans being revealed to the British, but Bose had continued to keep a speculative eye on Japan as a possible ally. Other than the military gains of Japan, Bose was aware of Rabindranath Tagore's journeys through Japan and the Indian national poet's enduring friendship with the Japanese curator and art historian, Okakura Tenshin. Bose had read Okakura and it was his writings which had "first turned his thoughts toward Japan".[65] Besides, with Japan's impressive victory in the Russo-Japanese war, nationalists from all over Asia had been looking at Japan as a role model against encroaching, and seemingly invincible, Western imperialism. Sun Yat-sen had been to Japan during his exile from China and so had Vietnamese nationalist, Phan Boi Chau; Japan had extended political asylum to Indian nationalist Rashbehari Bose as well. As Subhas Bose himself conceded at a press conference held at Tokyo on 19 June 1943, Japan, since her defeat of Russia in 1905, was the "point of departure" for Asia: "Forty years ago when I was attending primary school, the news of a small nation in the Orient defeating a big European power [ie., Russia] was widely reported and this gave a fillip to the freedom movement. The air was full of tales of Japanese exploits in the war. It was since then that we in India began to respect Admiral Togo and General Nogi."[66]

This positive image of Japan was further reinforced by the Japanese foreign minister, Matsuoka Yosuke's proclamation of the Greater East Asia Co-Prosperity Sphere on 1 August 1940, just before Japan signed the tripartite agreement with Germany and Italy.

The Greater East Asia Co-Prosperity Sphere

The Japanese Prime Minister, Fumimaro Konoe, conceived of the Greater East Asia Co-Prosperity Sphere as a bloc of Asian nations, led by Japan, to counter Western domination. It was to comprise primarily Japan, Manchukuo, China and parts of Southeast Asia and address the apparent plurality of Asia. As a natural fallout of the Russo-Japanese war, Japan came to take on itself the leadership role in awakening Asian nations to a common political destiny. Scholars point out that the Sphere was an imperative strategic initiative for Japan in the Pacific, both from military and naval standpoints: "With no risk whatever and almost no fighting Japan has established a semicircle of bases" which could be used to counter the combined American and British forces based in Singapore from cutting Japan's lines of communication.[67] By linking Japan, Manchukuo, China and parts of the Southern Pacific region, particularly the Dutch East Indies, French Indo-China and the Philippines, a formidable economic bloc had been envisaged against Anglo-American stratagems. But apart from military and economic considerations, there was another very significant ingredient to this concept: that of an idealist Meiji "Pan-Asianism". Politician and philosopher, Okawa Shumei, saw in it a means to achieve the spiritual and cultural unity of Asia: an awakening of a New Order which would overturn colonial control without corrupting indigenous social traditions.[68] Japan's Foreign Minister, Arita Hachiro, claimed the Greater East Asia Sphere was devoid of any national selfishness and instead helped small nations to "maintain a respectable existence with the great Powers".[69] And the Japanese Premier Tojo later held out the promise of freedom to the Philippines and Burma as equal partners in the Co-Prosperity Sphere.[70]

For Subhas Chandra Bose this New Order of Pan-Asian nationalism was an inspiring concept. He had run out of options of prospective war allies: Italy, though enthusiastic about India's liberty, had always been militarily the weakest of the tripartite powers. He had witnessed the end of Hitler's Asian dreams as Germany faced reverses at Stalingrad, while the Soviet Russia had turned pro-British. It is to this notion of Asian co-prosperity that he referred to time and again during his speech at the Greater East Asia Conference held in Tokyo towards the beginning of November 1943. At the conference Ba Maw, Burma's Prime Minister, had already argued vehemently for Indian independence, saying that there could be no liberation for Asia without the liberation of India. Thereafter Bose spoke with great eloquence of a new world, of a new Greater Asia that would prosper in freedom and referred to the Joint Declaration of the Greater East Asia Conference as a new "charter of liberty" for the year 1943 and beyond: "This is an assembly of liberated nations, an assembly that is out to create a new order in this part of the world, on the basis of the sacred principles of justice, national sovereignty, reciprocity in international relations and mutual aid and assistance. I do not think that it is an accident that this Assembly has been convened in the Land of the Rising Sun."[71]

Bose was not unaware of Japan's dark history of war atrocities, particularly in respect to China. The Marco Polo bridge incident of 1937, which led to the Battle of Beiping-Tianjin and the Battle of Shanghai in the same year, was still fresh in everyone's minds. Chiang Kai-shek's National Revolutionary Army had never recovered from this urban battle fought out in downtown Shanghai and on the roads to China's capital, Nanjing. The aftermath had seen America swing into action in China's aid and China formally joining the Allies in December 1941.

Subhas Chandra Bose had been concerned about the fate of China, and in 1938, while he was the President of the Indian National Congress, had sent a medical mission to Chungking as a token of sympathy for the Chinese people. In 1940 he had expressed a wish to visit China as well, but had been debarred by the British. At the end of the Greater East Asia Conference, on 18 November 1943, Bose travelled to Nanjing at the invitation of Wang Jing Wei, President of the Reformed Government of the Republic of China, with whom he had formed a relationship of mutual admiration. The latter had been a close associate of Sun Yat-sen and after a political fallout with Chiang Kai-shek had been responsible for establishing the Japanese-sponsored collaborative government at Nanjing. Bose utilized his stay in China to address the Chungking government and convey his message of friendship to the Chinese people. In two radio messages, broadcast from Shanghai on 20 and 21 November, he spoke of his early admiration for China and the peaceful revolution undertaken by the Chinese people against the Manchu dynasty in 1911, which, like the Russo-Japanese war, had left a lasting impression on him. He spoke at length of Sun Yat-sen and his belief in the liberation of Asia and Asian unity.

Speaking of Japan and her new role as champion of the "weaker and smaller countries of Asia" against the onslaught of European Imperialism, he mentioned: "Since then [ie., December 1941 when Japan declared war on the Anglo-American forces] a great change has taken place in Japan ... A new consciousness has taken possession of the spirit of the Japanese people. Today's Japan is not the same Japan of five years ago."[72] In support of his argument, he cited the examples of Burma and the Philippines which had been declared independent and the commitment from Japan of the return of the Andaman and Nicobar Islands to the Provisional Government of Azad Hind. He emphasized the need for the Asian nations to unify against British colonialism and urged the Chiang Kai-shek government to forget their differences with Nippon, because, unless Britain was defeated, "you can never have peace in China or East Asia."[73]

Like Gandhi and Tagore before him, Subhas Bose could not condone the Japanese "dismembering" of "the Chinese Republic" and the humiliation of this "proud, cultured and ancient race". And yet, he was impelled in his Japanese alliance by an optimistic faith in Japan's professed Asian universalism on one hand, and his own firm faith that India's liberation could not be achieved without foreign aid on the other: if there was nothing wrong in Britain seeking assistance from America, Australia, Chungking China and East and West Africa, then India could also accept help from the tripartite powers without the need to defend what they "have done or may do in future".[74] But significantly, despite accepting Japanese assistance, Bose was consistently wary of his allies and vigilant in maintaining the INA's independent stature. He firmly refused to walk on "stilts lent by others".[75] Instead he insisted that, "The first drop of blood shed on Indian soil must be that of a soldier of the INA", because freedom secured through Japanese sacrifices would be worse than slavery.[76]

The INA and the Japanese

The INA-Japanese alliance from the start was a contentious one and was marked by periods of intense differences. While he argued steadfastly for the Indian cause, Bose himself earned quite a reputation in the Japanese camp for being obstinate and difficult to mollify. Even during the much coveted first meeting with Tojo on 10 December 1943, he was careful in asking for "unconditional help" to Indian independence and hastened to ensure that there were "no strings attached to Japanese aid".[77] The strength of Bose's convictions was tested early on when he had to convince the Japanese to part with precious military resources to train the women of the Rani of Jhansi Regiment. This initial incident set the tone of his subsequent differences with the Japanese military.

Soon after Bose's arrival in Southeast Asia, he met Field Marshal Count Terauchi, commander of the Southern Army. The latter explained that the Japanese offensive into India would be led by the Japanese forces and all that they sought from Bose was personal cooperation in enlisting the sympathy of the Indian people. Bose was quick to take umbrage and explained in this meeting and later that the only role acceptable to the INA was at the head of the column as the army marched onto Indian soil.[78] Bose continued to wrangle with the Japanese on the stature of the INA as an allied army under Japanese operational command and managed to exact concessions from the Army Chief-of-Staff, Sugiyama, in November 1943: a second INA division would be raised and a third planned, while INA cadets would be sent to the War College in Tokyo for military training like their Japanese counterparts.[79]

As 1943 ended and the Japanese campaign in India became imminent, confrontations between the allies intensified. At the Imperial General Headquarters (IGHQ), Southern Army Headquarters and Burma Area Army Headquarters (BAA) of the Japanese there was doubt about the combat-readiness of the INA and the prevalent opinion was that the Indian men should only be used for guerilla warfare and intelligence work. But Bose's view finally prevailed and the commander of the Japanese BAA, General Kawabe agreed to the INA troops fighting directly under Indian commanders in units of regimental size, though the INA would ultimately be under Japanese command.[80] Bose insisted that one front in the offensive against India should be allotted to the INA and it was also his dearest wish that Chittagong should be the first target. As a result of his arguments, in August 1943, the Southern Army was coerced into making amendments in their strategic plans: "... a new plan emerged according to which the extreme left flank of the Japanese 15th Army which was in charge of Operation U, being an area south of a certain point of the front would be entrusted to the INA. The idea was to form a wedge here and attack Chittagong which was Bose's main target."[81] Even after this, niggling problems persisted: the issue of exchange of military courtesy between the INA and Japanese officials had to be handled diplomatically since it had led to incidents of bitter confrontations earlier. After January 1944, it was decided courtesy would be exchanged based on seniority and the authority of the notorious Japanese military police over Indian troops would be restricted to a minimum.[82]

Throughout his interactions with the Japanese, Bose was careful in maintaining the independence of the Provisional Government. The latter issued IOUs whenever receiving any Japanese loans, but Bose, dissatisfied with this system, wanted a more formal agreement to be instituted so that even his worst enemies would not be able to point a finger and say, "... we have bartered the future of our country."[83] What Bose was fighting for was complete liberty for India and not quasi-independence on borrowed resources: it had to be an Indian initiative from start to finish so that at the end of the struggle there would not be any moral obligation to accept Japanese interventions. This is borne out in his proposed discussions with Lt. General Renya Mutaguchi, commander of the 15th Army, on the takeover of Manipur as the first Indian administrative region under Bose's jurisdiction: the government as well as the people, property and public buildings of such occupied areas were to be turned over to the Provisional Government who would also issue special currency for use in these areas rather than Japanese military currency. In fact, keeping this in mind, Bose had announced the formation of the National Bank of Azad Hind on 5 April 1944, much against the wishes of the Japanese and by early-April, sample currency notes were being printed for use in the liberated zones. Once the INA's much coveted entry into India occurred, a party of civilian administrators, trained in military discipline, called the "Azad Hind Dal" was organized and a Chief Administrator of the Liberated Territories was appointed to prepare for setting up a civil administration.[84]

The Japanese Alliance: Conclusion

At the Greater East Asia Conference, Subhas Chandra Bose had hailed the Joint Declaration of the East Asian nations as the "new charter of liberty", and spoken with conviction of a new united Asia rising against the "mid-summer madness" of Western Imperialism. Till the end he stood firm in his belief in this new spirit of Pan-Asian nationalism. On the one hand, just as he withstood Japanese pressure to bomb his native city of Calcutta, he also refused Japanese attempts at utilizing the INA in suppressing the indigenous nationalist movement of Burma.[85] With the Japanese he struck a delicate balance: he could not commit India's future or his Provisional Government to Japanese jurisdiction and yet he could neither forget his gratefulness to his allies. It was this sense of gratefulness which took him to General Tojo's doorstep in November 1944. By then the tides of the war had turned and the once popular General of the Japanese Imperial Army lived, bereft of any military powers, in suburban Tokyo. Bose need not have come to pay him a visit but he came because he could not forget that without Tojo's consent neither the Provisional Government of Azad Hind nor the INA's participation in Operation U would have been possible.[86]

THE TRIAL AT RED FORT AND THE AFTERMATH

In Krishna Bose's writings of the INA, there is a story of the Thimayya brothers. After the fall of Japan Bose departed from Rangoon. But before departing he left detailed instructions with his subalterns so that the surrender, when it happened, could be smoothly executed. Major General A. D. Loganathan was in charge of the Azad Hind Government in Rangoon while Colonel Thimayya was his deputy. The British Occupation Force sent their representative, another Colonel Thimayya, to negotiate the surrender terms with the INA after the war and he was surprised to find his own brother on the side of the enemy. The two brothers, who had been fighting the war at different battle fronts during the war, met after a long while.[87] In another incident, Colonel Prem Kumar Sahgal of the INA reminiscences: after the British captured him near Alammyo, he was separated from his men and driven to Magwe in a truck with two British NCOs and a Punjabi Muslim *Naik* [Sepoy] as escorts. On the way the *Naik* got talking to him, he had already heard about the INA and "... was particularly impressed when he discovered" that one of the battalion commanders of the INA was Banta Singh, who in turn had been his commander in the British Indian Army.[88] It was this blurring of the dividing lines between the British Army and the rebellious INA which in the long run proved to be the most menacing for the British and finally succeeded in subverting Indian loyalty to the British Army. Hugh Toye, an officer in charge of the screening of the INA men wrote: "In the eleven months which had then elapsed since the first contact of the Indian Army, Navy and Air Force with the men of the INA in Rangoon, there had been widespread fraternization ... contact with the INA often meant re-union of close relatives separated since 1941. Its result was a political consciousness which the Indian servicemen had never before possessed."[89]

With the Japanese surrender on 15 August 1945, the scene of action for the INA shifted to India. The British took large numbers of the disbanded INA men prisoners and repatriated them to India. Around 17,000 of them were imprisoned in the Red Fort and the Kabul Lines of the New Delhi Cantonment.[90] In total around ten courts-martial were held but the most celebrated by far was the first — a joint court-martial of Colonel Prem Sahgal, Colonel G. S. Dhillon and Major General Shah Nawaz Khan — coincidentally a Hindu, a Sikh and a Muslim. In the meantime, the Congress leaders and workers had been finally released after the Quit India movement in June 1945. They emerged after their long hiatus, determined to make up for lost time. The Working Committee met in Pune in September and decided to take up the issue of the release of the captured INA men aggressively and what followed was of course history in the making.[91] The Indian population, restive since the last nationalist intervention had been quelled, took up the Red Fort trials as a popular agenda and led violent protests and demonstrations censuring the British stance on the INA. Nirad C. Chaudhuri writes: "The writer has witnessed other climactic outbreaks of nationalist agitation, but never greater popular excitement and passion."[92] On the question of the INA, the Congress and the Muslim League forgot their normal belligerence and united for the last time. Nehru donned his barrister's robe after thirty years and the INA Defense Committee consisted of revered names like Asaf Ali and Bhulabhai Desai. The trials opened on 5 November 1945 and Shah Nawaz Khan declared: "Born in traditions of loyalty to the British Crown, I had known India only through the eyes of young British officers. When I met Netaji and heard his speeches for the first time in my life, I saw India through the eyes of an Indian ... The question before me was — the king or the country. I decided to be loyal to my country ..."[93] Tales of Netaji and the valour and sacrifice of his soldiers did the rounds in every Indian home. Krishna Bose recalls watching hastily rigged up plays on the INA and hearing its rousing patriotic anthems on the streets of Calcutta.[94] In the course of a speech, Nehru also acceded: "The INA trial has created a mass upheaval. Wherever I went, even in the remotest village, there have been anxious enquiries about the INA men. There are profuse sympathies for these brave men, and all, irrespective of caste, colour and creed, have liberally contributed to their defense ..."[95]

The trials were the cynosure of all eyes for almost two months with the Indian populace hanging on every word and court transcripts being published every day. On 3 January 1946, the final verdict was announced. The court-martial found all the three INA officers guilty of waging war against the king and sentenced them to cashiering and transportation for life. But in an unprecedented reversal the Army Chief, Claude Auchinleck, commuted the sentence, and remitting the life sentence, only sentenced them to cashiering and forfeiture of arrears of pay. The result of the first trial made a "farce of the whole affair".[96] The final defeat of the British in the Red Fort trials was hinged on this first retreat and its significance would slowly dawn on the British and Asians alike: the British king was no longer the legitimate sovereign of India and Indian patriots could no longer be condemned as traitors. Major General Kiani writes of the British change of heart when he was held prisoner at the Kabul Lines:

> This was very different from the treatment meted out to members of the INA who were among the first to be captured during the fighting. Some of them were shot ... some found life in the underground cells in the Red Fort so unbearable that they made suicidal attacks on their armed guards, to have themselves killed. Several others went through the gruelling interrogation by the British ... The change in the attitude of the captors most certainly came about because the Indian people as a whole had identified themselves with our cause.[97]

He also mentions the "very powerful voices" which had begun to be raised in their support, because of which, by February 1946, the British had to release nearly 11,000 INA prisoners.[98]

What was more disconcerting for the British, as a corollary to the trials, the British Indian armed forces at this time witnessed large-scale mutinies and wavering support for the Raj. And most strangely the first manifestation of it was in the units of the Royal Air Force which was a purely British formation.[99] In mid-January 1946, some 5,200 RIAF personnel went on strike in protest against the living conditions and in sympathy for the INA.[100] And on 18 February a revolt began on *HMS Talwar*, a training ship of the Royal Indian Navy moored off Bombay. They were joined the next day by 20,000 ratings from the shore establishments. The strikes continued and developed into a pitched battle between the ratings and the British troops. By nightfall of the 20th, virtually the whole of the RIN was in open rebellion: the various ports of India, including Bombay, Karachi, Madras, Vizag, Calcutta, Cochin and even in Andaman were affected — nearly all ships and shore establishments were on strike and the Union Jack was hauled down. Complete chaos reigned on the streets of the cities where the RIN was on strike — naval trucks which went around asking the strikers to observe discipline bore the letters INN (Indian National Navy) and flew the Congress tricolour.[101] In a sickening reiteration of the 1857 mutiny for the British, attempts were made in Bombay by the ratings to take possession of the armory inside the Castle Barracks. Finally when truce was reached on the advice of the Congress, they surrendered with a declaration: "We surrender to India and not to Britain."[102] The rebellion spread like wildfire in the other units of the armed forces. Between 22 and 25 February the RIAF in Bombay and Madras went on strike and on the 27th Indian soldiers from Jabalpur followed. Nehru would soon declare: "The INA episode and the recent Royal Indian Air Force and Royal Indian Navy strikes have rendered the country a very great service. The gulf that separated the people from the armed forces has once and for all been bridged. The people and the soldier have come very close to each other."[103] In his broadcast on 25 February 1946, General Auchinleck would sound disturbed about the obvious political connection of the strikes: "In my position as Commander-in-Chief, I have nothing whatever to do with politics and I will not countenance political intrigue in the armed forces in India."[104] But despite British bravado and warnings, workers from railway workshops and textile mills in Bombay, Calcutta and Madras would take up the spirit of revolt and the strikes would threaten to spill over to the civilian population with sympathy spreading rapidly among the student bodies. It is rather ironical that, as evident by his speech at a mass rally in Singapore on 9 July 1943, this is exactly the scenario that Bose had envisaged: "When we do so, a revolution will break out, not only among the civil population at home, but also between the Indian Army, which is now standing under the British flag. When the British Government is thus attacked from both sides — from inside India and from outside — it will collapse and the Indian people will regain their liberty."[105] In his speech on the eve of leaving Burma, in April 1945, Bose again mentioned this intermingling of troops and warned of things to come: "Whatever reverses we have suffered during a campaign of about fifteen months ... There is, however, one silver lining ... Soldiers of the Azad Hind Fauj have had numerous opportunities of coming into close contact with members of the British Indian Army ... The effect of this experience on the British Indian Army, and all other Indians, who have come into Burma alongside of the British, is bound to be great in the days to come."[106]

Wilfred Russel, a British businessman who was in Bombay during those perilous days and who had come very close to mortal danger when the gun turret of the ship *Hindustan* was trained on the Yacht Club from where he was watching the proceedings, would observe: "I don't know whether it is a coincidence that full-blooded British rule in India began with a mutiny in the Army and ended with a mutiny in the Navy."[107] But for the troops on either side of the battle lines there was a sense of completing a full circle.

The inception of the British Indian Army in its modern avatar had been triggered by the 1857 rebellion. Prior to the British Crown taking control, precursor units of the army were under the East India Company. During the first half of the twentieth century, particularly after the establishment of the Military College in Dehradun and the subsequent Indianization of the Indian Army Officer Corps, the armed forces had seen a dramatic transition from being a glorified police force to evolving into a state-of-art, modern institution. Over the years the British had grown increasingly dependent on it for survival. It was an essential weapon for putting down local rebellions and had been extensively used across colonial Asia. By the time World War II broke out, India was the largest colonial contributor to the British war effort and the army numbers stood at around 205,000 men. During the war, with further recruitments, the ranks swelled and the Indian Army became the largest all-volunteer force in history. It was in the eastern theatre, rather than on the western front, that the Indian

Armoured Corps (IAC) came of age and Southeast Asia witnessed the largest use of Indian troops during the war.

The INA inspired strikes struck a blow to this crucial power-tool that connected the Raj with its subject nations. By the end of January 1946, there was a series of protests at Royal Air Force bases across the Southeast Asian crescent. They involved "perhaps fourteen stations and 50,000 men" and seemed to have begun in Karachi and rapidly spread across India and Singapore, creating a connecting wave of conflict across the crescent.[108] The apparent cause was poor food and living conditions and the enforced return to pre-war discipline. But in reality, the vast Indian army demoralized by continuous service at distant battlefronts during the war, was already struggling with a massive psychological dysfunction. The Red Fort trials of army men who had been their comrades-in-arms in the not-too-distant past and the subsequent enforced waiver of the British legislation was just the motivation required to spark off a full-scale mutiny. In Singapore, it began at Seletar and by next morning had spread to the Kallang aerodrome.[109] By summer, dissent had spread to the frontline troops: men from the Parachute Regiment, stationed at Malaya, protested against their living conditions and refused to obey the commanding officers' orders. The men were brought to trial en masse and sentenced to three to five years of penal servitude which was later commuted to two years' hard labour — "It was the British Army's Red Fort Trials".[110] Similar incidents happened across the theatre — each short-lived but increasingly connected. It was becoming progressively more obvious to the British that this loyal device which had helped perpetuate their supremacy through the two great wars was finally deserting them.

At the same time, it was clear that the Asian war would not end with the defeat of the Japanese in 1945. As radical and nationalist forces surfaced across the crescent, the SACSEA (Supreme Allied Commander of Southeast Asia) struggled to regain control. It was determined to deploy Indian troops not only in Burma, Malaya and Singapore, but also in Thailand and what had been French Indo-China and Dutch Indonesia. It was at this juncture that the SEAC (Southeast Asia Command) had become "more and more a purely British-Indian affair" started showing the first signs of cracking up.[111] Unfortunately, almost simultaneously, Vietnam and Indonesia proclaimed their independence during this period of interregnum and post-war power vacuum. While Sukarno and Hatta, under political pressure from the radical *permuda* groups, declared Indonesia to be independent on 17 August 1945; the *Viet Minh*, a communist and nationalist group, seized Hanoi and declared an independent provisional government on 2 September of the same year. The Indian National Congress, representing Indian public opinion, sent word supporting the two emerging nations. In October 1945, Lord Wavell, Viceroy of India, urged that the Indian troops be withdrawn from Vietnam and Indonesia as Nehru and Menon (V. K. Krishna Menon — Indian nationalist and Nehru's confidante) tried to rouse international opinion against British and French advances. On the battle lines in Vietnam, *Viet Minh* and communist cadres tried to win over the Indian army men to their side. Leaflets appeared denouncing the British: "You and your countrymen are struggling for independence as we are doing. Why are we struggling against each other?"[112] Like the INA, they decided the success of their revolution lay in the fast-widening lines of difference within the British army.

The British troops landed at Indonesia in October 1945. Of the battalions at the disposal of Mountbatten, only four were British. Reports on SEAC units in 1946 spoke of a "growing sympathy" for the INA and a deep dislike for the Dutch, who treated the sepoys as "natives".[113] One such Indian officer was S. K. Sinha, an ECIO (Emergency Commissioned Indian Officer) who was part of the G-3 Operations and attached to the HQ 15th Indian Corps at Jakarta, Indonesia. The original purpose of this corps was to take over from the Japanese forces and release Allied POWs and the civilian European captives. However, the mission soon turned into a war against Indonesian nationalist forces led by Sukarno. Sinha records feelings of unease and guilt at the role of Indian troops in subduing Indonesian nationalists while India herself was on the threshold of independence.[114] Whatever the outcome of the war at Vietnam or Indonesia, it was evident that the British Indian army was showing clear signs of unravelling.

The Red Fort trials and the aftermath impacted the subcontinent and the rest of Asia in different ways. It hit India when following the Quit India movement, the nationalist struggle was going through a period of torpor. The strikes in the armed forces and the great surge of patriotism that the trials unleashed propelled the country towards independence. But freedom was achieved at the cost of partition and the loss of thousands of innocent lives in the communal riots. What Nehru advocated as India's tryst with destiny, became the subcontinent's tryst with pain and loss. Poets on either side of the newly created border wrote of this bloody dawn. The partition left its wretched trail in the stories of Amrita Pritam and Manto and in the poetry of Faiz Ahmed Faiz.

Faiz writes movingly in *Subh-e-aazaadii*:

> ... We are told: our new dawn is already here;
> Your tired feet need journey no more
> Our rulers whisper seductively
> Why this constant struggle? Why, this perpetual search?
> ... This is yet no relief in the darkness of the night
> No liberation yet of our souls and minds
> So let us keep marching, my tiring friends
> We have yet to find our elusive dawn.

While the debate about the INA men raged on, thousands of Indian troops remained stationed across the Southeast Asian crescent under British command. They were a tired lot and had fought many wars. It did not take them long to realize the days of the colonial empire were waning. In a blurring of the lines of authority, they identified themselves with the nationalist struggle that was rapidly spreading across Asia. As 1946 wore on, the British too realized that the days of using the Indian Army as an instrument of British power were coming to an end. Local movements of national liberation in Burma could no longer be suppressed using Indian troops like before. The Red Fort trials' final verdict gave a new legitimacy to the INA which was mirrored in Aung San's BNA (Burma National Army) as well. Mustapha Hussain of KRIS in Malaya, had been arrested by the British for his collaboration with the Japanese. In 1946, he was released without a trial after 400 former Malay Regiment soldiers appealed on his behalf.[115] He had helped save their lives during the occupation period and now it was their turn to reciprocate. Incidents such as these spoke of a new rapprochement between soldiers and the local nationalist movements.

Across the crescent, the era of SACSEA authority was rapidly coming to an end. The founding of the new social order would take many years and the men and women from the disbanded INA would come to play a key role in this long process.

Notes

1. Clive J. Christie, *South East Asia in the Twentieth Century* (London: Tauris, 1998), Introduction.
2. "One of the most dramatic effects of the coming war was the way it forged the crescent into a bloodstained unity." Christopher Bayly and Tim Harper, *Forgotten Armies: Britain's Asian Empire and the War with Japan* (Penguin Books, 2005), p. 34.

3. Amartya Sen, *Poverty and Famines: An Essay on Entitlement and Deprivation* (Oxford: Clarendon Press, 1981), p. 58.
4. *Forgotten Armies*, p. 284.
5. Leonard A. Gordon, *Brothers Against the Raj: A Biography of Indian Nationalists* (New Delhi: Rupa & Co., 2008), p. 504.
6. Mrs Vijay Lakshmi Pandit — an Indian diplomat and politician, the first Indian woman to hold a Cabinet post, Nehru's sister, married to R. S. Pandit.
7. *Statesman*, India, 2 October 1943.
8. Subhas Chandra Bose, *Selected Speeches of Subhas Chandra Bose* (New Delhi: Government of India Publication Division, 1962), p. 206.
9. According to Gordon, *Brothers Against the Raj*, Bose was aware that the British were not only involved in blacking out the picture but also in negative propaganda against the INA, but given the wartime censorship and the fact that many of his supporters were in jail, he could not do much about it, p. 514.
10. *Syonan Times*, Malaya, 19 June 1943.
11. Ibid., 21 June 1943.
12. Sisir K. Bose and Sugata Bose, eds., *Chalo Delhi, 1943–1945,* Netaji Collected Works, vol. XII (Calcutta/New Delhi: Netaji Research Bureau/Permanent Black, 2007), pp. 45–48.
13. S. R. Nathan, *An Unexpected Journey: Path to the Presidency* (Singapore: EDM: 2011), p. 105.
14. Sugata Bose, *His Majesty's Opponent: Subhas Chandra Bose and India's Struggle Against Empire* (Cambridge MA: Harvard University Press, 2011), p. 246.
15. Ibid., p. 251.
16. *Chalo Delhi*, p. 117.
17. William Slim, *Defeat into Victory* (London: Cassell, 1956), pp. 150–51.
18. *Chalo Delhi*, p. 269.
19. *Chalo Delhi*, p. 324.
20. *Syonan Shinbun*, Malaya, 3 July 1945 to 10 July 1945.
21. Jan Becka, "Subhas Chandra Bose and the Burmese Freedom Movement", in *Netaji and India's Freedom*, edited by Sisir Kr Bose (Calcutta: Netaji Research Bureau, 1975), p. 55.

22. Sisir K. Bose, ed., *In Burmese Prisons, Correspondence May 1923–July 1926*, Netaji Collected Works, vol. III (Calcutta/New Delhi: Netaji Research Bureau/Permanent Black, 2009), p. 260.
23. Ibid., Letter to Dilip K. Roy, 11 September 1925.
24. *Forgotten Armies*, p. 11.
25. Rivers Salween, Sittang and Irrawady.
26. *Forgotten Armies*, p. 170.
27. Thet Lwin, "Indians in Myanmar", in *Rising India and Indian Communities in East Asia*, edited by K. Kesavapany, A. Mani and P. Ramaswamy (Singapore: Institute of Southeast Asian Studies, 2008), p. 487.
28. Tin Maung Maung Than, "Some Aspects of Indians in Rangoon", in *Indian Communities in Southeast Asia*, edited by K. S. Sandhu and A. Mani (Singapore: Institute of Southeast Asian Studies, 2006), p. 586.
29. Ibid., p. 586.
30. *Forgotten Armies*, p. 9.
31. Khin Maung Kyi, "Indians in Burma, Problems of an Alien Subculture in a Highly Integrated Society", in *Indian Communities in Southeast Asia*, edited by K. S. Sandhu and A. Mani, p. 635.
32. *Rangoon Times*, 15 August 1941.
33. *Forgotten Armies*, p. 167.
34. Tin Maung Maung Than, "Some Aspects of Indians in Rangoon", in *Indian Communities in Southeast Asia*, edited by K. S. Sandhu and A. Mani, p. 595.
35. *Forgotten Armies*, p. 372.
36. Ba Maw, *Breakthrough in Burma, Memoirs of a Revolution, 1939–1946* (New Haven: Yale University Press, 1968), pp. 329–30.
37. Jan Becka, "Subhas Chandra Bose and the Burmese Freedom Movement", p. 61.
38. Colonel G. S. Dhillon, "The Indo-Burman Relations during World War II", *The Oracle*, vol. VII, no. 3 (July 1985): 16.
39. Ba Maw, "The Great Asian Dreamer", *The Oracle*, vol. II, no. 1 (January 1980): 9.
40. Ibid., p. 10.
41. Lipi Ghosh, "Indian Revolutionaries and Subhas Chandra Bose in

Thailand: The Era of Plaek Pibulsongkram", in *Netaji and India's Freedom*, edited by Sisir Kr Bose (Calcutta: Netaji Research Bureau, 1975), p. 160.
42. Anne Boothe, *Colonial Legacies: Economic and Social Development in East and Southeast Asia* (Honululu: University of Hawaii Press, 2007), p. 122.
43. According to A. Mani in "Indians in Thailand", in *Indian Communities in Southeast Asia*, edited by K. S. Sandhu and A. Mani, p. 910, there is no available consensus but it is estimated that there were around 20,764 Indians in 1921 and according to the 1947 Census around 11,189 Indians in Thailand of whom 3,388 were females.
44. At this time the IIL in Thailand was primarily a Sikh organization linked to the Ghadr Party while the TBCL had a more eclectic mix of Indians.
45. Joyce Chapman Lebra, "Bose's Influence on the Formulation of Japanese Policy Toward India and the INA", in *Netaji and India's Freedom*, edited by Sisir Kr Bose (Calcutta: Netaji Research Bureau, 1975), p. 317.
46. At the Bangkok Conference, an invitation was extended to Subhas Chandra Bose to come to Asia and take over the reins of the freedom movement, Government of Japan, "4th Section, Asian Bureau, Ministry of Foreign Affairs", August 1956, p. 351.
47. Lipi Ghosh, "Indian Revolutionaries and Subhas Chandra Bose in Thailand: The Era of Plaek Pibulsongkram", p. 171.
48. Krishna Bose, *Charan Rekha Taba*, Bengali book (Calcutta: Ananda Publishers Pvt Limited, 1996), p. 180.
49. Jomo Kwame Sundaram, "Plantation Capital And Indian Labor in Colonial Malaya", in *Indian Communities in Southeast Asia*, edited by K. S. Sandhu and A. Mani, p. 288.
50. Ibid., p. 288.
51. Mohamed Amin and M. Caldwell, eds., *War, Boom and Depression, from Malaya: The Making of a Neo-Colony* (London: Spokesman Books, 1977), p. 32.

52. K. S. Sandhu, *Indians in Malaya: Immigration and Settlement, 1786–1957* (Great Britain: Cambridge University Press, 1969), p. 97.
53. Ibid., p. 159.
54. K. S. Sandhu, "The Coming of the Indians to Malaysia", in *Indian Communities in Southeast Asia*, edited by K. S. Sandhu and A. Mani, p. 151.
55. M. Stenson, *Industrial Conflict in Malaya* (London, New York: Oxford University Press, 1970), p. 17.
56. *Forgotten Armies*, p. 43.
57. J. N. Parmer, *Colonial Labor Policy and Administration: A History of Labor in the Rubber Plantation Industry in Malaya (1910–1941)* (New York: J. J. Augustin Incorporated Publisher, Locust Valley, 1960), p. 278.
58. J. K. Sundaram, "Plantation Capital and Indian Labor in Colonial Malaya", in *Indian Communities in Southeast Asia*, edited by K. S. Sandhu and A. Mani, p. 301.
59. S. Arasaratnam, *South Indians in Malaysia and Singapore* (London: Oxford University Press, 1970), p. 84.
60. Michael Stenson, *Class, Race and Colonialism in West Malaysia: The Indian Case* (St. Lucia [Australia]: University of Queensland Press; Hemel Hempstead, Eng., 1980), p. 70.
61. *Pinang Gazette and Straits Chronicle*, Malaya, 3 August 1936.
62. M. Stenson, *Industrial Conflict in Malaya* (London, New York: Oxford University Press, 1970), pp. 97–98.
63. Ellery C. Stowell, "Japan Joins the Axis", in *American Journal of International Law*, American Society of International Law, p. 711, <http://www.jstor.org.libproxy.nlb.gov.sg/stable/2192235> (accessed 20 November 2011).
64. Gordon, p. 461.
65. Joyce Chapman Lebra, *The Indian National Army and Japan* (Singapore: Institute of Southeast Asian Studies, 2008), p. 110.
66. Government of Japan, "4th Section, Asian Bureau, Ministry of Foreign Affairs", August 1956, pp. 340–41.
67. Joyce Chapman Lebra, ed., *Japan's Greater East Asia Co-Prosperity*

Sphere in World War II (Kuala Lumpur: Oxford University Press, 1975), p. 42.
68. Ibid., pp. 37–39.
69. Ibid., pp. 74–75.
70. Ibid., p. 80.
71. Government of Japan, "4th Section, Asian Bureau, Ministry of Foreign Affairs", pp. 360–63.
72. Ibid., p. 370.
73. *Chalo Delhi*, p. 162.
74. Subhas Chandra Bose, "The Cripps Mission II", *The Oracle*, vol. XVII, no. 3 (July 1995): 23.
75. Joyce Chapman Lebra, *The Indian National Army and Japan*, p. 143.
76. Ibid., p. 123.
77. Joyce Chapman Lebra, "Bose's Influence on the Formulation of Japanese Policy Toward India and the INA", in *Netaji and India's Freedom*, edited by Sisir Kr Bose (Calcutta: Netaji Research Bureau, 1975), p. 321. Professor Lebra quotes from Foreign Ministry, Asia Office, *Subhas Chandra Bose and Japan*, p. 100.
78. Joyce Chapman Lebra, *The Indian National Army and Japan*, pp. 123–24.
79. Ibid., p. 136.
80. Joyce Chapman Lebra, "Bose's Influence on the Formulation of Japanese Policy Toward India and the INA", pp. 324–25. Professor Lebra quotes from Foreign Ministry, Asia Office, *Subhas Chandra Bose and Japan*, p. 126.
81. Government of Japan, "4th Section, Asian Bureau, Ministry of Foreign Affairs", p. 381.
82. K. K. Ghosh, *The Indian National Army: Second Front of the Indian Independence Movement* (Meerut: Meenakshi Prakashan, 1969), p. 172.
83. Joyce Chapman Lebra, "Bose's Influence on the Formulation of Japanese Policy Toward India and the INA", p. 143.
84. K. K. Ghosh, *The Indian National Army, Second Front of the Indian Independence Movement*, p. 178.

85. Joyce Chapman Lebra, *The Indian National Army and Japan*, p. 174.
86. Krishna Bose, *Charan Rekha Taba*, pp. 64–66.
87. Ibid., p. 173.
88. Colonel P. K. Sahgal, "The Indian National Army", *The Oracle*, vol. XV, no. 1 (January 1993): 17, also cited in H. N. Pandit, *The Last Days of Netaji* (Delhi: Dariagunje, 1993), p. 79.
89. Hugh Toye, *The Springing Tiger: A Study of a Revolution* (Bombay: Jaico, 1959), p. 170.
90. S. A. Ayer, *Story of the INA* (New Delhi: National Book Trust, 1997), p. 82.
91. Ibid., p. 83.
92. Nirad C. Chaudhuri, "Subhas Chandra Bose, his Legacy and Legend", *Pacific Affairs*, vol. XXVI, no. 4 (December 1953): 350.
93. S. A. Ayer, *Story of the INA*, p. 87.
94. Krishna Bose, interview with the author in Calcutta, 28 March 2011.
95. *Selected Works of Nehru*, vol. XIV (New Delhi: Orient Longman, 1972), p. 279.
96. Nirad C. Chaudhuri, "Subhas Chandra Bose, His Legacy and Legend", *Pacific Affairs*, p. 352.
97. Mohammad Zaman Kiani, *India's Freedom Struggle and the Great INA, Memoirs of Maj Gen Mohammad Zaman Kiani* (New Delhi: Reliance Publishing House, 1994), pp. 179, 184.
98. Sugata Bose, *His Majesty's Opponent*, p. 7.
99. Colonel P. K. Sahgal, "Principles of Netaji's Strategy", *The Oracle*, vol. 1, no. 1 (January 1979): 40.
100. Mihir Bose, *The Lost Hero* (London, New York: Quartet Books, 1982), p. 263.
101. S. Ram and R. Kumar, *Role of INA and Indian Navy* (New Delhi: Commonwealth Publishers, 2008), p. 248.
102. Ibid., p. 216.
103. Ibid., p. 219, speech at Bombay, 26 February 1946, based on reports in *The Hindu*, 27 February 1946 and *National Herald*, India, 28 February 1946.

104. Ibid., p. 217.
105. *Chalo Delhi*, pp. 51–54.
106. Ibid., pp. 324–25.
107. Wilfred Russel, *Indian Summer* (Bombay: 1948), p. 12.
108. Christopher Bayly and Tim Harper, *Forgotten Wars, the End of the Britain's Asian Empire* (Penguin Books, 2008), p. 218.
109. Ibid., p. 219.
110. Ibid., p. 220.
111. Ibid., p. 139, words of Esler Dening, Mountbatten's political adviser.
112. Ibid., p. 155. The authors of *Forgotten Wars* quote from Gracey's Papers 4/20.
113. Ibid., p. 172. The authors of *Forgotten Wars* quote from Report on Morale of British, Indian and Colonial troops of ALFSEA, November 1945–January 1946, WO 203/4539, TNA.
114. P. Barua, Westport, *Gentlemen of the Raj, The Indian Army Officer's Corps, 1817–1949* (London: Conn. Praeger, 2003), p. 119.
115. Mustapha Hussain, *Malay Nationalism before UMNO: The Memoirs of Mustapha Hussain* (Kuala Lumpur: Utusan Publications & Distributors Sdn Bhd, 2005), p. 322. Earlier he writes of sharing food with an "old friend", Hamzah A. Cunard of the IIL at the Ipoh Central Police Station where they had been interned by the British Military Intelligence, p. 315.

Chapter 3

END OF A WAR, BEGINNING OF OTHERS

> "Though the days of the hero are o'er,
> ... He returns to Kinkora no more.
> That star of the field, which so often hath pour'd
> Its beam on the battle, is set;
> But enough of its glory remains on each sword,
> To light us to victory yet."
>
> — War Song, Thomas Moore

REPRESENTATIVE TENETS OF THE INA

The INA — Mercenaries or Patriots?

One of Krishna Bose's books, *Charana Rekha Taba* [In Your Footsteps] — which is a travelogue that doubles up as a historical narrative as the author traces Subhas Chandra Bose's footsteps across East Asia — recounts a rather memorable incident. The event occurred at Formosa (Taiwan). Bose was travelling to Tokyo, en route to possibly the Soviet Union on 17 August 1945. The Japanese Air Force bomber halted at the Taipei airport for refuelling. The engine of the aircraft had been giving trouble and soon after the plane was airborne again, there was a loud explosion and it tilted to the left and eventually crashed not far from the runway. The front of the plane caught fire and Bose and his sole Indian companion, Colonel Habibur Rahman, were badly burned. They pushed their way through the fire in the front because the way out towards the rear was already blocked. As the two men struggled out of the aircraft and lay down on the grass — exhausted and in intense pain, Bose turned towards his long-time friend and compatriot and asked in Hindustani, *"Aap ko zyada to nahin lagi?"* [Hope you are not too badly hurt?][1] Incidents such as these, when Bose expressed genuine concern for his colleagues are many; but this one, played out under a foreign sky, hours before he was to breathe his last, is perhaps the most poignant.

Another incident is narrated by Colonel Prem Kumar Sahgal, Military Secretary of the INA who, in the course of events, was tried for treason at the Red Fort. It was towards the end of battle in Burma, when the defeat of the Japanese and the INA loomed large on the horizon. The actual withdrawal from the war-front began on 9 April 1945. Units of No. 4 Guerilla Regiment were the first to withdraw. But on the morning of the 11th, British forces occupied Kyak-Padauo and the INA's direct line of retreat was cut off. Thereafter, it was decided that the Divisional Headquarters, the remainder of No. 4 Guerilla Regiment and No. 2 Infantry Regiment would attempt to break through the jungle route that night.

However, in the evening, the enemy attacked and surrounded one of the companies on outpost duty. Sahgal and his men's efforts to save those under siege, failed. Later Sahgal came to know from a British Intelligence Officer that the attacking forces had sent a note to the *Havildar* [a non-commissioned officer] commanding a platoon, asking him to surrender. But in reply, the *Havildar* had scribbled on the back of the note and sent it back, saying, "Mister, I do not come!" On that fateful night the entire platoon died fighting — right to the last man.[2]

The INA at various times has been castigated as a mercenary army which lacked political convictions. No doubt there were some number of men who would have joined to escape the wrath of the Samurai sword and it is also true that towards the end when the going got tough there were some who deserted to the British. There was Major B. J. S. Garewal, second-in-command of the Gandhi Brigade, and later some more officers from the second division who deserted to the British in the last confrontations at Mount Popa. They surrendered to the temptation of hope — the probability that they *might* escape British wrath rather than face the certainty of death and disease if they continued with the INA. But simultaneously, there are numerous tales like the one narrated by Colonel Sahgal, which speak of true patriotism and the spirit of sacrifice that permeated the army, from its leadership downwards.

There were some aspects of the operations of the INA and the Provisional Government of Azad Hind [Free India] which, without doubt, find resonance and perpetuation in the work of certain other Asian leaders. Key among these are perhaps the INA's egalitarian aspirations, the mass mobilization that it could achieve within the Indian community of Southeast Asia and the powerful and carefully planned publicity drive that it unleashed.

Religious and Regional Egalitarianism of the INA

Roman Script

Suniti Kumar Chatterjee, the famous Indian linguist and educationist who had travelled with Tagore on the poet's sojourn to the Southeast Asian islands, happened to be in Vienna in 1935.

He had already published his article on "A Roman Alphabet for India" in the *Calcutta University Journal* which had been the subject of much academic debate. One night, after an evening soiree at the Vetter residence, Subhas Chandra Bose took him to a nearby café. What ensued was a long, enthusiastic exchange of views on the Roman script. As the hands of the clock crept past midnight and the café staff got restive, Bose deliberated on the possibility of officially accepting the Roman script and using it to give India a unified, monolithic cultural structure. Chatterjee was convinced that the script was the least complicated and should be espoused in multi-lingual India.[3]

In fact, Bose, during his visit to Turkey in 1934, had been impressed with Kemal Ataturk's experiment with the Latin script. He felt that Persianized Hindustani was the natural lingua franca of Indians and its phonetic transcription in a universally recognized script, like the Roman one, would help Indians overcome apparently insurmountable language and racial barriers. Gandhi differed with Bose on this, and while accepting that a composite mixture of Urdu and Hindi worked well with the masses, advised Hindustani to be written in both the Devanagari and Urdu scripts to nurture a Hindu-Muslim bonding. Consequently, despite initial efforts by Nehru, the Roman script could not be popularized in India but Bose did use it as a powerful tool of communication in the INA of Southeast Asia. Every attempt was made to popularize Hindustani, right from the initial days, with classes for teaching the language being organized at the schools run by the INA Education and Culture department. The INA publications were in Hindustani, written in a Roman script, and so were the books meant for use by the students.[4] As a result of this concerted effort, the Tamil-speaking majority of Southeast Asia was very soon using both — the language and the new script. Captain Lakshmi Sahgal recalls, "Within three months illiterate recruits to the INA, those whose mother tongue was Tamil, Malayalam or Hindi, were able to read and write Roman Hindustani. It also proved to be a boon to the signaller who could train new recruits in the Morse code."[5] It proved to be a "boon" not only for the signaller but also for the INA at large, as it was one of the key unifying factors that would intimately integrate the diverse Indian community and hold it together through the thick of war.

Religious and Racial Unity

Abid Hasan, who had joined the INA movement while still an engineering student in Germany and had later accompanied Bose on the submarine journey to Asia, writes in his memoirs that while he and his men made their tortuous way back from Imphal, he wondered about the INA's multi-religious community. Moulmein, their immediate destination, seemed very far away as they crossed the Chindwin river, swollen with monsoon tide and trekked over the Karan hills. There was time for thought and retrospective dissection of their military campaign. He wondered what was the "force" that united the INA; what made the Tamilian, the Dogra, the Baluchi, the Assamese, the Bengali Brahmin, the Punjabi Muslim and the *Adivasi* [heterogeneous set of ethnic and tribal groups] come together as an indivisible whole?[6]

Bose, in the INA, was able to restructure communal relations and place them outside the traditional context of religious reference. Unlike Nehru, he did not interpret secularity as a dysfunction between state and religion but as a basis of building closer links between conflicting sectarian beliefs. According to him, the cultural and religious plurality of India could not be ignored but could definitely be overcome. The work he had started during his political career in India, took a more wholesome and practical shape in Southeast Asia. While firmly maintaining individual religious identities, he encouraged joint celebrations of religious festivals. For Diwali, the Muslim Officers would organize a *Bada Khana* [ceremonial feast], while for Id the Hindus would do the same for their Muslim colleagues. For Christmas there would be carol singing organized by the Rani of Jhansi girls despite there being very few Christians in the regiment.[7] But while religious beliefs and identities were respected, they never formed a part of the INA's public persona. The INA spirit expressed itself solely through its nationalist fervour. The strength of this conviction is borne out by the oft-narrated incident about the priests of the Chettyar temple at Singapore. Abid Hasan, who was to later append a *Safrani* denoting the Hindu colour saffron to his name as a mark of communal amity, recounts that the Chettyar priests invited Bose to the temple to celebrate *Dusshera* [Hindu festival]. The Chettyars were an affluent community and their generous donations did come in handy for the INA funds. However, Bose turned down the invite, saying he would not enter a place of worship where not only Indians of other faiths but even Hindus from lower castes were not allowed. Rather than taking affront, the Chettyars decided to organize a national rally on the day of *Dusshera*. The temple precincts were filled to capacity, with men in the INA uniform and South Indian Muslims in black caps. This time, Bose not only graced the occasion with his entire entourage, he also delivered a moving speech. However, while leaving, once he crossed the threshold of the temple, Bose wiped off the *tilak* [religious mark] that the priests had so reverently drawn on his forehead.[8] The message was clear to all — religion was for everybody, irrespective of race or caste, but it could never overshadow the nationalist ideology of the INA. In the same spirit, traditional greetings like "Jai Ram Ji Ki" and "Salaam Alaikum", with their religious connotations, were forsaken and the more patriotic "Jai Hind" evolved instead; the then prevalent national anthem "Vande Mataram" was abandoned, since Muslims could not identify with its spirit of mother worship, and instead, a simple Hindustani translation of Tagore's *"Jana Gana Mana"* was adopted, albeit with a more militaristic beat to it.

Bose was himself a believer and conceded the significance of religion in one's personal life, but was also aware of the fact that just as religion could be used to unite, it could also be manoeuvred to incite divisive sentiments.[9] As he proudly proclaimed at a press interview in June 1943, "In my National Movement the religious question does not exist. I have followers among all Indians, in particular among the Mohamedans who, according to the British, pursue separatist aims."[10] He strongly maintained that the multi-religious, multi-caste, multi-racial divides of India were a part of the "fable" created by British propaganda.[11] According to him, the Muslim problem was an artificial creation by them similar to the "Ulster problem in Ireland" or the "Jewish problem in Palestine".[12]

Major General Mohammad Zaman Kiani, the Chief-of-Staff of the INA, who after the partition of the Indian subcontinent would settle in Pakistan, mentions the existence of hostilities between the Sikhs and the Muslims while the INA was under the leadership of Mohan Singh. This was sometime before the Bangkok Conference, in June 1942, when Mohan Singh needed to build a clique of loyal supporters to bolster his leadership in his conflicts with not only the ageing IIL (Indian Independence League) leader, Rashbehari Bose, but also his arch rival, Lieutenant Colonel N. S. Gill. In Kiani's opinion, "The Muslim Officers were particularly suspect as, despite a sort of camaraderie brought about by regimental life, there was no love lost between the Sikhs and the Muslims." Mohan Singh felt that while the non-Muslims would remain with him, the Muslims would remain hostile at heart.[13] The feeling of distrust was reciprocated by the Muslim faction of the troops. At this time the Japanese reigned supreme in Southeast Asia and the Western Pacific and seemed poised for a siege on India. Under the circumstances, the Muslims faced a dilemma: "They were not at all happy to be placed under a Sikh [Mohan Singh], with almost unlimited power over them as POWs." At the same time, "They were apprehensive of a non-Muslim army marching into India with the Japanese"[14]

M. Sivaram, a journalist who would later handle the propaganda work for the INA, also mentions the diverse warring factions that tore apart the IIL in its earlier avatar, under the leadership of Rashbehari Bose. The Bangkok Conference of East Asia Indians held its formal opening session on 15 June 1942. And despite the flag-hoisting, the patriotic slogans and the life-sized portraits of Indian leaders which graced the walls, for N. Raghavan, presiding over these sessions, it was a trying experience to regulate the proceedings with some semblance of good order: "It produced a spicy fragment of Indian politics in all its complexity."[15] "Was it right to trust the Japanese?", asked one group; "Which territorial unit of the movement was most important — Japan, Thailand, Malaya or Burma?", asked another; "Weren't these military delegates mere mercenaries of the British until the other day?", asked a third.[16] It needed a leader of Subhas Chandra Bose's stature and international repute to sweep aside this petty bickering and focus on the key issue of India's freedom.

Subhas Chandra Bose's reputation preceded him and worked magic on the Southeast Asian imagination. For the common man of the migrant community, he was already larger than life. He had presented the Indian case to international leaders like Hitler, Mussolini and Tojo; he had worked in India with Gandhi and Nehru and was the bearer of Sri Aurobindo's message to Asia. He had staged an audacious escape from British bondage, in the tradition of Aurobindo and Rashbehari Bose himself. When he addressed the masses in chaste Hindustani and reached out to the minority groups, there could be no holding back. But it was not only his reputation and liaises with noted personalities; it was also the man himself. He was known for his singular efforts in India to work with minority communities. He had tried to execute the Bengal Pact with the Muslim population in all earnestness. In fact in 1940, at the time of his arrest and subsequent "Great Escape" to Europe while awaiting trial, he had been leading an all-out agitation to demolish the Holwell Monument, considered a slur on the name of Siraj-ud-dawla, the last independent Nawab of Bengal.[17] Like Gandhis' *Khilafat* movement, Bose's joint agitation with the Muslim League against this "Black Hole" of Calcutta had mobilized the masses. Much later, in Burma in 1943, when he stood before Bahadur Shah Zafar's tomb, he paid homage to the Indian emperor not only because he had given a "clarion call" to his countrymen to fight the British but because under his flag, "the Hindus, Sikhs" and "freedom loving Muslims" fought side by side in India's first war of independence.[18] Though multi-religious and multi-regional groups had enlisted in the INA prior to Bose's leadership, it was under Bose that they were welded together as a cohesive unit. The first unit of the INA, consisting of some 10,000 soldiers was placed under a Muslim — Mohammad Zaman Kiani. When he raised a new regiment for guerilla warfare, Bose selected a Muslim Officer, Shah Nawaz Khan, to command it, and when he left Southeast Asia on his ill-destined, final voyage, his sole companion was Habibur Rahman — again a Muslim. Gandhi remarked on this aspect of the INA when he said: "Though the INA failed in their immediate objective, they have a lot to their credit of which they might well be proud. The greatest among these was to gather together, under one banner, men from all religions and races of India, and infuse into them the spirit of solidarity and oneness to the utter exclusion of all communal and parochial sentiment."[19]

Mass Mobilization by the INA

Soon after he formally took over the mantle of Rashbehari Bose and assumed leadership, Bose gave the Indian civilians in Southeast Asia a new slogan: "Total Mobilization for a Total War". On 9 July 1943, at a mass rally in Singapore, he declared, "Friends! We have for a long time, been hearing so much of the Second Front in Europe. But our countrymen at home are now hard pressed, and they are demanding a Second Front. Give me Total Mobilization in East Asia and I promise you a second front — a real second front for the Indian struggle."[20] According to him, "half-hearted measures" would not do anymore; the time had come for the "three million Indians living in East Asia to mobilize all their available resources — including money and manpower". Unlike the earlier leadership's focus on the POWs from the British Indian Army, the emotional connect Bose built with the civilians was intense and comprehensive. The movement impacted all sections of society — the men joined the INA, the women the Rani of Jhansi Regiment and the youth the *Balak Sena* [youth wing]. The civilians who were declared physically infirm or unfit for the army, joined the numerous branch offices of the IIL in various capacities. No stones were left unturned to spread the nationalist message to the poor and marginalized as well — that section of the population who could neither enlist for the army nor contribute to the INA funds. John A. Thivy, who would later found the Malayan Indian Congress (MIC), reminiscences of the charitable work the INA's Health and Social Department did with the poor and the illiterate, who could be nothing but a "deadweight on the revolution".[21] In order to make it all the more popular, the

Provisional Government of Azad Hind's membership came with certain privileges. It was affordable to everybody — membership fee was a mere $1. Holding the small blue membership card entitled the member to uninterrupted movements within the country of his residence and to assistance from branches and sub-branches of the League, all over East Asia.[22] After the formation of the Provisional Government, each member took an oath of allegiance to faithfully serve the Provisional Government of Azad Hind under the leadership of Subhas Chandra Bose. On 21 October 1943, the first one to take the oath of allegiance was Bose himself. He committed himself to serve India with the last drop of his blood and fight for the liberty of his 380 million fellow-countrymen. The ceremony was a solemn one, charged with high emotions. After him, it was the turn of the Ministers and Advisers of the Provisional Government to step up to the Head of State and take their oaths. In the days that followed, the Office-bearers and the staff of the League took their oaths. Later it was the turn of the public. All members of the movement took the oath at mass meetings specially organized for this purpose. Each person received a card with the words of the oath written on it: "I, a member of the Azad Hind Sangh [Indian Independence League], do hereby solemnly promise in the name of God and take this holy oath that I will be absolutely loyal and faithful to the Provisional Government of Azad Hind, and shall be always prepared for any sacrifice for the cause of the freedom of our motherland, under the leadership of Subhas Chandra Bose." By dint of this oath, the Indians domiciled abroad became free citizens of India. The card was signed by both the recipient as well as the League Officer who administered it.[23] What Bose sought to achieve through this elaborately orchestrated oath-taking ceremony, cascading over each hierarchical tier of the movement, was an emotional commitment to the cause. By June

1944, 230,000 Indians took the written oath in Malaya alone.²⁴ It was a one-on-one connect that Bose sought between the vast migrant population and the cause to which they were now very consciously committing themselves.

After taking over, Bose went about reorganizing the League Headquarters. What he achieved was a vast structure with an extensive network of State Branches and Sub-Branches which reported to the Territorial Branch Departments while the Territorial Branches in turn, acted as liaison departments between the Headquarters and the Units. The Branch and Sub-Branch Training and Recruitment Departments took in not only those who by age and physique were fit to join the army but also office-bearers, merchants, shopkeepers and clerical staff working with the local governments. They were given training as per their skill set and provided opportunities in the various departments of the League or the back-room support groups of the army. This meant an all-enveloping influence of the movement. Even those not directly involved, were exposed to the INA via the mass rallies and radio and print campaigns. Some members of the Ceylonese community were also inspired to join the struggle, particularly in Malaya. Subsequently, a Ceylon Department was started at the INA Headquarters and then at the Branch and Sub-Branch Offices in localities which were Ceylonese. Later, a Lanka Unit was formed to train Ceylonese boys and girls to join the INA and the RJR, though all along Bose ensured that the Ceylonese members had the option of joining the Indian or Ceylonese departments of the League, according to personal predilection.²⁵

With his policy of "Total Mobilization" Bose endeavored to engage the hearts and minds of the entire Indian population. He had witnessed the inexorable power that mass sentiments could unleash during Gandhi's famous *Dandi* March. Gandhi had successfully forged an emotive connect with the masses over the symbolic salt tax laws back in India in the 1930s. As a result an entire country had been galvanized into supporting the Civil Disobedience movement, casting aside the traditional barriers of class, religion or gender. That Bose was aware of the consequences of effectively handling mass emotion is evident in one of his speeches: "Mass consciousness has been roused in India, thanks to the extensive and intensive propaganda undertaken during the non-cooperation movement; and the mass movement cannot possibly be checked now."[26] And more than just physical numbers, it is this mass movement, this emotional juggernaut that he wanted to set into motion against the overpowering British hegemony in Asia.

The INA's Propaganda War

M. Sivaram had worked as a journalist all over the world as well as with Reuters in London. After he joined the League, he held a position of eminence in the League's Publicity Department as the Director of the Azad Hind [Free India] Broadcasting Station and the Chief Editor of the Azad Hind newspapers. Sivaram recounts innumerable evenings which he spent along with S. A. Ayer, Minister for Publicity and Propaganda with the Azad Hind Government, at Bose's Meyer Road bungalow in Singapore. This was just after Bose had taken over charge in 1943 and they would sit discussing the INA's propaganda strategy into the early hours of the morning. Countless cigarettes would be smoked as they tried to stave off the slumber induced by the warm sea breeze. Bose was indefatigable in his enthusiasm and single-minded focus on mass communication. On one such evening he advised, "Propaganda must be bumptious to be really effective. We must always be thinking up new things to hold the interest of the people."[27] This would remain the underlying theme of the INA's publicity campaigns: they would consistently reach out to the last man in the crowd, be aggressive enough to rivet public interest and always be larger than life to capture popular imagination.

Subhas Bose had once said that he envied the British most for their special skill in propaganda, which was at times more powerful than "howitzers".[28] Sure enough, the propaganda war that ensued between the INA and the British was no less intense than their actual battle for physical supremacy. Right from the time when the IIL was initiated, British propaganda from New Delhi made a conscious effort to obscure it from public vision. In the earlier stages, New Delhi remained silent, and later, when it was impossible to ignore the League any longer, they were ambiguous enough in their reporting to confound public opinion. Bose's arrival from Germany to East Asia sparked global interest and yet the British propaganda machinery in India either maintained its quiescence or slandered Bose as a Japanese puppet. It was a time of internal disturbance in India, following the Quit India movement. Lord Wavell had succeeded Lord Linlithgow as the Viceroy and preparations were in full swing for the Anglo-American war efforts in which India would be a powerful Allied base. Under the circumstances, the British, for obvious reasons, chose to deliberately mislead public opinion about trouble brewing across the border under the popular leadership of Subhas Chandra Bose. Initially, Bose and his team often wondered about the stoic silence that the British-controlled All India Radio (Bose in his broadcasts chose to call it the "anti-India Radio" and the BBC the "Bluff and Bluster Corporation") maintained about the very existence of the INA. He once supposedly said with a twinkle in his eye, "Probably, Gandhiji will wire me his congratulations when we reach Calcutta."[29] In August 1944 Bose mentioned, "I have been keenly watching the methods employed by Allied propagandists … When the formation of the Indian National Army was first announced they were discreetly silent. When they realized that the news was known, they stated that it was a nominal army of war prisoners compelled by Japan to fight against their own people."³⁰ Consequently, Bose was all the more aggressive in his propaganda strategy. He not only needed to arouse the civilian Indian population of Southeast Asia from their customary apathy and move towards his objective of "Total Mobilization", but also had to cut through the wartime smokescreen imposed by the British and convey his message to India. In a broadcast, on 12 July 1944, he cited from books like *Secrets of Crew House* and Posenby's *Wartime Falsehoods* to illustrate the falsities that the British propagandists were capable of. In the same speech he also referred to British attempts at darkening his reputation: now that he was working with the Japanese, the All India Radio reported fictitious fallouts between him and the Japanese Government and earlier when he had travelled to Southeast Asia they said he had been compelled to do so because of differences with the German Government, but, "the public reply to that lie was given when the German Government gave its wholehearted support to the Provisional Government of Azad Hind ..."³¹

While on one hand, he needed to alert his countrymen to the dangers of British propaganda, Bose also devoted a substantial part of the publicity campaign to infiltrating the British Indian Army. He took forward the vigorous campaign launched by Pritam Singh and Mohan Singh in spreading the message of nationalism among the Indian soldiers of the British Army. The dropping of propaganda leaflets in different languages on the army from Japanese planes had been in prevalence since early 1941 and had yielded some results. During Bose's time, regular broadcasts from some of the key army personnel like Lieutenant Colonel Loganathan, Lieutenant Colonel Aziz Ahmad, Major Bishen Singh would be aired on the Azad Hind Radio to impel the Indian soldiers to cross over and join the INA.[32] Bose was aware that the eventual fate of the INA would depend on a shift in loyalties among these soldiers.

Bose did not take much time to swing the propaganda machinery into action in Southeast Asia because he had had adequate experience in the past. Even when he joined Indian politics, under the mentorship of C. R. Das, he had been assigned stewardship role for the Bengali nationalist daily, *Banglar Katha* and soon afterwards, the publicity work for the Bengal Provincial Congress Committee as well.[33] *Banglar Katha* was not the sole example. There were others, like the more ambitious English daily, *Forward* and the Bengali *Atma Sakti* — both of which were started under the leadership of Das and were later managed by Bose. In Germany too, from the Free India Centre, headquartered at Lichtensteinallee, he had taken India's message to the world.

Fully aware of the art of modern mass communication, soon after he took over IIL, Bose ensured there were some reshuffling in the League: out of the first five departments to be announced, two were for Publicity/Propaganda and Intelligence.[34] The Publicity Department which was already in existence, was rechristened Department of Publicity, Press and Propaganda, to convey its new and largely amplified role and S. A. Ayer was appointed the Minister for Publicity and Propaganda by the Provisional Government of Azad Hind.[35] The hierarchical pyramid of the Propaganda Department was huge with propaganda squads attached to every unit of the INA at the grass-roots level and with a multi-layered team at the state and territorial levels.

Bose's sensitizing campaign in Asia started soon after his reaching Tokyo in May 1943. In fact it had been under gestation during the long submarine voyage which had been spent in writing speeches and discussing the forthcoming meeting with the Japanese Premier. Once he reached Tokyo, he met a range of Japanese officials before his actual one-on-one with Tojo. According to Abid Hasan, during these initial meetings he was preparing ground and working on creating a "Subhas Lobby" of sorts, which would later help him in garnering support for his work in East Asia.[36] Bose remained in Tokyo for nearly a fortnight and he made sure that he hit the headlines almost every day, with press conferences, radio broadcasts, interviews with the Japanese Ministers, official banquets, public speeches and roundtable discussions on the Indian problem. This whirlwind of publicity remained unabated after he arrived at Singapore on 2 July. Very soon the Indian population not only had a new leader but a new war cry "Chalo Delhi", a new slogan "Total Mobilization for a Total War" and eventually a new Provisional Government. There was no way the activities of the League could be ignored. In these initial stages, Bose's purpose was to raise awareness levels and help in opinion building among the masses: the publicity campaigns were a sustained education drive on India. He sought to trace the history of Britain's true motives in India as well as sensitize the public of the real aims of the INA. He spoke of how under British rule communal differences were fostered in India, how her economy had been crippled and how ruthlessly India's first war of independence in 1857 had been crushed. The same message was carried by the Education and Culture Department to the schools and at the stage performances of the League workers. It was a time when hitherto obscure names of India's war heroes — Bahadur Shah Zafar, Tantia Tope, Tipu Sultan, Peshwa Baji Rao, Rani Laxmibai of Jhansi — gained in popularity and the illiterate masses could make an informed choice between Gandhi's Civil Disobedience and the INA's armed struggle. The money and gold that flowed into the INA coffers, as a result of this awareness drive, also served Bose's ultimate aim of reducing the movement's dependence on the financial aid from Japan.

With the contributions he would set up the National Bank of Azad Hind in Rangoon for bearing, at least partially, the expenses of the INA's war efforts.

This unrelenting propaganda continued till the very end. Towards the end, the campaigns were more so that Bose could carry public opinion with him and strengthen the spirits of his people during the time of crisis. If Bose "was worried, he did not reveal his thoughts and feeling, even to his closest associates".[37] Instead, "Netaji Week" was celebrated between 4 and 10 July 1945 to commemorate his taking over leadership of the Indian independence movement in Asia. It was a grand show with military parades, mass rallies and demonstrations. Gallantry awards like the "Sevak-e-Hind" and "Veer-e-Hind" were presented and there was a general round of promotions in the League and the army. The celebrations received widespread publicity in the newspapers of the time.[38] Even when the INA's victory march to Delhi was obviously over and Japan had been conclusively defeated, Bose coined a new slogan for the INA which held out new hope for its members: "But the roads to Delhi are many, like the roads to Rome. And along one of these many roads we shall travel and ultimately reach our destination, the metropolis of India."[39]

Public Rallies

In the endless publicity drives, Subhas Chandra Bose's own personality as a towering military leader played a key role. Sivaram recounts that Rashbehari Bose had envisaged the title of *Deshsevak*, meaning one who serves his country, for Bose. He concluded his speech, introducing the younger Bose at the first public meeting held at Singapore, with the slogan "Deshsevak Subhas Ki Jai".[40] But, unknown to Rashbehari Bose, serious thought had already been given to the title *Netaji* meaning a revered leader, by

Bose and his senior colleagues. And in this difference in epithet lies the key. Bose wanted to consciously discard the traditional Indian image conveying humility and servitude, popularized by Gandhi. Instead he sought to project himself as a martial leader who could inspire confidence in his people and take on the mighty British in mortal combat.

On 4 July 1943, Bose made his first public appearance at the Cathay Theatre in Singapore. This first public appearance was also the last time that Bose donned civilian dress in East Asia as he formally accepted the leadership of the Indian Independence League from the veteran leader, Rashbehari Bose. The following day, on 5 July, he appeared at the Singapore Padang to address a gathering of thousands of Indian soldiers and civilians. The 5 July parade would set an important precedent in Southeast Asia. On this day he would change to military greens and top boots and the metamorphoses would have a remarkable impact on his army officials as well as the common Indian. It was almost like he was holding himself up to public view as a symbol of Indian aspiration. The persona of a triumphant military leader was borne out by the grand scale of the mass rallies: Japanese military trucks with mounted machine guns and a fleet of cars carrying his personal staff, all flying the Indian tricolour, escorted Bose in his campaigns across Southeast Asia. He would often drive into these mass rallies, standing upright in an open military jeep, smilingly acknowledging the cheers of the jubilant crowd — it was a show orchestrated to inspire pride and confidence in the long persecuted Indians' feeble hearts.

Public Speeches

The tone of the INA's publicity campaigns was set by Subhas Bose's own political speeches. He never missed the opportunity of any public gathering, be it mass meetings, conferences, or interviews to communicate INA's message to the external world. He had learned the art of debating in his early years at Presidency College, as Secretary of the Philosophical Society of the Scottish Church College and at the Indian "Majlis" at Cambridge. Later, he had had plenty of scope to hone this skill, first at the Congress summits and then as India's emissary-in-bondage, during the years of forced exile in Europe. Bose, in his writing or his speeches was never flamboyant in his choice of expressions. Rather, he was more intuitive in his feel for the English language and understood its subtle nuances well. His book *The Indian Struggle* had already garnered praise in international circles. The *Manchester Guardian* had hailed it as the, "most interesting book which has yet been written by an Indian politician on Indian politics", while the *Sunday Times* had admitted, it had a point of view which was hard to ignore.[41] As far as Hindustani was concerned, initially he had grappled with it, much to the amusement of his Hindi-speaking colleagues, but later gained better control in not only the basic language but in the charming Urdu embellishments which added to its delicacy and appeal. His speeches have been compared in their political eloquence to the tradition of Pericles or Churchill. Though according to Girija Mukherjee, his long-term associate in Europe, Bose was not a particularly great orator — his delivery being slow and his choice of words being far from dynamic; however, the honesty and conviction with which he spoke was what set him apart. Recalling his first public speech in Singapore, Captain Lakshmi Sahgal also wrote that he had completely convinced all with his "utter sincerity and iron determination".[42] This earnest simplicity of his arguments combined with the grandiose scale of the INA mass rallies proved to be a potent formula, the alchemy of which never failed to generate vigorous enthusiasm among the people.

Print Media

Besides the public platform, the INA also used the print media well. Soon after Bose took over, Indian newspapers like *Kerala Bandhu* and *Tamil Murasu* became the mouthpieces of the movement. Besides, the pre-war daily, *Strait Times*, which had been rechristened the *Syonan Times* after the British surrender in 1942, was majorly used as a major publicity vehicle. Apart from the existing newspapers, the League also ran newspaper offices of its own, both at the central and territorial levels. News dailies, periodicals and bulletins were edited and published at these offices in English, Hindustani, Tamil and Malayalam. The *Azad Hind*, selling at 5 cents a copy and also with a Tamil edition, was a leading example. Sivaram, who went to Rangoon as a part of the advance party to set up the Field Propaganda Unit in Burma before the advent of war, recalls starting an English daily in Burma called *Azad Hind* on the lines of the Singapore model and two other dailies in Hindustani and Tamil. He had as many as 300 young men training under him for this purpose.[43] The message was clear: the propaganda unit had as much to contribute to the military campaign as the front-line soldiers.

Radio

During the war the radio was the only channel of news exchange between countries. Though under shadow of heavy censorship, Bose made optimum use of the radio and wireless to spread his message. He had established the Azad Hind Radio in Germany and by early 1942, broadcasts were made from there in English, Hindustani and half a dozen other Indian languages with Bose as the representative voice. A powerful Philips transmitter at Huizen, in Netherlands, was used to air the broadcasts to India. It was from this radio station that Bose had announced to his countrymen that despite contrary reports, he had surfaced alive in Berlin after his hazardous escape from his home in Calcutta. Later, he had launched the Azad Muslim Radio to voice the views of the nationalist Muslims and counter separatist activities. The INA continued to harness the power of wartime radio broadcasts in Asia as well. Stations were set up in Thailand, Burma, Malaya, Indo-China and Japan — each with its own staff of writers, commentators and announcers. Besides, the League enjoyed its special hour on the local Japanese-controlled broadcasting stations. Other than news and news commentaries, there was light entertainment to tempt the Indian audience. The Azad Hind Radio was also often used by Southeast Asian Indians to convey messages to their loved ones back in India as many families were traumatized by wartime separations. Gerald de Cruz, working at the Free India Radio Station at Saigon (Gerald would later join the left-wing student movement at the University of Malaya), recalls sending a message to his sister, Hazel, who had been sent away to live with relatives in India to protect her from the Japanese. Otherwise, Gerald's principal job was to write the anti-British talks which were broadcast to India on a weekly basis.[44]

During the war in Burma, Bose would broadcast on the radio almost daily, exhorting the Indians in Southeast Asia and trying to penetrate British censorship to reach out to India and solicit his country's support for the campaign. But unfortunately, thanks to British efforts, the outreach of his propaganda would remain woefully low in India and not until the Red Fort Trials would Indians be aware of the true magnitude of the INA campaign.

The publicity machinery that the INA built up was colossal, and Bose played a pivotal role in not only conceptualizing it in its entirety but in lending his own charismatic personality to add to the popular appeal. He was a personification of all that the INA campaigned for — military courage, patriotism and the spirit of sacrifice. But what was remarkable was that, at a certain point, Bose remained untouched by the furore of activity that surrounded him — the public persona could never subsume the real man. All through the turbulence of war and the disenchantment of defeat, he remained true to his personal spiritual beliefs; never failing to retire to the cloistered calm of his room or a certain monastery in Singapore for prayers and meditation. Major Takahashi of the *Hikari Kikan* recounts, during the retreat from Burma, punctuated with talks with his troops exhorting them to carry on the struggle and discussions with his army commanders on the future course of the battle, there were interludes when Bose would pick up a book on the Irish independence struggle. One night in Pyinmina, where he reached on 27 February 1945 and from where he endeavored to launch his "last battle against the British", he said: "The book on Irish independence says that, at the beginning of the campaign ... all the patriots were killed ... But after some decades, people ... followed the line of those patriots and finally won independence. Now we face [such a] situation. And I am prepared to die in my last fight ..."[45] The incident happened when publicly he had still not relinquished his desire for victory and was yet to declare, "But the roads to Delhi are many ..." Yet in his wistful death-wish he sounds strangely detached, echoing the convictions of early youth when he would write to his mother expressing a strong desire to die a martyr for the cause. It is almost as if he sought an escape to the purity of adolescent faith, when his mission lay before him, untarnished by the complexities of an external adult world. The futility of it all strikes him, as it did many other thinkers of the time:

> Ganga was sunken, and the limp leaves
> Waited for rain, while the black clouds
> Gathered far distant, over Himavant.

> The jungle crouched, humped in silence.
> Then spoke the thunder
> *Da*
> *Datta*: what have we given?
> My friend, blood shaking my heart
> The awful daring of a moment's surrender
> Which an age of prudence can never retract[46]

THE POLITICAL LEGACY OF BOSE IN BURMA

Indo-Burmese relations during the years of the two countries' nationalist struggle flowed in two distinctly different and mutually exclusive patterns. The two streams flow concurrently and at times, one eclipses but can never obliterate the other. The first gravitates round the majority-minority issue of the Burmese and Indian populations. This conflict had been raging in Burma since the inception of British dominion and placed the Burmese and migrant Indians in hostile camps. While the second, focused on the Indian and Burmese nationalist movements. This one is a more positive relationship with the Burmese at times looking on the Indians for ideological direction and implementation strategies. The Indian National Congress and Gandhi had influenced Burmese nationalists since the 1920s. Gandhi's non-cooperation movement had been adopted by some Burmese and activists like the monks, U Ottama and U Wisara, popularized the wearing of *pinni*, a handspun indigenous cloth similar to the *khadi* in India. They also fostered boycotts and home rule campaigns. But with time, the Burmese faith in non-violence as a practical means of countering imperialism seemed to be eroding. The 1930s was an era of severe economic depression and the Burmese freedom struggle at this time was led by the Dobama Asi-Ayon (DAA or the We Burmans Association). The *Thakins* of the Dobama Asi-

Ayon believed in the supremacy of the Burmans and the DAA was born after the *Saya San* revolutions and the ensuing massacre of Indian dockyard workers by the Burmese who felt Indians had usurped their jobs. Ironically enough, in the later years the DAA came to be influenced by the Indian Congress in their resistance strategy. By 1938, the new generation radical leaders of DAA regularly sent delegates to the Congress sessions. Communism was a new entrant in Burma and the *Thakins* found natural affinity with the left-wing of the Congress. The Communist Party of Burma was formally established in August 1939 and the young party also looked for ideological and political mentoring. Besides, during the 1930s, the *Thakins* had experimented with Gandhian methods of Civil Disobedience but by 1938–39 realized that these constitutional campaigns did not accomplish anything substantial for their cause. Instead, in 1940, there were large-scale arrests of nationalist by the British on charges of sedition. Consequently, the *Thakins* were drawn closer to the radical views of Subhas Chandra Bose and were increasingly convinced that the armed struggle advocated by him was a viable and perhaps more pragmatic alternative to the Gandhian ideology of non-violence. As the President of the Indian National Congress (INC) and then the leader of Forward Bloc, Bose was a familiar figure among the young DAA leadership. With war breaking out in Europe, like Bose, a faction of the Burmese leaders strongly felt the global scenario could be used to their advantage — both toyed with the idea of striking an alliance with a foreign power and opening yet another war front against the British. A *Thakin* delegation met Bose twice in 1940, while attending the Ramgarh session of the INC in India.[47] However, before any closer connections between the parties could be worked out, British reprisals started with renewed vigour and large numbers of nationalist activists from both countries, including Bose, were interned. It was left to the ingenuity of the leaders of both countries to escape British vigilance and discover new ways to take their struggle forward.

Bose and Ba Maw

According to Ba Maw, the premier of the nominally independent Burma from 1 August 1943, there was yet another reason why the DAA gravitated towards a policy of armed intervention and hence towards Subhas Bose. He held responsible an inherent trait in the Burmese people: they cannot think of a "mass revolutionary struggle" being successful "without revolutionary violence" and it was but natural that a "figure like Subhas Chandra Bose, young, brilliant, revolutionary, should appeal to them, and in particular to the youth".[48] Like any other historical event, the causes that led up to the sense of kinship between the *Thakins* and Bose were multi-layered. And consequently when he physically arrived at Southeast Asia, he was already a familiar figure, in name if not in form, to the Burmese leadership. Ba Maw writes, "... even before his dramatic appearance in Singapore ... his name had travelled widely in the region, so much so that when people thought of India, they thought of him more than anyone else."[49] With Ba Maw, Bose would share a different relationship than with the much younger Aung San. To the former, Bose was a comrade-in-arms, fighting with the same allies — the Japanese, against a common enemy — the British; while for Aung San he was more of a political veteran and inspiration.

Bose's formal introduction to Asia was at the Greater East Asia Conference in Tokyo hosted by the Japanese on 5–6 November 1943. Called a "family party" by Bose, the conference was essentially a celebration of the new spirit of unity that the Asians were rediscovering. Ba Maw attended as the head of state for the newly independent Burma while Bose was present as an observer, since the Provisional Government of Azad Hind at that time did not have administrative control over any territory. The former writes of the applause that Bose drew from the crowds that had gathered at the Hibiya Park in Tokyo and subsequently, at the conference. In his opening speech at the conference, Bose would reinforce the spirit of Asian nationalism: "This is not a conference for dividing the spoils among the conquerors. This is not a conference for hatching a conspiracy to victimize a weak power, nor is it a conference for trying to defraud a weak neighbor. This is an assembly of liberated nations, an assembly that is out to create a new order in this part of the world ..."[50] His speeches would be an instant hit with the other Asian leaders, including national heads of states like Japan, China, Thailand, Manchukuo and the Philippines. For Ba Maw, Bose would come to personify the spirit of the "long and passionate Indian revolution", and axiomatic of the "wider Asian revolution" which was about to change the face of Asia.[51]

This note of open admiration for Bose would remain with Ba Maw during the next two years of intense interaction, despite the presence of some trying situations which fostered misunderstandings. He would closely watch, as Bose straddled victory with defeat, and note the man's iron will and unmoving dedication to his cause. To illustrate this, Ba Maw writes that when Bose came to Burma, Ba Maw asked him casually what he wanted to do next. Bose stared at him for a moment and said, "Why, fight of course." His last meeting with Bose was after the INA's defeat, before he was to start the long trek back from Rangoon to Bangkok. Ba Maw asked him of his future plans. Bose's unblinking reply, yet again, was, "Start again and go on fighting ... what else can we do?"[52]

Bose was caught in a delicate situation when he decided to wage war from the frontiers of Burma using Japanese alliance. By then anti-Japanese sentiments were running high in Burma. The INA had to strike a difficult balance between the Japanese who were to provide them with the resource and the Burmese whose country's infrastructure they would need. The INA would fight on eight sectors using the entire Burmese frontier stretching for 800 miles from Arakan in the south to the Chin hills in the north; wide-scale recruitment and training of soldiers would happen in Burma which entailed setting up military bases and League offices; holding mass rallies and fund collection drives, using the Rangoon radio and Burmese press for propaganda. This large-scale military operation was possible because of the genuine rapport shared by the leaders. In an attempt to foster good relations with the Burmese, Bose sought Ba Maw's permission before shifting the INA headquarters to Rangoon. The latter writes, "He had no need to tell me that he must operate from a base as close as possible to India. I openly welcomed him ... Netaji and I met often and discussed our common problems, and did our utmost to help each other."[53] The leading members of both governments and commanders of the BIA (Burma Independence Army) and the INA would be put in touch with each other for ease of administration and this sense of closeness would percolate down to the grass root levels. INA veterans cite many incidents when headmen of Burmese villages provided food and shelter to the Indian troops, while Indian commanders, in their turn, would share the army rations with the villagers, hit by wartime shortages. Colonel G. S. Dhillon, commander of the Nehru Brigade, recalls a young girl called Maiyee whom he met at Nwebyin, the battalion headquarters. She was well informed and they had a long discussion on the freedom fighters of India. On a later visit she would adopt him as her brother and tie a sacred armlet on him to ensure safety.[54]

There were moments of discord between the Provisional Government and the Burmese Government on issues like the ownership of land left by the Indian evacuees that initially fell under the control of the INA and were later confiscated by the Japanese, much against the wishes of the Burmese; or on the question of citizenship of the migrant Indians. The Azad Hind Government was of the opinion, that legal protection should be extended to the naturalized Indian Muslim citizens but the Burmese insisted on maintaining a common status for all.[55] But in most cases an amicable consensus could be reached and unlike the racial bloodbaths of the *Saya San* revolutions of the 1930s, during the war period there were no open confrontations between the two communities. This was largely because of Bose's repeated efforts at integrating the immigrant Indians to their adopted land. He "exhorted Burmese Indians to adjust themselves to the new conditions and not to expect special privileges".[56] To him, as always, the nationalist cause was of paramount importance and superseded any of these petty squabbles.

This loyalty to his cause would be tested yet again by the Japanese. After the INA moved to Burma, i.e., in December 1944, the anti-Japanese sentiments among the BIA came to a head. The Japanese would subsequently issue orders to the INA to assist them in suppressing the *Thakin* revolution. The leaders of the Burmese AFPFL (Anti-Fascist People's Freedom League) in their turn tried to persuade the INA to join their side or in the least remain neutral. Bose would not surrender to the demands of either of the hostile parties — he would not go against the Burmese because he truly believed they were compatriots in their struggle for freedom and he was grateful to them for hosting the INA; neither would he go against the Japanese because he could not allow himself to digress from his chosen path of routing the British. This strategic neutrality would be remembered with gratitude both by the Burmese and the Japanese.[57]

Aung San and Ba Maw would go through mutual differences in taking an anti-Japanese stance and yet both in their own way would remember Bose with fondness and admiration. Ba Maw first met Bose in Singapore in July 1943 and, before parting, the two leaders decided that the war was theirs in every sense of the term and there would be no going back in the days to come: "That was the beginning of our comradeship, and without any need to talk further we adhered to the words we had spoken to the very end."[58] In April 1945, Bose himself was unwilling to relinquish the fight and leave Burma. Finally when his ministers convinced him of the perils of staying on in an enemy-infested land, he left with a sentimental message to the Burmese. Thanking them for their cooperation and help, he said, "The day will come when free India will repay that debt of gratitude in a generous measure."[59]

Bose and Aung San

It is believed that Aung San told Bo Let Ya, a close friend from his student days who would later help him put together the "Thirty Comrades", "I should like to know English better, and perhaps even take a shot at the examinations for the Indian Civil Service. After I pass, I could throw the job away, as Subhas Chandra Bose did, and go into politics. Then the country as well as the Government would look up to me for my education as well as my dedicated purpose."[60] At the time Aung San was poised at the fulcrum of his political career which would, in time, shape the future face of the Burmese nation. The two friends, Aung San and Bo Let Ya, were in the midst of the student strikes of 1936, camping, for a protracted period of time, in the precincts of Shwedagon Pagoda. Of course, for Aung San, life would take other turns — he would not have the opportunity to pursue the ICS and instead plunge in headlong into the student movement which would bring him to the forefront of Burmese politics.

The old socio-political connections between India and Burma cannot be denied and Aung San too could not escape the political influence of India, particularly of the rebellious nationalist circles of Bengal. These were the men and women who were making political history at the time and like many other young Burmese, Aung San was influenced by their thoughts and ideals. He had grown up hearing of their exploits and had occasion to meet the forerunners of the Indian National Congress — Gandhi, Nehru and Bose. In March 1940, immediately before the war, he travelled to India leading a team of delegates from the Dobama Asi-Ayon (DAA). The DAA, established in 1931, was particularly popular among the young Burmese and the organization members called themselves the *Thakins* or masters, in open challenge to British authority. Aung San and his team attended the session of the Indian National Congress in 1940 at Ramgarh, Bihar. By then the rift in the Congress had already occurred: the Forward Bloc had been formed and the high point in the Gandhi-Bose drama been played out. Bose, along with other radical thinkers on the Indian political scene, continued to believe that the 1935 Government of India Act had merely served in enhancing the clout of the landlord elites who would finally surrender to the British authorities. Therefore at Ramgarh in March, while the Congress session was chaired by President Maulana Azad, at a neighbouring premise, Bose held an Anti-Compromise Conference.[61] At the end of the Congress session, Aung San had the opportunity to meet Bose. He, along with his team, also addressed some Indian gatherings, speaking to the audience about the Burmese nationalist struggle. Compared to the century-old resistance to the British in India, in Burma it was more of a late awakening. Burmese nationalism had burst onto the scene only with the peasant revolts of the 1930s which were rapidly followed by the student agitations of 1936–37. Aung San spoke of the mortal sacrifices that the independence struggle would demand and presented the DAA manifesto at the conference. In the manifesto, like Bose, the overarching theme was of the "complete independence" that the Burmese people demanded. Independence would include the, "areas excluded under the 1935 Government of Burma Act", would mean freedom "from the present imperialist domination and exploitation" and would denote the "introduction of a free, independent people's democratic republic".[62] During this sojourn in India, Aung San discussed the possibility of closer synergies between the Burmese and Indian movements and the strategic implications of a joint opposition front and later, in May 1941, Bose would attempt a clandestine contact with the DAA, though nothing would come of it. This meeting in India in 1940 between the two leaders, Bose and Aung San, would be followed by a long hiatus till January 1944, when the advance headquarters of the INA moved to Rangoon.

In fact, the similarities in the lives of Bose and Aung San are manifold and one cannot help but agree with the historian Christopher Bayly when he calls the latter, Bose's "Burmese alter ego".[63] Though, unlike Bose, who was always known for his oratory skills and cut an impressive figure in international circles, Aung San, who had learnt English under difficult circumstances was less eloquent and yet managed to wrangle much more out of the British than perhaps his more urbane contemporaries — Nehru or Jinnah — ever did.[64]

Bose and Aung San, both changed to military garb during the course of their political career and are better known as *Netaji* and *Bogyoke* respectively — epithets conferred on them by their followers. Around these two Asian leaders many myths circulate and at times seem to engulf the real men. Both of them grew up with a fiery patriotic passion and single-mindedly drove their countries towards freedom till a premature and unnatural death overcame them. Both men's romantic involvement and subsequent marriage were treated with incredulity by their followers and both left behind infant children who would grow up with no living memory of their fathers. Both got their initial taste of politics while students and Aung San is strongly reminiscent of Bose when at a speech to his fellow students in high school he says, if so-called nationalist students remained engrossed only in their studies and do not take an interest in the affairs of their country, they do not fulfill their national duty.⁶⁵ It echoes of the same spirit of dedication and sacrifice that inspired Bose to forego the ICS and return from Cambridge to join the Indian political milieu.

Bose actively sought out a foreign alliance from as early as 1938 and his sojourn to Europe helped him raise the initial structure of the Azad Hind Fauj [Free India Army] and forge a connection between the freedom struggle and a military intervention that he had long dreamed of. In Aung San's case, by late 1939, the DAA formed an underground organization called the People's Revolutionary Party (PRP). The leaders of PRP chose *Thakin* Mya and *Thakin* Aung San as the foreign liaison and initiated plans for an armed uprising against the British. The Japanese, who were undertaking covert operations to identify indigenous resistance movements, came into contact with the Burmese nationalist leaders by 1940. As a result the "Thirty Comrades" came about and 1941 saw the Minami Kikan and the PRP underground outfit smuggling men out of Burma. In the meantime, with war breaking out in Europe, the British announced Burma to be a belligerent state without consulting the Burmese nationalists. The DAA became more aggressive in its nationalist message and like Bose, Aung San argued that Burma would not cooperate with the British in their war efforts and instead would use it to their own advantage to wrest freedom.⁶⁶ As a part of the effort to unite Burmese political opinion against the British, Aung San approached Ba Maw, leader of the peasant party and the future premier. By end 1939, an alliance was forged between the DAA and Ba Maw's Sinyetha Party and the Freedom Bloc was formed which was close in political ideology to the Forward Bloc raised by Bose in India in May 1939.

Bose had envisaged the Forward Bloc as a rallying point for the left-wing with equal representation from all leftist factions. It represented "the greatest common measure of agreement among radicals of all shades of opinion".[67] What was interesting was, the Forward Bloc did not preach doctrinaire communism. Instead, it was a loose consolidation of radical opinions while maintaining the individuality of each school and aimed at providing an alternate leadership within the Congress. The Bloc urged the people towards an armed struggle against the British and thereafter to build a "socialist India". Similarly, the Freedom Bloc in Burma emerged as a collective body of different political opinions — uniting the various political parties while allowing them to maintain their individual characters and campaigned for complete, unconditional independence, non-cooperation with the British during war and a socialist form of government in the post-independence scenario.[68]

In 1942 Aung San led the BIA into Burma as vanguard to the Japanese army. Like Bose, Aung San too worked on the premise that once the BIA entered Burma, Burmese nationals from the British Army would shift loyalty and join the nationalist army: "I counted then upon the coming over of the troops belonging to the British Government to our side, particularly the non-British section."[69] The BIA, like the INA, would be able to attract a large number of civilians to its folds. For the Burmans, Aung San held out the promise of reviving the Burmese military tradition which had been largely exterminated because, like some Indian communities, they were considered non-martial under British military tutelage. With the BIA's successful recruitment drive, its strength increased progressively and by the time it had reached Rangoon in March 1942, it was an intimidating column of more than 10,000 men.[70]

But right from its inception, the Burmese-Japanese alliance sat uneasy on Aung San. Like Bose, he had already envisaged a situation when the Japanese would forcibly invade Burma and decided that in that case it would be the BIA's task to offer stiff resistance: "I also visualized the possibility of a Japanese invasion of Burma ... we would try to forestall a Japanese invasion, set up our own independent state, and would try to negotiate with Japan before it came into Burma."[71] The frictions with the Japanese would grow, as the promised Burmese independence turned out to be merely a notional one, nothing more than the home rule proposed by the British. Eventually, with the much-touted Japanese co-prosperity sphere floundering towards its termination and the BIA getting increasingly restive, Aung San would decide to turn against the Japanese and forge an alliance with the returning British. This last move would have been incomprehensible to Bose, had he lived to see it, but as it turned out Aung San's tryst with the British would be brief and soon devolve into bickering over the clauses of the "White Paper": "Our deal is total independence for Burma ... No doubt that is out of the question at present, so we shall be a self-governing Dominion ... If the British refuse to grant us one or the other, then we will fight them too."[72]

Thus, Aung San and Bose's lives flowed in somewhat parallel streams — at times marked by decisions which bore striking semblance to each other, at others they were governed by the individual circumstances in which destiny had placed them. In Aung San's decision to form the Freedom Bloc of Burma, there is immediate evidence of Bose's influence on the *Bogyoke*'s political life. In the other aspects of Aung San's political philosophy, like his continued belief in armed resistance, his emphasis on equal rights for the minority groups and his vision of a socialist state, it is interesting to note the similarities of the two leaders' viewpoints.

Use of Voluntary Army and Belief in Armed Resistance

In December 1945, towards the end of his turbulent political career, Aung San was instrumental in forming yet another people's army, called the People's Volunteer Organisation (PVO). By then the BIA had gone through its fourth name change and metamorphosed into the Patriotic Burmese Forces (PBF), a carefully selected section of the PBF had participated in the victory parade along with the Karens, Kachins, Burma Rifles and other auxiliary forces of the British Army. As a part of the Kandy Agreement, a limited number of the PBF was absorbed into the regular Burma Army with a promise of further recruitments when the army expanded. In September 1945, Aung San himself had written to Mountbatten resigning from the military and opting to go back to politics. The "White Paper" policy had been published in May 1945 and negotiations regarding the rehabilitation of Burma were coming to a head. The formation of the PVO helped to strengthen the position of the popular *Bogyoke* even further — he was not only the undisputed political leader as the head of AFPFL, he could also flex a military muscle against the British Governor with the PVO. Burma's previous Governor, Dorman Smith, who had recently returned from exile, was caught between two trying situations: on one hand was this united front of political and military clout, and on the other, was the Indian National Congress' decision, since the provincial elections of 1946, that Indian troops could not be used to suppress the nationalist resistance in Burma. This meant Governor Smith had to find a solution to the Burmese problem and yet had no resources placed at his disposal to do so.

While apparently not espousing violence, Aung San's PVO continued their training and drills with dummy rifles and Bren guns. By May 1946, the PVO had nearly 6,500 members and was a prominent participant in the Resistance Day parade.[73] Dorman Smith, perceiving the impending threat that the organization represented, attempted to circumscribe its powers. In response, Aung San at a press interview, openly threatened the British Governor with PVO-executed violence. This was followed shortly by the police shoot-out in the town of Tantabin, in the Insein District, on a procession of several thousand people demonstrating against the arrest of members of the Tantabin PVO. The bloody police action killed three and wounded many and coincided with a week-long AFPFL Supreme Council meeting convened by Aung San. In his opening address, Aung San threatened the use of extra-legal struggle which he defined as "mass civil disobedience combined with mass non-payment of taxes and mass strikes".[74] The Tantabin incident would have a far-reaching impact — it would force Dorman Smith, already pushed into a corner over the possibility of a mass armed uprising, to forego his plans of a political coalition with Aung San's rival, U Saw, and climb down. Hubert Rance would replace him as the new Governor, and like Mountbatten, would be far more open to working in tandem with the nationalists. The veracity of Aung San's belief in using armed resistance against the British would again be proven to the Burmese people.

Bose too had initiated the Volunteer Corps in Bengal, back in 1928, with much the same purpose — he had envisaged a people's army raised from the provinces of Bengal which would eventually spread to the other states of India and, with training, could be used to counter colonial control.

Socialist Philosophy

Like Bose, Aung San was born at a time when Asia was in transition. It was a time when nationalists were actively seeking alternate political strategies which would help them counter British colonialism. Like Bose too, Aung San was an avid reader and since his student days had fed his appetite on a healthy diet of Marx, Lenin, Stalin, Trotsky, Mussolini and Hitler and like Bose, he had been greatly inspired by the Sinn Fein movement of Ireland. The books that could not be found on the shelves of the Bernard Free Library due to British vigilance, would be made available to him at *Thakin* Nu's bookstore. *Thakin* Nu, Aung San's close associate and future premier, had opened the Red Dragon bookshop just off the university campus to sell leftist literature. Thus, Aung San was exposed to the various shades of radical thought including communism, socialism and fascism. In addition, like other young Burmese of the time, he read the works of Asian leaders like Sun Yat-sen, Gandhi, Nehru and Bose. These were the personalities who were making news at the time while the political systems advocated by Russia, Italy or Germany seemed tempting alternatives to the British and French colonialism that Asia had seen for the last centuries.

Aung San's association with Marxism was early, if short-lived. *Thakin* Thein Pe, his university associate, had studied for a while in Calcutta and while there had come in contact with leaders of the Indian Communist Party. He, along with other *Thakins*, brought communism to Burma and the first communist cell was formed in 1939, with Aung San as Secretary General. But the latter dropped out of the group soon after its formation and though there was another flare up of interest in communism in 1944, Aung San was never a doctrinaire Marxist. The association finally came to an end in 1946, when his communist comrades threatened the unity of AFPFL, and he was compelled to expel the Communist

Party from the AFPFL alliance. However, during his career he expressed continued interest in non-communist socialism as a political form and when it came to framing the constitution of independent Burma, he advocated socialism as a future strategy. In 1940, when he fled the British, his original plan was to seek help of the Chinese Communist Party. But later, while clarifying his communist stance to the Japanese, he said: "To the question of our attitude towards the 'China Incident' I pointed out that we were more concerned with our national struggle and whoever opposed our enemy was our friend."[75]

This is distinctly reminiscent of the political path that Bose had trodden. Fascism was never a viable option for him and he could never accept Japan's aggression towards China. On an earlier occasion he had wondered why the Japanese Renaissance could not be achieved "without Imperialism, without dismembering the Chinese republic, without humiliating another proud, cultured and ancient race?"[76] For both men, the Japanese alliance was more for tactical reasons than inspired by an ideological faith in fascism. They baulked at the monarchical nationalism preached by Japan and when it came to their own country, were determined in snuffing out any traces of imperialism. Both were consistently cautious in retaining a balance of power with the Japanese. Like Aung San had vouchsafed for the communist "planned economy", Bose too admired the USSR because it had been home to the first people's revolution and was an example of a backward, agricultural land's move towards modernization.[77] They were pragmatic in their approach and political sagacity and interested in finding working-models which would help them achieve independence. In this context, Aung San Suu Kyi's character sketch of her father can be applied with ease to both men: "But Aung San was not fanatical in his belief in communism or any other rigid ideology. He found much to attract him in the broad range of socialist theories, but his real quest was always for ideas and tactics that would bring freedom and unity to his country."⁷⁸ To both, Bose and Aung San, politics was not a static concept but had to be adapted to suit the changing needs of the country.

Secularity

Bose, during his political career in India had consistently avoided far-right Hindu ideologues, as he had tried to reason with Muslim extremists. Later, he had been equally vehement in retaining the secular framework of the INA. Like India, Burma too was an ancient culture and religion, where Buddhism was an inalienable part of Burmese national identity. With time Buddhist monks had come to play a decisive role in nationalist activity, some monks even claiming that it was impossible to achieve nirvana in a land ruled by Christians. In fact the pro-activism of the monks had proved to be an effective device in drawing rural support to the nationalist cause. And yet Buddhism, as a political stimulant, never inspired Aung San. Unlike his associate, *Thakin* Nu who was a practising Buddhist in his personal life and sought a Buddhist revival in Burma, Aung San advocated a disciplined severance between the state machinery and religion. But what was more remarkable was, like Bose, Aung San too did not banish religion from his scheme of things. He wrote, "Politics must see that the individual also has his rights, including the right to the freedom of religious worship. [But] here we must stop and draw the line definitely between politics and religion."⁷⁹ Elsewhere he said, "If we mix religion and politics, then we offend the spirit of religion itself."⁸⁰ He wanted the Buddhist message of charity and non-violence to be perpetuated among the people but simultaneously wanted the Buddhist *Sanghas* [associations] to retain their traditional roles and abstain from politics. Their contribution to nation building could be in spreading the message of brotherhood and freedom from fear but not in inflammatory communal politics. He showed no desire to announce Buddhism as a state religion and instead emphasized the need to accept the cultural and religious plurality of his country.

Equal Rights for Minority Groups

Subhas Chandra Bose was vociferous in deploring the British policy of divide-and-rule, which he felt threatened the organic unity of his country and made numerous efforts in rapprochement with the Muslims and other minority groups of India. Like Bose, Aung San discovered a Burma which had been divided on the lines of ethnicity and religion. Burma had been ceded to the British in stages — while most of central and lower Burma came to be ruled directly by the Chief Commissioner reporting to the Governor General of India, some of the areas in the mountainous regions of north and the plains and valleys south of the Himalayas continued to be ruled by the traditional chieftains. After 1897, all of lower Burma and large sections of central Burma, where the ethnic Burmans resided, came to be known as ministerial Burma while the Excluded Areas, comprising of around 15 per cent of the country's population, was inhabited by the hill people — the Karens, Kachins, Chin and Shans. British administration as well as Christian missionaries at work among the hill-tribes had actively encouraged the separatist tendencies of the frontier provinces and this trend continued, undeterred, through Japanese invasion.

Speaking on the unity of Burma, Aung San had mentioned, "The dream of a unified and free Burma has always haunted me ... In the past we shouted slogans: 'Our race, our religion, our language!' Those slogans have gone obsolete now ... We can preserve our own customs and cultures, enjoy our own freedom of belief, but on the broader national life we must be together."[81] The scale of the unity that Aung San and the AFPFL had achieved was borne out at the All Burma Congress organized by the League which was held at the Shwedagon Pagoda in January 1946. As many as 1,300 delegates attended, with representation from the fifteen most important political parties of Burma. The ethnic hill tribes along with the Buddhist *Pongyis* [monks] came under one roof as Aung San, in his presidential address, spoke of what had been achieved in the nationalist struggle so far and the "arduous way" that remained to be traversed which could be done only with the "active support and cooperation of a whole people".[82] This speech is crucial because it demonstrates the close link that he forged between nationalism and national unity. He could not envisage one without the other and for him nationalism was much more than mere disinterested coexistence — it was the development of common interests and a sense of community. Like Bose had done in the INA with communal eating and mutual celebration of festivals, Aung San too advocated an informed acceptance of plurality. In his "Defense of Burma" statement of January 1945, he mentioned that any "books, signs, symbols, names" which fostered racial or religious discrimination should be banned and minorities should enjoy a proper place in the state with their "political, economic and social rights definitely defined and accorded".[83] This is distinctly reminiscent of Bose, who in his inclusive ideology, did not hesitate to change the national anthem to accommodate the Muslims of the INA. It was this willingness to accept cultural and political differences of the minorities that was borne out at the Panglong Conference of February 1947. According to the Aung San-Attlee Agreement that had been signed in London, the British and Burmese were to work towards an "early unification of the frontier areas with ministerial Burma with the free consent of the inhabitants" of these areas.[84] Thus the Panglong Conference was to play an imperative role in accelerating the actual transfer of power to the Burmese and its failure could lead to the unraveling of the Aung San-Attlee Agreement. In the conference, held at the Shan

At the Singapore camp of the Rani of Jhansi Regiment, 1943.
Source: Courtesy of the Netaji Research Bureau.

The same part of Singapore as it stands today.
Source: Courtesy of Madan G. Kannuvakkam.

The house at Chancery Lane, Singapore, used by the Indian Independence League (IIL) as its office.
Source: Courtesy of the Netaji Research Bureau.

Chancery Lane as it stands today.
Source: Courtesy of Madan G. Kannuvakkam.

Wartime residence of Bose at Meyer Road, Singapore.
Source: Courtesy of the Netaji Research Bureau.

The condominium that stands at the site today.
Source: Courtesy of Madan G. Kannuvakkam.

At the inauguration of the boys' dormitory: Ramakrishna Mission, Singapore.
Source: Courtesy of the Ramakrishna Mission, Singapore.

The Ramakrishna Mission, Norris Road, Singapore, as it stands today.
Source: Courtesy of Madan G. Kannuvakkam.

Unity, Faith, Sacrifice: Bose laying the foundation stone of the INA War Memorial at Esplanade, Singapore, 8 July 1945.
Source: Courtesy of the Netaji Research Bureau.

Wreaths at the INA War Memorial which was completed after Bose left Singapore and before the British Military Administration (BMA) returned in September 1945.
Source: Reproduced with permission from the National Archives of Singapore.

The INA War Memorial demolished by the returning British Army, Singapore, 1945.
Source: Reproduced with permission from the National Archives of Singapore.

The site of the INA War Memorial which was marked by the National Heritage Board, Singapore, in 1995.
Source: Courtesy of Madan G. Kannuvakkam.

states, Aung San heard the wishes of the frontier people and was able to come to individual understandings with the groups. It was largely because of his earlier work and the trust he had earned from the hill people that the conference was a success. The Panglong Agreement promised autonomy to the frontier areas and though it did not yet commit the Shan, Chin and other groups to a permanent union with ministerial Burma, it would prove to be a cornerstone in the final step towards independence.

That Aung San was not paying mere lip-service to the idea of unity was borne out by the fourteen point resolution he placed before the AFPFL pre-constituent assembly in May 1947. He identified the various minority groups that coexisted in Burma — each with their own language, culture and traditions and proposed the formation of a Burmese union. The draft Constitution laid down that there would be a single citizenship for all people and yet it guaranteed a variety of rights to any group of citizens who were distinctly different from the majority in race, culture, language, historical traditions and formed at least 10 per cent of the population.

Burma would ultimately win independence on 4 January 1948, but not before Aung San lost his life to internal intrigue — the same people who he had laboured to unite would turn against him in a final treacherous confrontation. *Thakin* Nu would be his unwilling successor and according to Aung San's wishes a representative from an ethnic minority community would be the first President of the sovereign nation.

Sarat Bose's Visit to Burma

Long before Burma's independence, Subhas Chandra Bose had passed away in August 1945, leaving his grieving family and followers. His elder brother, Sarat Chandra Bose, who had been an island-of-calm in the turbulent waters of Bose's life, would visit Burma for a brief while in 1946. The two brothers had shared a deep bonding and had perfectly complemented each other — if Subhas was the rebel with a cause, Sarat was the cautious politician. The purpose of Sarat's visit to Burma was as much to help boost the morale of the INA which had been abruptly disbanded as also to personally experience the last living memories of Subhas. Aung San would receive Sarat warmly and extend help in commuting the pending trials of the ex-INA men. Sarat in his speech would address Burma as a "holy land", a land where patriots like Tilak, Lajpat Rai and Subhas Bose had been interned and speak of the commonality of cause between India and Burma. He would urge the Indian immigrants to throw in their lot with their country of adoption and identify themselves completely with the Burmese "struggle for freedom and in their work of reconstruction".[85] While Aung San, in one of his most unrestrained speeches about Bose, would give a candid account of the Indo-Burmese relations: he would open his speech by welcoming Sarat Bose as the "great brother of a great leader and patriot" and then continue with: "I knew Netaji, even before I met him for the first time in Calcutta in 1940 by reading various accounts of his life of sacrifice and struggle and, last of all, his own book *The Indian Struggle* which was in these days banned in India and Burma. I knew Netaji, as I came into close and frequent contacts with him during this recent World War ... Between him and myself, there was complete mutual trust." He would speak of their joint decision to not let their armies fight each other and the adherence to the decision through the twists and turns of war and end his speech with a solemn promise from the AFPFL to offer a safe refuge to the Indian community in Burma.[86] Thus, the chapter in the history of the Indian migrant community, which had started with distrust and bitter rivalry, would draw towards a somewhat amicable close.

Epilogue: Burmese Indian Community after Bose

The period 1943 to 1945 was a time when the anti-Indian sentiments in Burma were eclipsed by the sense of comradeship as the two nationalities fought their own battles of freedom. After Burmese independence the problems would emerge again but some of the goodwill would remain. The long pending issues regarding citizenship, vernacular education, remittance of money to homeland would return to plague the Indians. But this would be interspersed with periods of concurrence between the two communities. Soon after the return of the British, Governor Dorman Smith would appoint S. A. S. Tyabji, who had recently returned from India, as his adviser on Indian Affairs. This would provoke hostile criticism from both the Burmese and Indian camps because Tyabji was from the old school and had not witnessed the solidarity between the two communities during the war years. The nationalists would see it as an attempt to perpetuate the British policy of divide-and-rule.[87] Soon after the war, some Indians got together to form the All Burma Indian Congress (ABIC), somewhat on the lines of the Indian National Congress. The group members straddled Indians from both the old and new schools: there were some like Dadachanji and Dr R. S. Dugal who were nationalists who had returned to India during the war and now wanted to carry forward the old minority politics; while there were others like Zora Singh and Dina Nath, who had been associated with the IIL, and believed in Bose's philosophy of collaboration with the Burmese leadership. The differences in opinion soon led to a rift between the two groups: the neo-nationalists were of the opinion that all Indian peasants should become citizens of Burma, a stance aggressively opposed by Dadachanji. Zora Singh and Dina Nath would, within a couple of years, opt for Burmese citizenship themselves and withdraw from the ABIC.[88] The ABIC, unlike the MIC (Malaysian Indian Congress), would not be able to identify itself with the aspirations of independent Burma and degenerate into merely a cultural body, without any significant political role.

THE POLITICAL LEGACY OF BOSE IN MALAYA
Background: KMM and KRIS

The pre-war years had not seen political mobilization of any significance in Malaya. In the pluralist society of Malaya, the emotional connect between the Chinese, Indian and Malay was at best tenuous. To add to the complexity, national sentiments were born of and coloured by multi-ethnic needs and clung obdurately to political movements of ancestral homelands. The *Kesatuan Melayu Muda* (KMM), formed by the journalist Ibrahim Yaacob in 1938, was Malaya's first Malay political party. The second-in-command was Mustafa Hussain — the classic "armchair, pipe-smoking, left-wing intellectual". Besides, KMM brought together Idris Hakim, M. N. Othman, Ishak Haji Muhammad (Pak Sako) Abdul Samad, Ahmad Boestamam — men who would come to play decisive roles in shaping future Malaya. Like other Asian countries, Malay youth too, had been politicized by leftist literature. Most of them managed to smuggle in books from the Left Book Club against a few shilling annual membership fee and drew inspiration from world movements led by Gandhi, Mustafa Kemal Ataturk or the Irish rebellion. The Sultan Idris Training College for Malay Teachers (SITC) became a crucible of anti-colonial thought and fostered an explosion of nationalist journalism. Ibrahim, alum of SITC, and his group members operated from the KMM House, off Jalan Bukit Timah in Singapore.

Some of the young radicals joined forces with the Japanese in their invasion of Malaya and in the formation of the Japanese sponsored Malay Volunteer Force, the Malai Giyu Gun. Members of the *Giyu Gun* received some elementary training and weapons. Mustapha Hussain, KMM's Vice-President, recounts the excitement at the uniform fitting session with Pak Chik Ahmad, an elderly KMM member craving to be an "officer with a long sword trailing by his side".[89] Though the Malai Giyu Gun would never achieve the scale of the BIA of Burma or Bose's INA, it would be the first step in militarization of some sections of the otherwise peaceful Malay people, culturally inclined to farming and animal husbandry. However, the Malay alliance with the Japanese would be marred by distrust from the early stages. Mustapha, who had been the voice of the skeptic in the Japanese alliance, had told his optimistic colleagues at the end of the successful Japanese invasion, "The war is not over yet ... This victory is not our victory."[90] The disillusion would grow more pronounced when, in October 1943, the Japanese ceded the four northern Malaya states to Siam as an award for the initial rite of passage through Thailand. Kedah, Perlis, Kelantan and Trengganu comprised the rice bowl of Malaya and the cessation would accentuate the food shortages and escalating inflation of the occupation. But equally importantly, it would be a blow to the Malay dream of forming the Malay dominant "Indonesia Raya". Mustapha writes, "One of KMM's early objectives had been to regain control over the Strait Settlements of Singapore, Melaka and Penang. Now on top of those three, we had to strive to recover four states we once had."[91] Towards the end of the occupation, the Japanese in a last desperate attempt to counter their serial defeats in the Pacific Theatre, would attempt galvanizing Malay opinion against the Allies. KRIS would be formed under Ibrahim Yaacob's leadership to foster the message of independence. Fired by Indonesia's plans of independence which had been afoot for a while, Ibrahim would commit the Malays to Sukarno and Hatta's leadership and plan on the declaration of a "Greater Indonesia" in early-September 1945. But the plan would soon be aborted with the abrupt Japanese surrender, followed by the equally fortuitous declaration of independence on 17 August by Indonesia with no mention of Malaya. The Malay radicals would be overcome by a sense of futility and missed opportunity as Ibrahim fled to Indonesia on a Japanese aircraft, leaving the dreams of an early Malay independence unfulfilled. Even as British forces fanned out across Malaya, Indonesia and the French Indo-China, the Malay nationalists would be chased down and implicated as Japanese collaborators.

Formation of Malay Nationalist Party

Though the advent of the British effectively dispersed the Malay leadership, the movement was soon resurrected by some ex-KMM members. Ishak Haji Muhammad, Pak Chik Ahmad, Ahmad Boestamam who had managed to evade the British dragnet came together in 1945 to form the Malay Nationalist Party (MNP). MNP took shape in Perak, under the leadership of one Dr Burhanuddin Al-Helmi. Dr Burhanuddin was a devout Muslim, well known for his writings on Islam. His brand of nationalism was founded on an inclusive spiritualism that was not common at the time. The title Al-Helmi, appended to his name, conveyed his non-violent beliefs, in fact the police and Malayan Special Branch had taken to referring to him as the "Gandhi of Malaya".[92] Burhanuddin had been a first-hand witness to Gandhi's campaigns when he travelled to India to study medicine and it was this ethos that he perpetuated. During the occupation he was employed by the Japanese as an advisor on Malay customs and, though not a KMM member, had been politically active. Now, with the formation of the MNP, the Malay movement resurfaced but with a distinct difference. While it continued to use red and white — the colours of the Indonesian flag and sing the Indonesian anthem, it was more inward looking, less prone to fall back on Sukarno as the role model. Malay politics during the post-war years was in essence reactive as it grappled with the Malayan Union Scheme imported by the British and much that happened in the next couple of years was triggered by British intentions and attitudes. The preoccupation with "Indonesia Raya" was further diluted when the MNP alleged loyalty to the multi-ethnic AMCJA-*Putera* alliance. In fact, Mustapha Hussain claims that when he and Burhanuddin drafted the Constitution for independent Malaya in July 1945, there was no mention of a joint declaration or a geographical integration with Indonesia. Malaya's independence would be read out by Ibrahim and broadcast by the Penang Radio Station: "I want to repeat that the objective of KRIS was not to integrate Malaya with Indonesia but just to be under one union, with each having its own separate decision-making bodies."[93]

API: Ahmad Boestamam

While the Malay radicals gathered fresh reinforcements to counter the British and drifted away from their Indonesian beginnings, the post-war years saw the emergence of a whole new generation of Malay activists. Abdullah Sani bib Raja Kechil who operated with the *nom de plume*, Ahmad Boestamam, was one of them. A self-professed follower of Subhas Chandra Bose's political philosophy and oratory style, Boestamam went to the extent of adopting the Indian leader's family name as a part of his own pseudonym[94] — an alias that would remain with him in his later life when he emerged as one of the most charismatic leaders Malaya would know.

In the thirteenth chapter of his memoir, Boestamam reminiscences of an INA mass rally attended by him at the Padang Club, Ipoh.[95] Subhas Chandra Bose was to arrive to address the audience by five in the evening but was slightly delayed. He describes the eager anticipation with which the large crowd which had gathered in the field awaited Bose. Boestamam was accompanied by Dilbagh Rei, an Indian Independence League worker. Because of his fair skin, Boestamam was easily noticeable in the crowd and some from the audience asked Dilbagh what was a non-Indian doing in their midst. To this Dilbagh replied, since Boestamam worshipped Subhas Chandra Bose [may be more than many Indians themselves], he had come to attend the rally. In response, those who had asked the question came forward and embraced Boestamam.

Bose arrived at the rally around half an hour late, at 5.30 p.m. He was accompanied by a large convoy of personal guards and on seeing him the crowd broke out in spontaneous applause, cheering cries of "Jai Hind" and "Inqilab Zindabad" rending the air. Bose spoke for about an hour, in Urdu [possibly Hindustani]. Boestamam did not comprehend much of the Urdu words but was nevertheless impressed by the stirring speech and the "handsome" Indian leader's oratorical style.

Towards the end of the chapter, Boestamam writes that this episode at Ipoh taught him important lessons in how to be a good leader. In the foreword to the same biography, written by noted Malaysian journalist and writer, A. Samad Ismail, there is mention of an interview done by Boestamam of Bose for the Japanese-supported newspaper, *Berita Malai* (of which Samad was the editor for some time). Samad mentions the repeated references to Bose in Boestamam's writings and wonders why the IIL and Subhas Chandra Bose find repeated mention while Boestamam is comparatively silent about Sukarno, Ho Chi Minh or Atau Jose Rizal — the other contemporary leaders of Southeast Asia, particularly Indonesia.[96]

Ahmad Boestamam was a late entrant to KMM, joining shortly before Japanese occupation, but by then he was a past master in handling the propaganda machinery. His involvement with the Malay cause had started earlier, when, as a young subaltern, he had co-edited "Majlis" with Ibrahim Yaacob. His columns had been known for their unreserved radical views and he had shot to fame in Malay journalist circles. Later, during the post-war days, he was the leading light of the newspaper — *Suara Rakyat* or the Voice of the People. During his career as a journalist, he had come to know well the strength of the written word in forming public opinion. In the context of his editorials in *Suara Rakyat* and other political writings, he mentions Subhas Chandra Bose's speeches as a source of influence.[97] The speeches had exposed him to new political concepts like imperialism, capitalism, socialism etc. and guided him in his critique of British governance. He would actively read up Bose's speeches not only for his columns or articles but also to prepare himself for any anti-British debate.[98]

Besides handling the propaganda machinery for KMM, Boestamam had been trained by the Japanese military. At the end of the war he emerged as a self-styled *pemuda* [young nationalist] and set the Malayan stage ablaze with his fiery speeches. Like Bose, his public persona was an important devise in conveying the militant spirit of the movement. Reminiscent of the combative young revolutionaries of the Indonesian *pemuda*, Boestamam's aggressive speech and military attire added a distinctly different flavour to the MNP. Unlike the non-violent, spiritual Burhanuddin, he represented the new generation of a more volatile, defiant, anti-authoritarian leadership. Consequently, API (Angkatan Pemuda Insaf or the Generation of Aware Youth), the youth wing of MNP, led by Boestamam also emerged with a singularly militant character that was different from and at times tended to overshadow the parent body. With Boestamam, INA style larger-than-life mass rallies became common which were often followed by fund collection drives. Like the INA, garlands worn by MNP leaders were auctioned to the highest bidder.⁹⁹ The red-and-white *Sang Saka Merah Putih* flag would be hoisted while the API youth lustily sang the national anthem. With Japanese sponsorship gone, the MNP would not be able to afford the military cavalcade flaunted by the INA but red and white flags would abound everywhere and the leaders' cars would be painted in the MNP colours. The API was given a military structure with the young rebels wearing uniforms and arm bands with the API insignia. A large number of these young men had received military training from the Japanese and now continued to participate in drills and carried indigenous weapons. The API became axiomatic of the new invincible spirit of the rebellion and like the INA had done with the Indian community, was aimed at infusing the Malays with a new found confidence and steer them away from the peaceful *kampong* life they had grown accustomed to.

In his book, *Carving the Path to the Summit*, which was initially published as a series of articles in *Berita Minggu* — a Strait Times Group publication, Boestamam writes: "Within the space of a month or two the MNP had become a strong political party with no small support from the people. Some didn't trust it. And to convince those who didn't, a show of strength had to be arranged."¹⁰⁰ That like Bose, Boestamam believed in the convincing power of the uniform was evident when this "show of strength" took the form of the hastily-put-together API. Within the span of a few days, he would manage to assemble as many as nearly 500 Malay youths, to be trained and paraded at the Jubilee Park of Ipoh. Realizing the API's potent strength, MNP would make it into a permanent front and later at the MNP conference in Malacca, it would be formally separated from the parent party. This was the second conference of the MNP, organized in December 1946. At this gathering, Burhanuddin would declare his personal manifesto, clearly delineating MNP's objectives which were so different from the more parochial UMNO. Following his non-communal philosophy, Boestamam would say: "Whoever was loyal to the country and who was willing to call himself *'Melayu'* was part of 'independent Malaya'."[101] This anti-elitist, anti-capitalist ideology which refused to acknowledge any "purity of blood" would form the basis of his speeches in the future campaign trail. His strident rhetoric would bring the crowds to a fevered pitch of enthusiasm. As Mustapha writes, "Had he ordered, 'set this house ablaze', the youths would have done so without question: such was Boestamam's oratorical power."[102] With the API battle cry of "Freedom through Blood" [*Merdeka dengan Darah*], again reminiscent of Bose's very popular, "Give me blood and I promise you freedom", he would manage to captivate the imagination of the rural Malays while the UMNO would continue to be dominant in the cities. The API's mass appeal would be such that, in July 1947, when the British started its ban on leftist Malay and non-Malay parties, the API would be the first to be debarred, even before the MNP. Boestamam himself would be interned during the Emergency and would resurface again, only several years later, to form a new socialist, secular party, Partai Rakyat, though he would never attain the political stature he had enjoyed before.

THE POLITICAL LEGACY OF BOSE IN THE INDIAN COMMUNITY OF MALAYA: JOHN A. THIVY

Background: Malayan Union Scheme

In August 1945 the Second World War came to an abrupt end with the bombing of Hiroshima and Nagasaki. But like in the rest of Asia, in Malaya too, this end merely heralded the beginning of yet another and perhaps more bloody battle — the final encounter with the returning colonial powers for national independence.

In Malaya this final struggle would stretch over the next decade, throwing up much bitterness and acrimony. The communist insurgency would be followed by an equally brutal counter-insurgency and the eventual declaration of the Malayan Emergency on 18 June 1948. The communities of the pluralist Malayan society would come to the fore with nationalist leaders and ideologies of their own. The first British policy, that would disrupt the uneasy calm following the landing of the Allied troops in Malaya and elicit passionate reactions from the Malays, would be the British constitutional order, named the Malayan Union Scheme, initiated in October 1945.

The Malayan Union sought to confer political rights on the non-Malay communities. It was conceived by Sir Edward Gent, a trusted British officer, and was buttressed by the support of the ruling Labor Party. The Scheme was intended as the initial step in preparing Malaya for eventual self-government. Under it, Penang, Malacca, Province Wellesley and the Malay States formed a single entity which in essence meant a reversal of earlier Anglo-Malay agreements to maintain the Peninsular states as sovereign units under overall British control. Singapore would be segregated and would form an independent crown colony. Apparently the separation of the Strait Settlements was planned to appease Malay sentiments by keeping the large Chinese community settled in Singapore, out of the Malayan Union. But in all possibility, Singapore was intended to be the next defense base for the British following the decolonization of India and Burma. A clause under the scheme qualified all inhabitants of Malaya, who fulfilled certain domicile conditions with automatic citizenship. This implied a naturalized citizenship under the new Constitution for a majority of the non-Malays and stirred intense Malay belligerence. Malay opposition crystallized under the leadership of Dato Onn bin Ja'afar who formed the United Malay National

Organization (UMNO) in March 1946. UMNO sought to establish that Malaya was constitutionally a Malay state with only restrictive concessions allowed to non-Malays and signified the restoration of sovereignty to the Malay sultans. To counter the conservative Malays of UMNO and the Anglo-Malay proposal of a Malayan Union, radical opinion came together under the AMCJA (All Malayan Council of Joint Action) and Putera (Pusat Tenaga Rakyat) — a loose coalition of largely communist-front organizations of both Malay and non-Malay origin. The AMCJA-Putera coalition would present the People's Constitution in September 1947. While providing for the socio-political advancement of the Malays and establishing Malay as the national language, it proposed a united Malaya including Singapore, a popularly elected Central Government and State Councils and Malay rulers invested with real sovereign powers but, at the same time, responsible to the people of Malaya through popularly elected State Councils. To the reactive issue of citizenship, it proposed conferring equal political rights to domiciled non-Malays.

Indian Reaction to the Malayan Union

The end of the war found the Indian community in Malaya in a state of disarray. Those who had returned to India during the Japanese occupation, now came back to find their homes trespassed and means of livelihood largely dwindled. The few who came back from the Burma-Siam railway construction sites were a battered lot. Prices of essential commodities were spiralling out of control while the trade and economic networks had all but collapsed. Most of the educated professionals had identified with the nationalist cause during the occupation and now faced British reprisal. With key figures like N. Raghavan, John Thivy, V. J. Somasundaram and M. K. Lukshumeyah arrested by the BMA (British Military

Administration), the community found itself virtually leaderless. The ensuing sense of insecurity and material need fostered sub-communal separatism which was further enhanced by British policy. Instead of electoral politics, the British announced the revival of nominated advisory councils which sought to "bring into consultation the various communities in the country".[103] However, these councils were envisaged as a continuation of the earlier social order and sub-communities vied with each other to gain British favour. The various factions of the Indian community formed independent associations "with the express objective of gaining official recognition for representational purposes".[104] Besides, the Hindu-Muslim rivalry festering in India was echoed in Muslim separatism in Malaya as well and branches of the Indian Muslim League were established in the main cities. Simmering Tamil sentiments of the pre-war times came to the fore again seeking to revive Dravidian nationalism. Radical Tamils held separate celebrations of the Indian Independence Day while G. V. Thaver revived the Malayan Indian Association in Singapore. As the community imploded in disintegrated factions, the response of Indians to the proposal of the Malayan Union was understandably weak. Though the Central Indian Association of Malaya (CIAM) invited comments on the proposals, only the Selangor Indian Association and a few scattered individuals responded.[105] The Indian community and press remained fragmented in their opinion on the Union: while some moderate minorities like the Punjabis, Malayalees, Chettyars and some factions of the Indian Muslims extended a tentative acceptance, the left-wing Indian organizations opposed the scheme.

Malayan Indian Congress (MIC): John A. Thivy

The overall sense of despondency in the splintered Indian community was somewhat alleviated with Nehru's state visit in March 1946. At mass rallies, Nehru was greeted by cheering crowds, large numbers of whom still wore their INA uniforms and forage caps. After months of being hounded by the British as fascist collaborators, this was a solitary moment of redeemed self-esteem for the League workers. Like Bose, Nehru represented the voice of the educated, nationalist leadership of Asia and somewhat revived the sense of lost pride amongst Indians. Nehru was instrumental in organizing an Indian Relief Committee under the leadership of INA stalwarts such as N. Raghavan and Brahmachari Kailasam and later, this panel would be led by John Thivy.[106]

John Aloysius Thivy was a lawyer by profession who had trained at London and returned to practice in Malaya. His active interest in the Indian independence movement since his London days drove him to join the INA and he rose to be a minister in the Provisional Government of Azad Hind. Thivy had served at the Burma front and since the end of the Japanese occupation been interned at the Changi prison. He was released with Nehru's intervention along with several others in Malaya and Singapore. At Nehru's behest, he took up the leadership of the Relief Committee and worked towards forging a communal nationalist movement. He operated out of the Relief Committee Office leased at the Sri Mariamman Temple premises in Kuala Lumpur. The same office would be used by him for the next sixteen months as he, as the organizational President, laboured to give shape to the Malayan Indian Congress (MIC). Thivy got in touch with his earlier colleagues of the INA and it was decided a united political front needed to be established for the Indian community. But the initial efforts were met with stiff opposition — the pre-war CIAM leadership was markedly apathetic to the MIC since they would prefer a revival of their own organization. Also, there was the constant British surveillance to be handled since they were understandably skeptical of any seditious coming together of INA veterans.

MIC for the Indians

In August 1946, the first All Malaya Indian Political Conference was convened at the Chettyar Hall in Kuala Lumpur. Thivy, true to the multi-racial egalitarian precedence of the INA, attempted to provide a fair representation to all existing Indian bodies though there were accusations of over representation of North Indians and Malayalees and of the Tamils being marginalized. The same note of dissension had marked the earlier All Malayan Hindustani Conference on adopting Hindustani as the Indian national language.[107] Such sectarian divides would plague the MIC in the years to come as well. However, after a preliminary discussion the delegates drew up a draft proposal for the MIC Constitution: it would aim to safeguard and promote the varied interests of the Indian community, would prevent inter-communal dissensions and misunderstandings in their struggle for independence, would cooperate with other Asian communities on matters common to all and in the establishment of a peaceful and independent Malaya.[108] Under the thirty-three-page draft Constitution, MIC also planned to have certain departments: Labour — which would focus on building sound Indian trade unions; Political — to study local reactions to the Malayan Union and to build contacts with Indian representatives of various local governments and public bodies; Trade — to coalesce business efforts of Indians, study economic interests at various localities and liaison with Malayan trading bodies.[109] Membership to the MIC would be open to all Indians above the age of eighteen who subscribed to its aims and objectives, irrespective of their country of domicile. The prime focus was thus the Indian migrant community: the MIC was to function as a local representative of the INC and be the voice of the Indians in Malaya. It would strive to promote the Indian interest and political-economic advancement by coalescing with other local communities, while nurturing sub-communal unity.

MIC's Response to the Malayan Union: Malayan-Indian Sensibilities of Thivy

True to its objectives, the MIC initially focused on celebration of Indian national events and the propagation of Hindustani. The INA anniversaries were celebrated with particular aplomb since a majority of the MIC members had been associated with the movement. In continuation of the INA tradition of building a casteless society, it also worked towards the social uplift of the community by opening up Hindu temples to accept worship by lower castes and removing caste discrimination from Hindu burial practices.[110] But soon enough, the MIC leadership became deeply involved in the debate over the Malayan Union which was raging at the time and pledged loyalty to the AMCJA-Putera coalition. Unlike the more conservative Malay UMNO, the AMCJA-Putera coalition represented left-wing multi-ethnic interests: the AMCJA was a non-Malay body acting for the Federation of Trade Unions, the MDU and the Democratic Youth League while Putera represented essentially the Malay youth, women and peasant groups. There was a perpetuation of the Bose legacy in the MIC's stepping beyond the self-assigned role of representing the Indian community and actively participating in the campaign for a truly democratic, non-communal constitution for Malaya. A solid core of the MIC would remain committed to the ideology of the AMCJA-Putera during the coming years, despite its waning power with the declaration of Emergency.

Thivy played a key role in this transition of MIC loyalties. The evolution over time in Thivy's stance towards India *vis-à-vis* Malaya is interesting to note. In one of his speeches commemorating an INA anniversary in July 1946, he begins with, "The fact that month by month you are observing Azad Hind Day proves that though the form may be destroyed yet the spirit lives." And he then continues to outline the role of the immigrant community: "The Indians in East Asia are the Ambassadors of India. Therefore we are to safeguard the honor and prestige of India by our conduct, organization and culture."[111] It is obvious that he identifies himself and his community, foremost as Indians: the umbilical cord connecting the motherland with her people is yet to be severed. But in a few months' time, at yet another gathering, he comments, "As for the Indians, the best assurance they can give to the Malays will be to declare unequivocally for a single citizenship and declare this land the object of their undivided loyalty. Although the idea of dual citizenship is very tantalizing, I have always felt that single citizenship would be the correct and logical stance."[112] This time the emergence of a Malayan-Indian loyalty is evident and like Bose, the emphasis is on rising above communal differences to focus on national cohesiveness.

Though personally, Thivy would return to India to pursue a career in the Indian diplomatic services, organizationally, he would steer the MIC towards a united front of Malayan resistance. In doing this he would be going against some factions of popular opinion in the Indian community. While earlier the community's response to the proposal of the Malayan Union had been feeble, now with MIC taking up the issue, the Indian opinion finally made itself heard. But unfortunately, MIC's position was severely undermined by factional politics which primarily stemmed from skepticism between migrant Indians and local-born Indians. The Indo-Malayan Association, representing the local Indians, warned the MIC to steer clear of local politics and "dismissed the Congress' comments on the Malayan Union as 'being very mischievous' ".[113] The community was divided in their support of the Union — while the labour unions, influenced by radical opinion, rejected the constitutional proposals, the more conservative elite, led by the CIAM, were mildly approving. But cutting through all the dissension, Thivy and consequently the MIC, remained consistent in support of the Malays and Malay rights throughout this period. Thus, in December 1946, Thivy would assure the Malays that the Indians would "never appeal over the heads of the Malays to the British for any particular right or privilege in the task of establishing a constitution for Malaya" for, if they were to do so, it would sow the seeds of communal dissension.[114] The focus was to be on non-violating the unity of Malaya and the rights of the Malays who were, "by common consent the true inhabitants" of the country. The course of events in India and the ensuing communal violence would also nudge the MIC towards the decision of single citizenship for migrant Indians.

The MIC's stance towards the constitutional proposals was characterized, first, by its opposition to the British in order to protect the sanctity of the Malayan people and then, against the ultra-nationalism of the more conservative UMNO. The MIC found the Malayan Union Scheme unacceptable because of its basic unconstitutional nature — it had been formulated without any consultation of the Malayan leadership. It had been "decided upon in all its details before its return to Malaya" and could only hope to foster fear and suspicion.[115] And since it was unacceptable to the Malays, it could not be condoned by the migrant Indians either. Initially MIC extended a conciliatory hand to the UMNO, urging the party and the Sultans to join the non-Malay struggle against the British. But the attitude changed by mid-1946 as Thivy realized that by dint of a secret nexus with the Malay elite, the British was planning to replace the Malayan Union Scheme with an even more reactionary constitution. A Working Committee had been formed with representation from the UMNO, the Government and the Malay Sultans, completely ignoring the rival radical parties. The divide was as much between Malays and non-Malays as between conservative and radical ideologues.

Thivy would accuse UMNO of unscrupulously playing on Malay fears of "being overwhelmed by the immigrant population" and of being founded "on a narrow fascistic concept of racialism".[116] Subsequently, MIC would veer even more strongly towards the AMCJA-Putera ideology.

Thivy would spend the last months of 1946 and the first half of 1947 in campaigning for a People's Constitution. In his attempt to unite the Malay and non-Malay interests and resist conservative ideologues, he would tour the country, trying to build public opinion. Reminiscent of Bose's attempts at achieving a politically inclusive, non-communal society, he would push for a united Malaya, including Singapore; naturalized citizenship and equal political rights for Malays and non-Malays; special provisions for the advancement of Malays with the simultaneous formation of a Council of Races to prevent any discriminatory legislation based on ethnicity or religion; real sovereign powers for the Sultans who would be elected by popular councils. Thivy, perhaps rather unrealistically, hoped that swayed by the people's voice, the Sultans and UMNO would forego their unilateral negotiations with the British and instead, move towards democracy and greater good for a greater number of people. The People's Constitution proposals would be adopted by the AMCJA-Putera coalition and Thivy would comment: "There were many who thought that the communal unity of Malaya would not stand so severe a test. We have stood the test. ... There was always the specter of communal bargaining facing us ... This desire for unity was the anvil on which this constitution was forged."[117] However, the Constitutional Proposals would be revised by the Government Consultative Committee and published in July 1947. It would be evident that much of the original proposal had been ignored or altered leading to AMCJA and ACCC (Associated Chinese Chambers of Commerce) led strikes in protest. Initially the UMNO would be marginalized in its counter demonstrations. But the implementation of the Federation of Malaya Constitution in February 1948, based on the Revised Constitutional Proposals, would instigate the MCP towards an armed rebellion. Consequently, National Emergency would be declared, marking an end to the AMCJA-Putera coalition which had come to be dominated by the radical Chinese. Going forward, this would leave Malayan politics open to the pro-British conservative elements. In the midst of this turmoil, Thivy would retire to India and Sardar Budh Singh would take over his mantle at MIC. He would continue with the same stance of single citizenship-single nationality.

Thivy had called for seamless integration of Indian and Malayan aspirations at a time when few Indians were ready to forego their professional and commercial interests and do so. It was easier to come to terms with colonialism and return to normalcy after the long years of war. But for Thivy, committed to the INA's political tenets, any concession to the British was complete anathema and as a corollary, nationalism was synonymous with the triumph of non-communal cohesiveness. Just as in this choice he antagonized some members of his own community, ethnic conservative Malays too grew increasingly skeptical of the intents of MIC. He sought to negate the elitist culture perpetuated by the British through their advisory councils which were almost entirely composed of wealthy, English educated members known for their bonhomie with the British. In attempting to counter this trend, he began by reorganizing the newly formed Indian trade unions through the CIAM. But in this he earned the ire of the communist supported GLUs (General Labour Unions), who demanded a non-elitist, democratically elected representative body for Indians. Though he went ahead in attempting to create a mass base among Indian labour, he would find it difficult to reconcile the elitist leadership of the Indian Associations, placed as they were at the other end of the spectrum. Intra-communal suspicions between North and South Indian factions also returned to undermine MIC's fragile unity.

MIC After John Thivy

The path chosen by Thivy would seem increasingly intractable. This organizational dilemma between ideology and the realities of politics would remain with MIC. In 1953, the MIC was hard-pressed to decide between Dato Onn's IMP (Independence of Malaya Party) on one hand, which was theoretically non-communal and yet made no bones about soliciting Malay votes and joining a communal alliance on the other hand, which was ideologically different and yet pushing for early independence. Again under the leadership of K. L. Devaser, another MIC man who had been associated with the IIL and was also Tunku Abdul Rahman's friend from his London days, there would be the same internal impasse.[118] Given the choice between the ideal of non-communalism and joining the tripartite Alliance which represented a powerful electoral force and the future of independent Malaya, Devaser pushed for the latter. Independence would come to Malaya finally on the 31 August 1957 — a day when it rained incessantly since morning and yet the stadium at Kuala Lumpur was filled to capacity and reverberated with cries of *Merdeka*. As the Tunku mentioned, it was no mere coincidence that it had been one of his forefathers who had ceded the first islands of Malaya to the British and now, it was him, who had redeemed independence to the country — history had run its course and ultimately vindicated itself.[119]

BOSE'S POLITICAL LEGACY: CONCLUSION

When the British returned to Southeast Asia at the end of the war, they struggled to regain control as they were confronted by determined nationalist networks of resistance across the region. In this nationalist awakening, the INA and its leader Subhas Chandra Bose had played a key role. His speeches, the INA's public rallies and powerful propaganda drives combined with the mass mobilization that the movement achieved within the Indian community, created an atmosphere of aggression and swirling anti-British sentiments. The war years were a time of rapidly increasing political awareness among the common man and the subsequent period would witness the dawn of mass politics in the true sense of the term with anti-colonial agitation spreading among the plantation labourers and factory workers — both men and women.

By the time of his formal introduction to Asian leaders at the Greater East Asia Conference, Subhas Chandra Bose had already built an enviable reputation for himself. He had led a legendary life of the invincible patriot. Just as Aung San had grown up hearing stories of the Burmese war hero Bo Min Yaung or the Malays heard of Datuk Sagor and Sri Maharajalela, they had also heard of Subhas Chandra Bose and his charmed life. Bose's personal charisma and dexterity as a platform speaker was backed by the century-old tradition of India's political struggle. The message he delivered was too strong to be ignored by the next generation of Asian leaders — some, like Boestamam, adopted his propaganda techniques and oratory style to take his party's message to the masses and some, like Aung San, were influenced by his political philosophy. Perhaps one of the most important political legacies of Bose was his message of non-communalism: John Thivy would use this critical tool to set the direction of the Malayan Indian Congress and it would be endorsed more propitiously in pre-independent Burma. The message of national unity was particularly relevant at the time when freedom from the British, Dutch or the French was being brokered by the local nationalist bodies. And this message of non-communalism remains equally relevant today for the Asian continent whose borders have been repeatedly violated, where countries have been truncated and maps manoeuvred.

Notes

1. Krishna Bose, *Charan Rekha Taba*, Bengali book (Calcutta: Ananda Publishers Pvt Limited, 1996), p. 127.
2. Colonel Prem Sahgal, "Memoirs of an INA Officer", in *Netaji Subhas Chandra Bose: A Malaysian Perspective* (Kuala Lumpur: Netaji Centre, 1992), p. 124.
3. Suniti Kumar Chatterjee, "Netaji, National Unity, the Language Question and the Roman Script", *The Oracle*, vol. I, no. 1 (January 1979): 11.
4. John A. Thivy, *The Struggle in East Asia* (Calcutta: Netaji Research Bureau, 1971), p. 47.
5. Captain Lakshmi Sahgal, *A Revolutionary Life: Memoirs of a Political Activist* (New Delhi: Paul's Press, 1997), p. 64.
6. Abid Hasan Safrani, *The Men from Imphal* (Calcutta: Netaji Research Bureau, 1971), p. 9.
7. Reba Som, *Gandhi, Bose Nehru and the Making of the Modern Indian Mind* (New Delhi: Penguin Viking, 2004), p. 213.
8. Abid Hasan Safrani, *The Men from Imphal*, pp. 13–14.
9. Abid Hasan, "Netaji and the Indian Communal Question", *The Oracle*, vol. I, no. 1 (January 1979): 44.
10. Sisir K. Bose and Sugata Bose, eds., *Chalo Delhi, 1943–1945*, Netaji Collected Works, vol. XII (Calcutta/New Delhi: Netaji Research Bureau/Permanent Black, 2007), p. 35.
11. Ibid., p. 34.
12. Sisir K. Bose and Sugata Bose, eds., *Azad Hind — Subhas Chandra Bose: Writings and Speeches*, Netaji Collected Works, vol. XI (Calcutta/New Delhi: Netaji Research Bureau/Permanent Black, 2007), p. 153.

13. Maj. Gen. Mohammad Zaman Kiani, *India's Freedom Struggle and the Great INA, Memoirs of Maj. Gen. Mohammad Zaman Kiani* (New Delhi: Reliance Publishing House, 1994), p. 51.
14. Ibid., p. 57.
15. M. Sivaram, *The Road to Delhi* (Vermont and Tokyo: Publishers of Rutland, 1967), p. 71.
16. Ibid., p. 72.
17. The Black Hole of Calcutta was a dungeon in Fort William, Calcutta where British Prisoners had been held by Nawab Siraj-ud-dawla in 1756. Later one of the prisoners, John Z. Holwell, claimed that many prisoners had died in the cramped conditions. The British raised a monument in respect of the dead in one corner of Dalhousie Square in 1901.
18. *Chalo Delhi*, p. 98.
19. Ibid., p. 54.
20. D. G. Tendulkar, *Mahatma: Life of M K Gandhi* (New Delhi: Publications Divisions, Ministry of Information and Broadcasting, Government of India, 1963), pp. 107–8.
21. John A. Thivy, *The Struggle in East Asia*, p. 52.
22. Ibid., pp. 64–65.
23. Ibid., p. 66.
24. Sugata Bose, *His Majesty's Opponent: Subhas Chandra Bose and India's Struggle Against Empire* (Cambridge MA: Harvard University Press, 2011), p. 259.
25. John A. Thivy, *The Struggle in East Asia*, pp. 50–51. Letter from Subhas Chandra Bose to Secretary, Ceylon Department, Rear Headquarters, IIL, Syonan, written from Rangoon on 21 June 1944, *Chalo Delhi*, pp. 426–27.
26. Sisir Kumar Bose and Sugata Bose, eds., *The Essential Writings of Netaji Subhas Chandra Bose* (Calcutta/New Delhi: Netaji Research Bureau/Oxford University Press, 1997), p. 85.
27. M. Sivaram, *The Road to Delhi*, p. 133.
28. *Essential Writings of Netaji Subhas Chandra Bose*, p. 141.

29. M. Sivaram, *The Road to Delhi*, p. 139.
30. *Selected Speeches of Subhas Chandra Bose*, p. 268; cited in Dr Moti Lal Bhargava, *Netaji Subhas Chandra Bose in Southeast Asia and India's Liberation War (1943–45)* (Kerala and New Delhi: Vishwavidya Publishers, 1962), p. 164.
31. *Chalo Delhi*, pp. 255–56.
32. Dr Moti Lal Bhargava, *Netaji Subhas Chandra Bose in Southeast Asia and India's Liberation War (1943–45)*, p. 150.
33. Leonard A. Gordon, *Brothers Against the Raj: A Biography of Indian Nationalists* (New Delhi: Rupa & Co., 2008), p. 84.
34. Dr Moti Lal Bhargava, *Netaji Subhas Chandra Bose in Southeast Asia and India's Liberation War (1943–45)*, p. 149.
35. M. Sivaram, *The Road to Delhi*, p. 129.
36. Abid Hasan, "A Soldier Remembers", *The Oracle*, vol. VI, no. 1 (January 1984): 64.
37. M. Sivaram, *The Road to Delhi*, p. 205.
38. *Syonan Shinbun*, Singapore, 3 July–10 July 1945.
39. *Chalo Delhi*, p. 324.
40. Ibid., p. 123.
41. R. K. Dasgupta, "Subhas Chandra as a Writer", *The Oracle*, vol. VI, no. 1 (January 1984): 9.
42. Reba Som, *Gandhi, Bose Nehru and the Making of the Modern Indian Mind* (New Delhi: Penguin Viking, 2004), pp. 137–38.
43. M. Sivaram, *The Road to Delhi*, p. 151.
44. Gerald de Cruz, *Colliding Worlds: Memoirs of a Singapore Maverick* (Marshall Cavendish Editions, 2009), pp. 58–65.
45. Government of Japan, "4th Section, Asian Bureau, Ministry of Foreign Affairs", August 1956, p. 408. The incident is also quoted in Gordon, p. 522.
46. T. S. Eliot, *The Waste Land*.
47. Jan Becka, "Subhas Chandra Bose and the Burmese Freedom Movement", in *Netaji and India's Freedom*, edited by Sisir Kr Bose (Calcutta: Netaji Research Bureau, 1975), p. 57.

48. Ba Maw, "The Great Asian Dreamer", *The Oracle*, vol. II, no. 1 (January 1980): 9.
49. Ibid., p. 10.
50. Ba Maw, *Breakthrough in Burma, Memoirs of a Revolution, 1939–1946* (New Haven: Yale University Press, 1968), p. 345.
51. Ibid., p. 350.
52. Ibid., pp. 352 and 357.
53. Ibid., p. 352.
54. Colonel G. S. Dhillon, "The Nehru Holds the Irrawaddy", *The Oracle*, vol. VI, no. 1 (January 1984): 76–77.
55. Jan Becka, *Subhas Chandra Bose and the Burmese Freedom Movement*, p. 60.
56. Ibid., p. 61.
57. Ibid., p. 64.
58. Ba Maw, *Breakthrough in Burma*, p. 351.
59. S. A. Ayer, *Unto Him A Witness: The Story of Netaji Subhas Chandra Bose in East Asia* (Bombay: Thacker and Co., 1951), p. 319.
60. Angelene Naw, *Aung San and the Struggle for Burmese Independence* (Thailand: Silkworm Books, 2001), p. 36.
61. Gordon, *Brothers Against the Raj*, p. 409.
62. Surendra Prasad Singh, *Growth of Nationalism in Burma, 1900–1942* (Calcutta: Firma KLM Pvt. Ltd., 1980), p. 124.
63. Christopher A. Bayly, "The Eve of Independence: Subhas Bose and Aung San", in *Netaji Oration*, January 2007, <www.netaji.org-oracle_2008.pdf> (accessed 11 August 2011), p. 23.
64. The opinion is ratified in Hugh Tinker, *Men Who Overturned Empires, Fighters, Dreamers and Schemers* (Great Britain: Macmillan Press, 1987), pp. 97–98.
65. Angelene Naw, *Aung San and the Struggle for Burmese Independence*, p. 12.
66. Ibid., p. 48.
67. Gordon, *Brothers Against the Raj*, p. 390.

68. John F. Cady, *A History of Modern Burma*, 2nd ed. (New York: Cornell University Press, 1960), p. 146.
69. Josef Silverstein, ed., *The Political Legacy of Aung San* (New York: Southeast Asia Program Publications, 1993), pp. 45–46.
70. Angelene Naw, *Aung San and the Struggle for Burmese Independence*, p. 81.
71. Josef Silverstein, ed., *The Political Legacy of Aung San*, p. 46.
72. Louis Allen, *End of the War in Asia* (London: Hart-Davis MacGibbon, 1976), p. 18.
73. *The Burman*, 11 May 1946, cited in *Aung San and the Struggle for Burmese Independence*, p. 161.
74. *Burma Review*, vol. 1, 20 May 1946, p. 10, cited in *Aung San and the Struggle for Burmese Independence*, p. 162.
75. Ibid., p. 67.
76. *Essential Writings of Netaji Subhas Chandra Bose*, p. 190.
77. Angelene Naw, *Aung San and the Struggle for Burmese Independence*, p. 67.
78. *Aung San Suu Kyi, Aung San* (University of Queensland Press, Australia, Lawrence, Mass., USA; Distributed in the USA and Canada by Technical Impex Corp., 1984), p. 8.
79. Muang Muang U, *A Trial in Burma: The Assassination of Aung San* (The Hague: M. Nijhoff, 1962), p. 96; also cited in Josef Silverstein, ed., *The Political Legacy of Aung San*, p. 5.
80. Mikael Gravers, *Nationalism as Political Paranoia in Burma* (Great Britain: Curzon Press, 1999), p. 41.
81. Muang Muang U, ed., *Aung San of Burma*, pp. 123–24.
82. *The Burman*, 22 January 1946, cited in *Aung San and the Struggle for Burmese Independence*, p. 147.
83. Josef Silverstein, ed., *The Political Legacy of Aung San*, p. 10.
84. Angelene Naw, *Aung San and the Struggle for Burmese Independence*, p. 199.
85. Jan Becka, *Subhas Chandra Bose and the Burmese Freedom Movement*, pp. 73–75.

86. Aung San, "Welcome India", *Aung San of Burma*, 24 July 1946, <www.aungsan.com/Links.htm> (accessed 12 August 2011).
87. Usha Mahajani, *The Role of Indian Minorities in Burma and Malaya* (Bombay: Vora & Co., Ltd. for the Institute of Pacific Relations, 1960), p. 186.
88. Ibid., pp. 187–88.
89. Mustapha Hussain, *Malay Nationalism before UMNO: The Memoirs of Mustapha Hussain* (Kuala Lumpur: Utusan Publications & Distributors Sdn Bhd, 2005), p. 255.
90. Ibid., p. 207.
91. Ibid., p. 254.
92. Ibid., p. 339.
93. Ibid., p. 280.
94. Ramlah Adam, Malay book, *Ahmad Boestamam: Satu Biografi Politik, Dewan Bahasadan Pustaka, Kementerian Pendidikan* (Malaysia, Kuala Lumpur: 1994), p. 69 (BAB 4: Penglibatan A Boestamam Dalam). See note 12: Dari Nasionalis ke Sosialis, journal vol. 2, no. 23, February, p. 15.
95. Ahmad Boestamam, *Memoir Ahmad Boestamam: Merdeka dengan Darah dalam Api* (Penerbit Universiti Kebangsaan Malaysia: Malaysian Book Publishers Association, Bangi, 2004), pp. 92–97.
96. Mention of interview in *Kata Pengantar, oleh Tan Sri A Samad Ismail*, from Ahmad Boestamam, *Memoir Ahmad Boestamam: Merdeka dengan Darah dalam Api*, p. 18.
97. Ramlah Adam, *Ahmad Boestamam: Satu Biografi Politik*, pp. 68–69 (BAB 4: Penglibatan A Boestamam Dalam). Mention of Subhas Chandra Bose's influence on Boestamam in writing *Testament Politik* of API, in *Kata Pengantar, oleh Tan Sri A Samad Ismail*, from Ahmad Boestamam, Memoir Ahmad Boestamam: Merdeka dengan Darah dalam Api, p. 18.
98. Ramlah Adam, *Ahmad Boestamam: Satu Biografi Politik*, p. 4 (BAB 1: Tahun-tahun Awal Kehidupan, 1920–1939). Also see note 16:

Memoir Seorang Penulis, Kuala Lumpur, Dewan Bahasa dan Pustaka, p. 15.
99. Mustapha Hussain, *Malay Nationalism before UMNO: The Memoirs of Mustapha Hussain*, p. 331.
100. Ahmad Boestamam, *Carving the Path to the Summit* (Athens: Ohio University Press, 1979), p. 34.
101. Christopher Bayly and Tim Harper, *Forgotten Wars: The End of the Britain's Asian Empire* (Penguin Books, 2008), p. 353.
102. Mustapha Hussain, *Malay Nationalism before UMNO: The Memoirs of Mustapha Hussain*, p. 337.
103. Rajeswary Ampalavanar, *The Indian Minority and Political Change in Malaya, 1945–1957* (Kuala Lumpur: Oxford University Press, 1981), p. 106.
104. Michael Stenson, *Class, Race and Colonialism in West Malaysia: The Indian Case* (Australia: University of Queensland Press, St. Lucia, 1980), p. 142.
105. Rajeswary Ampalavanar, *The Indian Minority and Political Change in Malaya, 1945–1957*, p. 78.
106. *Netaji Subhas Chandra Bose: A Malaysian Perspective*, p. 4.
107. Michael Stenson, *Class, Race and Colonialism in West Malaysia: The Indian Case*, p. 158.
108. Draft Proposals for an All Malayan Indian Organisation, presented at the MIC conference, quoted in Usha Mahajani, *The Role of Indian Minorities in Burma and Malaya*, p. 219.
109. Ibid., p. 219.
110. Michael Stenson, *Class, Race and Colonialism in West Malaysia: The Indian Case*, p. 149.
111. John A. Thivy, *Indian Daily Mail, Malaya*, 28 July 1946.
112. Ibid., 16 January 1947.
113. Rajeswary Ampalavanar, *The Indian Minority and Political Change in Malaya, 1945–1957*, p. 83.
114. Presidential address by Thivy at the first annual session of MIC, Ibid., p. 83.

115. Thivy papers, 21 October 1946, quoted in Michael Stenson, *Class, Race and Colonialism in West Malaysia: The Indian Case*, p. 154.
116. MIC Working Committee, "The History of the Congress Association in the Constitutional Issue", Thivy Papers, Kuala Lumpur, 1948, pp. 6–7.
117. John A. Thivy, *Indian Daily Mail*, Malaya, 19 July 1946.
118. Devaser's League connection is mentioned in Usha Mahajani, *The Role of Indian Minorities in Burma and Malaya*, p. 245. The Selangor Indian Regional Congress was led by V. J. Somasundaram who had been a Major in the INA and a founder-member of the MIC.
119. Tunku Abdul Rahman, *As a Matter of Interest* (Kuala Lumpur; Singapore: Heinemann Asia, 1981), p. 15.

Chapter 4

WE ARE THE MULTITUDES

> "An odor has remained among the sugarcane:
> A mixture of blood and body ...
> Between the coconut palms the graves are full
> Of ruined bones ...
> The weeping cannot be seen, like a plant
> Whose seeds fall endlessly on the earth.
> Whose large blind leaves grow even without light."
> — The Dictators, Pablo Neruda

LABOUR LINES

In one of the books by an INA veteran, there is a description of a League meeting at a rubber plantation. The Indian Independence League's (IIL) message was conveyed to the plantations on the Malaya-Thailand border. It was a plantation like any other of this region. As the young representative of the League spoke, the Tamil workers gathered around him in silence. Their silence was emphasized by the rows and rows of tall, symmetrical rubber trees that surrounded them, effectively cutting them off from the world. The canopy of leaves over their heads was so dense that sunlight seemed never to have penetrated down below. The dampness of the forest floor seeped into their feet. In the distance stood the labour lines — *attap* huts with zinc roofs.

As he spoke of the nationalist struggle, a heavy shower broke out. Streaks of lightning could be seen far above their heads. And yet the labourers never spoke or moved away from the meeting place. After a quarter of an hour, droplets of rain trickled down — the thick foliage above did not permit any of the soaking downpour to find its way down. But once the *tup-tup* of the rain drops falling on the leafage began, it never seemed to stop. The speaker felt it would drive him frantic. And yet the workers stood around him in silence in the gloomy half-light — seemingly drinking in the words he spoke.[1]

BOSE AND TRADE UNIONS

Subhas Chandra Bose's interactions with trade unions and worker movements began early, under the tutelage of his political guru, Chittaranjan Das. The All India Trade Union Congress (AITUC) became active during the economic recession which tailed the First World War boom. C. R. Das served as the President of AITUC in 1922, and it was around this time that Bose too started taking an active interest in mass mobilization of labour. Though they did speak to peasants, as city dwellers, both Das and Bose initially addressed the concerns of urban workers. Following in Das' footsteps, Bose was President of the AITUC during the years 1930–31. He presided over a number of other worker unions as well — the unions of the Calcutta Corporation, the Bengal Oil and Petrol Workers' Union, Jamshedpur Labour Association, All Bengal Railway Indian Employees' Association were among them.[2] His message to the workers was akin to his message to the other groups he worked with — the youth, the professionals or the women. While addressing the economic grievances of the workers and urging them to form strong unions, he never forgot to emphasize on the wider issues of nationalism and the need to achieve independence. In his speeches he highlighted the British impact on the Indian economy — on losing indigenous resources and India's increasing dependence on foreign imports. He felt the workers could play an effective role in the economic revival of the country if *Swaraj* [self-rule] and labour movements could be brought together. Bose was never involved in day-to-day union building but consistently worked towards raising the levels of political awareness of the unions. With this purpose in mind, in 1929, he put together a small book called *Boycott of British Goods* which effectively linked *boycott* with *Swadeshi* or indigenous efforts of production.[3]

One of Bose's most intense involvements with unions was in the context of the business house of the Tatas. The Tata Iron and Steel Company (TISCO) was an important early venture with Indian capital and the likes of C. R. Das and Motilal Nehru had worked towards the recognition of its union. Bose was asked to intervene on behalf of the workers in the TISCO strikes of 1927–28. During the next few years, Bose continued to work as a mediator between the management and the union, trying to work out an understanding which would be advantageous to both parties. With the management playing off one labour group against another, Bose emphasized the need of worker solidarity. He tried to bring the warring factions of white-collar Bengalis with blue-collar non-Bengalis as well as the radical and more moderate groups of workers together. His involvement with TISCO and the associated industries continued to the 1930s when he was exiled to Europe. So we find him writing to Sir N. B. Saklatvala, Chairman of the Tata group, about the eviction of the Labour Association from their company-owned quarters, all the way from Vienna.[4]

Bose had to take on this role of a mediator, time and again, in his interactions with the AITUC as well. As the President, he struggled to balance the communist, socialist and the more conventional right-wing members of the federation. The first serious split in the AITUC occurred in December 1929, when Bose was taking over as President. At the Nagpur session, the radicals defeated the right on a number of issues, who as a result, staged a walk out from the AITUC Executive Committee. Bose published a statement, appealing to them to reconsider their decision: "... if they [i.e., the right wing] believe in democracy they cannot object to the growing importance of the Left Wing in the TUC, nor can they grudge the recognition granted to the Girni Kamgar union [a radical union from Bombay]."[5] He was caught again in a similar crossfire in 1931, with yet another serious dispute within the AITUC. This time at the AITUC, Calcutta session, the communist group led by the AITUC Secretary, S. V. Deshpande from Bombay, decided to split from the federation. Referring to the earlier split by the right wing, he commented, "On the other side there were the Moscow communists led by the Bombay group who followed blindly the dictates of Moscow in the matter of their ideals, methods and tactics." And he continued, "The Moscow Communists are a serious menace to the growth of healthy trade unionism in India and we cannot possibly leave the field to them."[6] Just as earlier, he had berated the right wing for rejecting the unanimous consensus of the Executive Committee, this time he was equally vocal in not accepting doctrinaire communism. For him what was of importance was addressing the real concerns of the beleaguered workers — the retrenchments, wage-cuts, unemployment that they faced every day. These issues needed to be ironed out so that they could focus on their real work of contributing to the economy and thereby helping in nation building. And for this, according to Bose, India would have to work out a solution that suited her best, independent of any political indoctrination. He concluded his AITUC address with a statement that leaves little space for conjecture: "... India should be able to evolve her own methods in keeping with her own needs and her own environment. In applying any theory to practice, you can never rule out geography or history. If you attempt it, you are bound to fail."[7]

INDIAN LABOUR IN MALAYA — PRE-WAR SCENARIO

In Malaya, during the pre-war years, though the need to mobilize the vast mass of Indian labour was felt, the actual process was still at a rudimentary level. In 1939, N. Raghavan was elected as the President of CIAM (Central Indian Association of Malaya) and he started actively encouraging the Indian Associations to expand their membership base. The reorganization of the Associations in the Selangor state was led by the likes of R. H. Nathan — an English-educated intellectual who was on the board of the popular Tamil newspaper, *Tamil Nesan*. In the Klang district, the work of two other nationalistic social reformers, Y. S. Menon and Y. K. Menon, had already emerged. These young men represented the CIAM elite. Along with other members of their group, they were part of the intelligentsia and believed in the ethos of socialism. However, their high status, combined with their mainly Malayalee origin precluded them from, "directly mobilizing the mass of the Indian population".[8]

The war and the attendant economic crisis intensified the exploitation of the Indian labour. While the production of rubber and its price went steadily up, there was no commensurate redress of grievances regarding the low wages or poor living conditions of the workers. During the inter-war years rubber had been the largest single U.S. dollar earning export of the sterling area. The value of the per capita output of rubber estate workers increased by over 55 per cent, between 1939 and 1940, which would seem to warrant an increase of the per day male tapper's wage to at least 75 cents.[9] The rubber companies, however, were adamant in holding the Indian labourer's wage at an average of 50 cents per day. Any allowances to cope with a higher cost of living were to be paid in rice or as a separate allowance not connected to the wage. It was at this time that the strikes in the Klang district of Selangor were actively encouraged by R. H. Nathan and his associates. Soon, Raghavan and other CIAM leaders stepped in and as a result of their negotiations, the Klang District Planting Associations conceded to an additional 5 cents cost-of-living allowance. Although, as a result of this announcement the strikes were called off, resentment simmered since not only was the increase too meager, the other demands of the workers had been completely ignored. Nathan continued speaking to the workers, telling them to wear what they liked, not to get off from their cycles when passing the estate officials and not to fear replacement by a Chinese or Javanese workforce. The British High Commissioner ordered Nathan's arrest on 5 May 1941 and the Punjab Regiment and other troops were called in to disperse demonstrators protesting against his arrest. A state of emergency was declared in the state of Selangor and by the end of May, around 300 workers were arrested, at least five killed and many others injured. While Y. K. Menon returned to India, Raghavan also left the country for a while, on a self-imposed exile.

The Indian leadership was caught completely off-guard as the British came down to ruthlessly suppress the strikes. They had failed to forge any connection with the Malayan Communist Party and the Chinese estate workers it represented. In fact there was only one Indian MCP activist in Selangor, R. K. Thangaiah.[10] A united front with a larger support base could have turned the tides in their favour. Though the Klang strikes failed, the sense of a failed mission remained with the workers, as did their accumulated rage at the British. Later, Raghavan wrote, the events of 1941, "tended to create a feeling of suppressed anger among Indians".[11] This sense of impotent fury was one of the key triggers for the widespread enthusiasm that the INA campaigns later generated.

CIAM AND IIL (INDIAN INDEPENDENCE LEAGUE)

With the advent of Rashbehari Bose's IIL in Southeast Asia, in the first half of 1942, it was all but natural for the CIAM leadership to throw in their lot with the new movement. Already deeply influenced by the Indian National Congress and the Indian political leaders, the CIAM elite, including N. Raghavan, K. P. S. Menon (as distinct from Y. K. Menon) and S. C. Goho, decided to join the various branches of the IIL that were established all over Malaya. However, all along they remained deeply suspicious of the Japanese motives and consequently of the Rashbehari Bose leadership, with its Japanese connections. In the East Asia Conference, held in Bangkok in 1942, they led the way in demanding complete autonomy of the League's operations and non-intervention by the Japanese. It was decided that the IIL would bear the cost of the INA and also the responsibility of recruitments. Japanese help would be sought only for arms, ammunitions and other equipments.[12] The CIAM leadership's skepticism only deepened since the Japanese was not forthcoming in their commitment and ultimately this rift led to the initial collapse of the League. Raghavan and K. P. S. Menon resigned over a fallout with the Japanese regarding the formation of the Indian Youth League. It was later, with Bose's taking over the reins of the IIL, that Raghavan would join back the ministry of the Provisional Government.

Unlike the CIAM elite who were presented with a viable option with the IIL, the Indian workers on the plantations found their strictly-regimented, routine-bound lives suddenly disrupted by the Japanese occupation. The Japanese followed up their invasion of Malaya with a period of chaotic brutality. The Chinese community suffered the maximum as anybody connected with the China Relief Fund or the communist party were savagely sought out and killed by the Japanese. On the plantations, the European managers had left, leaving the Asian estate staff in charge. In most cases this led to a dismantling of the hierarchical power structure with the workers openly challenging their authority and often using this opportunity to settle old scores. The deadly reprisals of the Japanese somewhat mellowed down by mid-1942, as they turned to govern their newly acquired territories. With the Japanese asserting authority, some of the rubber estates returned to production but total production ran at a mere fraction of pre-war levels.[13] As a result, a large number of the estate labourers found themselves unemployed. A substantial section of Indian labourers, along with Australian, Briton and American troops and Chinese and Malay workers were coerced into working on the infamous "Death Railway", where thousands died of disease and starvation. The Tamils, redundant on the estates now, were worst hit as the Japanese considered them entirely dispensable. There are horrific stories that the survivors from the "Death Railway" tell of Japanese atrocities against Asian workers, with cholera patients being buried alive and deaths on a large scale. The number of victims went up to as many as 150,000, over two years.[14] Later, Bose would send his emissary, Amar Singh from Bangkok, to investigate the situation and when the investigators confirmed the worst rumours, would take up the issue strongly with the Japanese army.[15]

With the destruction of the estate structures, most Indian labourers were left to fend for themselves and were hit hard by wartime scarcities. The employment market became even more irregular and inadequate and their experience of physical degradation reached an all-time low. M. Sivaram, a journalist who would join Bose later in his propaganda team, remarks: "It was difficult to see how Malaya, where people of all classes had enjoyed fairly high standards of living, had been reduced to such abject poverty and distress in a little over a year of Japanese military occupation ... in Malaya, the pivot of the co-prosperity sphere, the people had been living on semi-starvation rations."[16] As rice became more and more scarce, the Japanese made cultivation of tapioca compulsory and the rice-eating populace was advised to switch to tapioca. It was at this juncture that Subhas Chandra Bose appeared on the scene and not surprisingly was welcomed as a messiah who would redeem the Indians' fortune. As an onlooker described his mass rallies, which were to become such an important event for the Southeast Asian Indians: "Every man and woman in the audience feels that he is talking to him or her in particular. He indulges in no theatricals. No water to be sipped, nobody to fan him, not a scrap of notes to help memory, no fuss and no fluster ..."[17]

With the arrival of Bose, a large number of Indians from the previously formed Indian Associations joined the Indian Independence League. While the English-speaking members of the former Indian Associations provided the top leadership of the League and the INA, the lower leadership came from the clerks, Tamil *kanganies* and school teachers, and the rank-and-file was made up of the more politically conscious estates workers. A multitude of labourers came forward to join the nationalist cause. Even when some did not participate directly in the army, they were exposed to the mass rallies and fund-raising campaigns of the League. In contrast to their earlier isolated lives on the plantations, mostly cut-off from the Indian community life, this new mobilization opened up their worlds. The military training at the INA prepared them for taking up leadership roles: "In the course of the war, these latter groups [workers] gained experience in leadership and organization, acquired some of the discipline and skills of soldiers and became imbued with a sense of nationalist obligation for the upliftment of their community."[18] For the first time, there was better intermingling between the English-educated Indian elite, the petty bourgeoisie and the barely literate, Indian workers. Army life at the INA camps threw up a rich array of thoughts on not only nationalism but on other radical political schools like socialism, communism and the Dravidian reawakening. It was a time of introspecting and redefining one's ideas of freedom, a time of new learning with lectures and radio broadcasts on anti-imperialism by the IIL leaders. Pamphlets on subjects like "Religion", "Caste and War", "Poverty Amidst Plenty", were regularly circulated while the Tamil versions of the INA publications, *Free India* (daily) and *Young India* (weekly), were especially influential in heightening the political awareness of the Tamil workers.[19] Another powerful tool the INA used to shape the Indian mind was the *Balak Sena* or the youth wing. The Education and Culture Department of the IIL had a well planned scheme of National Education for the young children and under it, schools were opened with Tamil or Hindustani as the mediums of instruction. Soon, these National Schools became quite popular and students from these schools who were under fourteen joined the *Balak* or *Balika Senas* of the INA. They would attend public meetings, demonstrations and rallies and were trained physically, as well as taught patriotic songs. As John Thivy wrote: "They [the children] learnt national songs and sang them in their homes ... in their lusty voices to eventually find an answering echo in the mature but faltering voices of their parents and elders."[20] The INA movement helped the Indian community to look beyond immediate domestic realities and gain a new insight not only into their political past but also the world around them which was so rapidly changing.

INDIAN LABOUR — POST-WAR SCENARIO: THE INA AND INDIAN LABOUR UNIONS

While the Indian labour force was still finding its feet in the pre-war days, the Chinese community was far advanced in its labour mobilization. The Malayan Communist Party (MCP) had already been founded in the early 1930s. Though it was founded as a multi-ethnic organization, the membership was pre-eminently Chinese. The years 1936–41 was characterized by the party's remarkable breakthrough in the fields of labour and the national salvation movements. Amid the economic downturn of this period, the MCP went all out to organize and mobilize workers to strike against the key industries of British Malaya, including the Singapore Harbour Board, the Singapore Municipality, the construction works, the Batu Arang Collieries as well as the tin mines and rubber plantations of Malaya. By 1941, the Malayan General Labour Union (MGLU) and its affiliate organizations had a membership of 100,000 and the fact the MCP was able to, "strike at the economic heartland of British Malaya showed that the party had come of age with a deepened power base in labour unions".[21]

On the eve of the Japanese invasion of Malaya, in December 1941, the MCP had a solid mass base and the Malayan Communists were the only effective, "resistance army against the new Japanese conqueror in much of Malaya" to whom the British could turn for assistance.[22] In the last days before the fall of Singapore, the MCP put aside its struggle against British imperialism. Instead the British Special Operations Executive (SOE) began training the Chinese communists in guerilla warfare. They were left behind enemy lines in a bid to help build resistance and carry out sabotage missions against the Japanese. The invading Japanese in the first flush of victory was relentless in their witch-hunt of the communists. The Chinese were subjected to the notorious

Sook Ching — that is, a rounding up and weeding out of the alleged leftists and anti-Japanese elements. By late 1942, the Chinese nationalists and communists "simply disappeared into the Malayan jungle".[23] They started organizing themselves into camps and armed with the tommy guns and grenades the British had left them, prepared for the long-drawn-out war that was to ensue. The period of Japanese occupation enhanced the already strong trend of MCP as representative of Chinese nationalism and resulted in the widespread adaptation of the communist ideology among Chinese youth. They were the ones who provided the core of the Malayan People's Anti-Japanese Army (MPAJA) and its civilian wing, the Malayan People's Anti-Japanese Union (MPAJU), during the Japanese occupation.

At the end of the war, the MPAJA guerilla emerged as popular heroes among the Chinese. They had aided the British in a guerilla war against the Japanese and would eventually go on to attempt a red revolution against the returning British as well. In the meantime, the MPAJA had been joined by a young set of Malayan-born cadres and the movement came to take on a more Malayan outlook. During the Depression and the resultant lack of employment, a steady flow of workers had taken up residence in the forested areas behind the industrial belts. They had taken to cultivating their own food in small "market gardens" and in the eyes of the colonial law were the illegal "squatters".[24] Their numbers swelled to nearly a half-million during the war and they often took over defunct rubber estates to grow crops and tend livestock. These squatter colonies, away from the public eye, soon became congregation points for the MPAJA forces. They not only got their regular supplies from here but also used these colonies to set up their intelligence networks.

The war ended rather abruptly with the bombing of Hiroshima and Nagasaki in August 1945. The Japanese surrender was quickly followed by the proclamation of the British Military

Administration (BMA) in Malaya. The purpose of the BMA was to restore British authority after an absence of three-and-a-half years. Malaya would remain under the sway of the BMA till April 1946 and this interregnum was a period of painful discoveries as the true extent of Japanese atrocities unfolded. The jails of Singapore and Malaya were emptied of its thousands of European prisoners-of-war. Official sources listed close to 75,000 POWs in the Southeast Asian theatre alone.[25] Medical and hospital facilities were appalling and two days after the return of the British the Japanese banana money was declared worthless. Since this was the only currency in circulation, this declaration sent the already unstable economy spiralling out of control and black market prices soared. In this period of confusion, the INA found itself disbanded and leaderless. Large numbers of INA men were detained in various internment camps all over Southeast Asia while others were repatriated to India and then dishonourably discharged from the ranks without pay or provision. In one of its first operations, on 8 September 1945, the SEAC (Southeast Asia Command) pulled down the INA War Memorial in Esplanade, Singapore. Bose had laid its foundation stone only two months previously.

On the other hand, the Malay Peninsula was virtually taken over by the Chinese guerilla of the MCP. During the interregnum, the MPAJA set up indigenous courts of law in the inland towns and meted out justice of sorts to the Japanese collaborators. Their forces captured village police stations, arms and ammunition dumps left by the Japanese and seized transport.[26] It was also a time when the contact between the INA and the MPAJA grew, as many ex-INA men found their way to the squatter colonies near the industrial areas where they had been previously employed. The Janus face of the BMA revealed itself — they tried to appease the MCP without letting it intervene in their peacetime administration. Though the MCP was allowed to operate openly for the first time and the MPAJA was lavished with praise for their role during the

Japanese occupation, official recognition was held back. Initially the MCP leadership was divided on the issue of immediately leading a struggle against the British, however it did not take them long to organize themselves. Under MCP direction, People's Committees were set up in most towns and many villages. The pre-war General Labour Unions were revived and while earlier they had gone underground, now they set up new offices and set about mobilizing labour throughout the country. The INA men, seeing this as a continuation of their struggle against British hegemony, forged an alliance with the communists. While for the MCP, the INA personnel, indoctrinated in anti-British ideology, were attractive candidates for recruitment.

Former INA personnel took the lead in forming the Indian sections of the General Labour Unions (GLUs). Thus 1946 finally saw some kind of worker solidarity emerging with a new "Chinese/Indian working class alliance".[27] For the Indian community, demoralized after the sudden death of their leader, this was an articulation of their political awakening and a means to protect their newly discovered "dignity and self-respect".[28] Apart from the labour unions that were set up by the former INA men in collaboration with the MCP, there were other former INA and former IIL members who set up independent Indian labour unions of their own. Like the GLUs, these independent unions were set up in every district and took the various categories of Indian labour under their folds. Such unions were set up first in Negri Sembilan and Kedah and later, in Johore and Perak as well and most of the organizers were young former members of the INA.[29] There was the Perak Indian Labour Association, headed by M. C. P. Menon from the INA who could garner support from a large group of enthusiasts including women. By June 1946, the Association held sway over most of central Perak. The Negri Sembilan Indian Labour Union was headed by H. K. Choudhury and P. P. Narayanan — both English-speaking former members of the INA.[30] But perhaps the most remarkable was the Kedah Indian Labour Union, headed by A. M. Samy, a fifty-one-year-old estate shopkeeper and lorry driver who, though not a part of the INA, was nevertheless influenced by its anti-imperial philosophy.[31] Samy was remarkable because, unlike the other educated, elitist leaders, he rose from the estate ranks to voluntarily take up leadership of the labour movement.

The returning British planters were determined to reinforce the pre-war regimentation on the estates. For them it was a return to the relentless routine which had prevailed earlier with the ritualistic morning roll-call at 4.30 a.m. followed by the mandatory hoisting of the Union Jack. After this, the day would be set into motion with the tappers, weeders, the pest-and-drainage gangs each assigned their gruelling daily schedules. It was a mechanized world where the men and women operated as extensions of the geometrical lines of rubber trees they tapped — both performing a pre-determined role to enhance the commercial viability of the estates. The planter's control over the worker's mind and body was complete: "Managers and overseers competed to achieve a 'mathematic perfection of movement that does away with every redundant gesture; it even governed bodily necessities — labourers were encouraged to urinate in their buckets to prevent the latex coagulating."[32] Estates were still private property, with strict trespass laws and there was no chance for the workers to move freely between employers or collaborate with other estate workers for collective bargaining.

Thodar Pedai: Dublin Estate Strikes

A. M. Samy returned home after the war to the Harvard Estate, near Bedong in central Kedah. At the time, the burning issue was against the selling of *toddy* in the estate shops by the planters.

Toddy, like the old practice of opium sale and consumption in British or Dutch colonies, kept the workers docile and effectively silenced any spirit of rebellion. Samy set about reviving the civilian vigilance group that the British management had put together on the eve of Japanese invasion. He called it the *thodar pedai* or labourer's militia. Initially, they worked as a volunteer corps and helped the police maintain discipline at religious processions. But soon, the *thodar pedai* started campaigning against the sale of liquor and picketing toddy shops. In May 1946, the workers at the Harvard Estate stopped work, protesting against the reopening of the toddy shops on the estate and the strike was actively supported by the *thodar pedai*. Samy soon had a following of around 1,500 men who wore their old INA caps and trained in mock battles.[33] The leaders of the *thodar pedai* made impassioned speeches to the workers and Samy founded the Harvard Estate Labour Union and began negotiating for better working conditions and wages. He soon branched out to form unions on neighbouring estates and, by early 1947, had the support of around 13,000 labourers in Kedah.[34] With the mass base and support from the Kedah GLU for Samy, the rebellion came to a head and the managers and staff of the estates increasingly got the feeling that they were losing control.

It did not take long to alarm the authorities, and in February 1947, a crowd of *thodar pedai* picketing at a toddy shop in Bedong was assaulted by the police. A worker was clubbed to death and twelve leaders including Samy arrested. A series of protest strikes followed, spreading rapidly not only in central Kedah but also to Selangor and Johore. At the Dublin Estate in Kedah, Chinese workers came out, supporting the Indian labour union. The *thodar pedai* moved close to the radical Pan-Malayan Federation of Trade Unions led by another INA veteran S. A. Ganapathy. During the Emergency both the Federation as well the *thodar pedai* would be banned. Ganapathy would be accused of carrying arms and sentenced to death. Appeals for clemency by Indian leaders would go unheard and he would be hanged at the Pudu jail in 1949.

Similar youth associations like the *thodar pedai* were organized amongst different groups of Indian workers, particularly on estates.[35] The overarching sentiment of these groups was of Indian nationalism and the leaders would make impassioned speeches invoking the achievements of the INC in India and the INA in Southeast Asia. The workers would be incited to assert their independence and demand better economic and general working conditions.[36] Along with the basic amenities, the Indian unions as well as the GLUs, demanded better educational facilities on the estates. At this time, the Indian labourers took the lead in establishing schools in Penang and other parts of Malaya for the estate children.

Militancy amongst the Indian workers of the rubber industry did not die down with the arrest of the Kedah leaders. The Federation of Trade Unions (FTUs), led by the Selangor Estate Workers' Trade Unions, was in the process of forging a country-wide agreement on behalf of estate workers which included demands like: a 100 per cent increase for all Indian workers, a war bonus or rehabilitation grant, sick pay, better quarters and living conditions, longer notice before eviction and the removal of trespass restrictions.[37] The agreement also intended to address the existing disparity between the pay of Chinese and Indian workers. The Kedah incident proved to be a powerful turning point: while the Indian community was incensed by the government's handling of it, the estate officials on the other hand were anxious to put an end to the unrest and initiate bargaining procedures. It was a time of labour shortage, high costs and declining rubber prices. Faced with this grim economic scenario, the United Planters' Association of Malaya (UPAM) used every tactic possible to first avoid meeting the unionists and then in granting the concessions they demanded. The negotiations went through many twists and turns with the UPAM attempting to weaken the worker alliance and questioning the legal status of the negotiating union bodies. The final agreement, reached in 1948, would be a compromise decision with the demands of the Indian workers only partially met. The radical struggle would bring the Indians a modicum of dignity: by the 1950s, estates workers were no longer compelled to dismount from their bicycles when a manager passed by or were not subject to physical assault. The labour movement would continue with armed struggle breaking out across industrial sectors and, by June 1948, Emergency would be declared in Malaya. The period of Emergency would be war in another name with the fury of counter-insurgency dragging on past the 1950s. The trauma of arrests, detentions, deportations would tear apart the community of unionists. The MCP would again withdraw into the jungles and continue to wage war through sabotage missions.

JAMES PUTHUCHEARY

James J. Puthucheary (1923–2000) returned from two harrowing years at the Burma war-front and a subsequent period spent in Calcutta and then Santiniketan, the university founded by poet Rabindranath Tagore, to Singapore in 1948 with two overriding principles that would change his life forever — a strong anti-colonial fervour and a new capacity to look beyond parochial politics. His father was from South India who had later settled at Johor Bahru, Malaya. James was all of twenty and had just completed his secondary education when he joined Subhas Chandra Bose's INA. He was yet another former INA loyalist who later crossed over to join the worker movement in Singapore. In 1955, he was appointed one of the secretaries of the Singapore Factory and Shop Workers' Union, the largest trade union in Singapore. What was remarkable about James was, with time, he came to represent the intellectual left of Malayan nationalism, a part of a small exclusive group that would be dubbed the "English speaking intelligentsia or ESI" by colonial authorities. He was an economist, a trade unionist and later, a lawyer, who was a founding member of the People's Action Party (PAP) and then broke away from the PAP to join the opposing Barisan Sosialis in 1961, as part of the "Big Six" trade unionists.

James was a part of the guerilla outfit of the third regiment of the INA's first division, the Azad Brigade commanded by Gulzara Singh, which had played a key role in the Imphal-Kohima offensive. He had been stationed at Palel, on the outskirts of Imphal, and seen fierce fighting along the Tamu-Moreh-Palel-Imphal road during the month of May 1944. By the third week of June, early monsoons swept away the INA's advantage and effectively cut off supply lines. James was a part of the humiliating and physically exhausting retreat from Burma which commenced in July. Lack of food and medicines took a heavy toll on the regiments of the INA's first division and James was the only one of his platoon to have survived the cruel journey.[38] At the end of the war, in an attempt to continue the struggle, he flew to Calcutta with help from Indian officers of the Royal Air Force. He spent several months hidden in Subhas Chandra Bose's ancestral home and then joined the liberation movement of India. It was the time of the INA trials and nationalist emotions were at a fevered pitch. James returned to Singapore only in 1948, after India had gained her long sought after independence, to find his homeland greatly changed.

In Malaya, the INA had left behind an overarching sense of political awakening among the Indian working class. James had already been baptized into Marxist literature at the INA battle front and his belief in left-wing politics had only been reinforced during the time spent in Calcutta. On return it would have been easy for him to be swept away by the pro-communist winds of change. Many of his friends from the MNP or API had decided to take up arms to continue the anti-colonial struggle. But James, instead of entering the jungles with other communists, became a part of the intellectual zymosis at work in the Raffles College of Singapore. By 1948, there was already a left-wing student movement at the Raffles College with links to the Anti-British League and the Malayan Democratic Union (MDU). He soon became actively involved in student politics and, by May 1949, was instrumental in the formation of the Malayan Student's Party. The party actively campaigned for developing a Malayan culture and consciousness. In their bid to realize a Malayan nation, they propounded sacrificing narrow racial identities and embracing a larger national identity. This led to his first arrest in January 1951, by the Singapore Special Branch. James was detained for one-and-a-half years without a trial.

But despite his multiple arrests and detentions (though like his earlier political inspiration, Bose, he used these periods of solitary imprisonment well — in study and introspection), the anti-colonial stance would remain with James as would his intellectual preoccupation with multi-racial politics — both of which had been the founding tenets of the INA movement. He spent the three years of his second detention in 1956 at the Changi prison, researching and putting together a book called, *Ownership and Control in the Malayan Economy*. In it James argues that the Singaporean and Malayan economies were controlled by a tightly-knit web of European "agency houses". These agency houses played a central role in controlling most of the country's imports and exports as well as represented most of the insurance and shipping companies operating in the country. In James' economic analysis, what stands out is his belief that labour organized under the exploitative economic system fostered by colonial rule was not conducive to racial cooperation.

He deflects the contemporary spotlight on Chinese capitalists and mentions: "The idea that Chinese capitalists dominate the economy of Malaya is an optical illusion, which results from seeing a very large number of Chinese traders as independent operators, and not as agents of exporters and importers. It is really European capital that dominates Malaya's economy."[39] According to him, creating a class of Malay capitalists to counter the presence of Chinese capitalists would not solve the problem of Malaya's poverty. His analysis of the political economy of Malaya would shape his political ideology as well and he would propose a socialist state, instead of political parties based on communalism, and state intervention to redress economic anomalies. Years earlier, Bose had declared that the, "... salvation of India as of the world, depends on socialism".[40] James too would foresee socialism as the "definite future in Malaya" and the "only possible solution to the country's problems".[41] But he would also emphasize the need to adapt socialism to the indigenous needs of his country. The racial distribution of Malaya's population and the unique problems it posed could not be solved or even understood within the experiences of foreign socialist movements. According to him, "To go on mouthing imported slogans, without examining their relevance to the Malaysian situation, is not only futile, but also dangerous."[42] In the years from 1928 onwards, Bose too had spoken openly on socialism but had reinforced the need of an Indian brand of socialism which was not born from the books of Karl Marx but in the "thought and culture of India".[43]

In February 1963 James was again arrested by the Singapore Special Branch in a security raid called "Operation Coldstore". This time he was banned from entering Singapore. He established himself as a lawyer but also worked closely with the Malaysian government on reform measures for the economy and bringing in government-funded interventions through public corporations.

CONCLUSION

Historians are divided in their opinion on the true cause of the communist insurrection in Malaya. Some feel that the Malayan uprising was a part of the concerted communist revolt that rocked India, Burma, Indonesia and the Philippines at this time. It was a part of the same chain of events — integral to the Stalinist strategy which began across the Southeast Asian crescent in 1948 and also saw the communists capturing power in Eastern Europe.[44] On the other hand, others, like Michael Stenson, feel the communist insurgency was inherent in the political confusion and physical hardships of the time. It was a time when industry-based trade unions were numerous; the MCP was legal and very active.[45] For the otherwise docile Indian community of workers, perhaps it was a combination of both factors. Inflation and the after-war prices of necessities had skyrocketed: the "Interim Report on Prices and Wages", by McFadzean, stated, that while the monthly budget of the average Indian worker in Penang was only $7.11 in December 1939, by October 1945 it had leapt up to $59.05.[46] Wartime distress and economic desperation were the most obvious and immediate causes, which under the influence of the prevalent communist ideology of the MCP, led to the tremendous upsurge of militant unionism during the pre-1948 period. This coming together was catalyzed by the INA for the Indian community. Anti-British indoctrination, combined with a sense of nationalist pride, made the average Indian worker extremely resentful of the returning British authority and in no mood to revert to the pre-war conditions of abiding servility. Like the women's movement, the labour movement too, at first coalesced with the Indian nationalist struggle and the community's search for a collective identity. As John A. Thivy explained, the wage struggle of the Indian workers would assist in the general struggle of "politico-economic domination" for it was a fight against a common enemy — British imperialism.[47] The movement was spearheaded predominantly by former INA and IIL members and as early as in the middle of 1946, an overriding majority of the Indian workers were affiliated to trade unions and had already experienced the successful staging of a strike. This period also saw a rare concord in the fragmented Indian community, triggered by the shared nationalist mission, as well as a new solidarity on the Indian and Chinese worker fronts which significantly reinforced their bargaining abilities.

During the Emergency, Indian estate workers were forcibly regrouped into more centralized labour lines and isolated from the influence of communist trade unionists. Estate managers were given special powers to supervise the workers more closely; the labour lines were surrounded by barbed wire, effectively locking them in for the night.[48] Any concerted effort by the MCP to infiltrate into the labourer lines came to a halt. The impact was felt immediately on the wage levels — they were held at the 1948 rates till 1950, when the price of rubber went up considerably. The wages, as a result, went up to an extent but was quickly reduced again in 1952, when rubber prices fell. P. P. Narayanan, former INA and unionist, estimates: in May 1951, while the average Indian contract worker earned less that M$2 per day, he produced rubber worth M$30.[49] Moderate unions which countered the communist influence and were approved by the Registrar of Trade Unions flourished. The fragile Indo-Chinese worker alliance was effectively broken.

But on the flip side of the coin, was the snowballing effect of the strikes which had held the economy at ransom between the years 1946 and 1948. Stoppages in one sector could easily lead to general strikes in other sectors. Public services and business in general, ground to a halt. In the financial year 1946–47, there was a loss of 713,000 workdays in Malaya while in Singapore as many as 1,173,000 man-days were lost.[50] The situation worsened in 1948, with the premeditated use of strikes as a weapon of disruption. In Singapore, where the workforce was concentrated in the city, it was easier to organize strikes at a short notice. Consequently, by April 1948, once the GLUs decided on a policy of militancy, the city came to a virtual standstill. In the peninsula, with the workforce scattered on estates across the country, it was May 1948 by the time the strikes broke out on the labour scene. In May alone, 179,539 work-days were lost. Often, the strikes were a part of a coordinated effort to create pressure on vital sectors of the economy and were unduly prolonged. The workers inadvertently found themselves to have become, "an organizational tool to be forged and manipulated by the Pan-Malayan GLU for the long-term political objectives of the MCP".[51] Like Subhas Chandra Bose's experience with the communists who had become a "serious menace to the growth of healthy trade unionism in India", in Malaya too, it was a case of the communist "cause" looming larger than the actual welfare of the workers. What had initially been a completely legitimate struggle for worker rights, had mutated into an oppressive force that seriously hindered economic progress.

The Kedah strikes had been one of the key triggers for the declaration of Emergency, which first affected Perak and parts of Johore but soon extended to the entire peninsula. In June 1948, it was viewed as a temporary gesture but would last for more than the next decade. The draconian powers of the British government were effectively used to remove an entire generation of communist leaders and senior cadres from the scene. The carefully orchestrated campaign to win over the "hearts and minds" of the Malayan people was launched and the British consciously worked towards building a non-communist alternative leadership. While the labour scene of peninsular Malaya remained comparatively calm, communist-instigated agitation resumed in Singapore during the 1950s.[52] Essential services including the waterworks, the bus service, post and telecommunications and even the picking up of the "nightsoil" buckets were sabotaged.[53] It would take time and concerted effort for organizations like the National Trade Union Congress (NTUC) to develop which aimed primarily at improving the working conditions of workers through negotiations. As Ho See Beng, President and Secretary General of NTUC, explained: "Our strategy was to use legal means, all done properly and above board. We would negotiate, failing which we would fight their case in the Arbitration Court instead of in the streets or through the media."[54]

With the INA and the spread of Indian nationalism, the archetypal "Ramasamy" of the Malayan estates had gained a new voice. He had been exposed to new political thought and learnt to articulate his needs. For him the struggle to improve his economic condition was synonymous with the far more emotionally charged struggle of regaining his national identity. As the INA veteran and unionist, S. A. Ganapathy, repeatedly emphasized, "The fight for a democratic constitution is a fight for better food and clothing." For most activists, there was no fine line dividing the economic and political needs of the time. As a continuation of their struggle, Indian workers did not hesitate to arm themselves for the confrontation, as they had done on the battlefields of Burma. The movement degenerated into disruptive militancy and would take years to emerge out of the shadows of pro-communism. But in the meantime, Indian political opinion had travelled far beyond the elite and the bourgeoisie, reaching the labouring multitudes:

> We the inheritors of the earth
> The producers of wealth.
> ... We the toilers in the factories
> The tillers of the soil.
> We are the multitudes
> But leave no footprints on the sand.[55]

Notes

1. Description from *Jai Hind: The Diary of a Rebel Daughter of India with the Rani of Jhansi Regiment* (Bombay: Janmabhoomi Prakashan Mandir, 1945), p. 31.
2. Leonard A. Gordon, *Brothers Against the Raj: A Biography of Indian Nationalists*, pp. 238, 248.
3. Ibid., p. 206.
4. Bose to Saklatvala, 15 November 1935, Ibid., p. 300.
5. *Liberty*, Calcutta, 6 December 1929.
6. *Liberty*, Calcutta, 11 July 1931.
7. Ibid.
8. Michael Stenson, *Class, Race and Colonialism in West Malaysia: The Indian Case* (St. Lucia, Australia: University of Queensland Press, 1980), p. 55.
9. Ibid., p. 62.
10. Ibid., p. 56.
11. N. Raghavan, *India and Malaya: A Study* (London: McGraw Hill Far Eastern Publishers, 1954), p. 68.
12. K. K. Ghosh, *The Indian National Army: Second Front of Indian Independence Movement* (Meerut: Meenakshi Prakasan, 1969), p. 40.
13. Michael Stenson, *Class, Race and Colonialism in West Malaysia: The Indian Case*, p. 90.
14. Christopher Bayly and Tim Harper, *Forgotten Armies: Britain's Asian Empire and the War with Japan*, p. 407.
15. S. A. Ayer, *Unto him a Witness: The Story of Netaji Subhas Chandra Bose in East Asia* (Bombay: Thacker, 1951), p. 200.

16. M. Sivaram, *Road to Delhi* (Vermont and Tokyo: Rutland, 1967), p. 104.
17. *Jai Hind: The Diary of a Rebel Daughter of India with the Rani of Jhansi Regiment*, p. 45.
18. Michael R. Stenson, *Industrial Conflict in Malaya: Prelude to the Communist Revolt of 1948* (Oxford University Press, 1970), p. 57.
19. See note 28 of Michael Stenson, *Class, Race and Colonialism in West Malaysia: The Indian Case*, p. 104.
20. John A. Thivy, *The Struggle in East Asia*, edited by Sisir Kumar Bose (Calcutta: Netaji Research Bureau, 1971), p. 49.
21. C. F. Yong, *The Origins of Malayan Communism* (Singapore: South Sea Society, 1997), p. 274.
22. Ibid.
23. Romen Bose, *The End of the War: Singapore's Liberation and the Aftermath of the Second World War* (Singapore: Marshall Cavendish Editions, 2005), p. 27.
24. *Forgotten Armies*, p. 42.
25. Romen Bose, *The End of the War: Singapore's Liberation and the Aftermath of the Second World War*, pp. 93–94.
26. *Forgotten Wars*, pp. 40–41. MPAJA activities corroborated by veterans of the INA (Girish Kothari, Interview with the author, Singapore, 12 September 2011) (Kuppusamy Ramiah, Interview with the author, Singapore, 16 September 2011).
27. Michael Stenson, *Class, Race and Colonialism in West Malaysia: The Indian Case*, p. 107.
28. S. K. Chettur, *Malayan Adventure* (Mangalore: Basel Mission Press, 1948).
29. Michael R. Stenson, *Industrial Conflict in Malaya: Prelude to the Communist Revolt of 1948*, p. 100.
30. Michael Stenson, *Class, Race and Colonialism in West Malaysia: The Indian Case*, p. 135.
31. Though some books like Kalaimuthu K., *Malaysian Indians: Towards a New Paradigm* (Ipoh: Kalaimuthu K., 2008), p. 201, do mention A. M. Samy as a former INA, but it is safer to go with Christopher

Bayly, Tim Harper and M. R. Stenson who say he was never a formal participant of the INA but influenced by the INA ideology.
32. Pierre Boulle, *Sacrilege in Malaya* (Kuala Lumpur: 1983), cited in *Forgotten Wars*, p. 335.
33. The description from *Forgotten Wars*, p. 338, also in the writings of M. R. Stenson.
34. Ibid., *Forgotten Wars*.
35. Michael Stenson, *Class, Race and Colonialism in West Malaysia: The Indian Case*, p. 136.
36. Michael R. Stenson, *Industrial Conflict in Malaya: Prelude to the Communist Revolt of 1948*, p. 118.
37. Ibid., p. 183.
38. *No Cowardly Past, James Puthucheary: Writings, Poems, Commentaries*, 2nd ed., edited by Dominic Puthucheary and Jomo K. S. (Petaling Jaya: Strategic Information and Research Development Center, 2010), p. 25.
39. James Puthucheary, "Who Owns Malaya", Ibid., p. 122.
40. *Liberty*, Calcutta, 11 July 1931.
41. James Puthucheary, "Statement of political belief", *No Cowardly Past, James Puthucheary: Writings, Poems, Commentaries*, p. 197.
42. James Puthucheary, "On the Future of Socialism in Malaya", Ibid., p. 173.
43. Subhas Chandra Bose, *Selected Speeches of Subhas Chandra Bose* (New Delhi: Government of India Publication Division, 1962), p. 50.
44. Gerald de Cruz, "The 1948 Communist Revolt in Malaya, A Note on Historical Sources and Interpretation", *ISEAS: Occasional Paper* no. 9, 1971.
45. Michael R. Stenson, *Repression and Revolt: The Origins of the 1948 Communist Insurrection in Malaya and Singapore*, Papers in International Studies, Southeast Asia Series no. 10.
46. Charles Gamba, *The Origins of Trade Unionism in Malaya* (Singapore: Eastern Universities Press Ltd., 1962), p. 44.
47. John A. Thivy, *Sunday Tribune*, Malaya, 29 September 1946.

48. Michael Stenson, *Class, Race and Colonialism in West Malaysia: The Indian Case*, p. 168.
49. Charles Gamba, *The National Union of Plantation Workers: The History of the Plantation Workers of Malaya, 1946–1958* (Singapore: Eastern Universities Press, 1962), p. 45.
50. Khong Kim Hoong, *Merdeka! British Rule and the Struggle for Independence in Malaysia, 1945–1957* (Petaling Jaya: Strategic Information and Research Development Center, 1984), p. 190.
51. Michael R. Stenson, *Industrial Conflict in Malaya: Prelude to the Communist Revolt of 1948*, p. 108.
52. S. R. Nathan, *Winning Against the Odds: The Labor Research Unit in NTUC's Founding* (Singapore: Straits Times Press, 2011), p. 20.
53. Ibid., p. 34.
54. Ibid., pp. 39–40.
55. James Puthucheary, "Song of the Workers", *No Cowardly Past, James Puthucheary: Writings, Poems, Commentaries*, p. 234.

Chapter 5

"THEY HAVE DONE ENOUGH AT HOME": ESCAPE FROM THE SHADOWS

> "With a houseful of hungry men to feed
> I guess you'd find ... It seems to me
> I can't express my feelings anymore
> Than I can raise my voice or want to lift
> My hand ... It's got so I don't even know for sure
> Whether I am glad, sorry or anything.
> There's nothing but a voice-like left inside
> That seems to tell me how I ought to feel ... the place is the asylum."
> — A Servant to Servants, Robert Frost

THE BACKGROUND

Muthammal Palanisamy's story unfolds across three generations on a rubber estate at Malaya. The plantation, called Sungai Wangi, is in a lesser-known district of Perak, peopled by men and women who are lost in history today. Muthammal's biography is peppered with female protagonists — daughters, wives, mothers who had willingly or unwillingly migrated from India in the wake of their menfolk, to find themselves in an unfamiliar and often hostile world. There is Saraswathy, born out of wedlock of a Scottish father and a Tamil mother. With her Caucasian good looks, it did not take long for Saraswathy to be noticed and one Mr Grant, a manager of a neighbouring estate, chose her for his wife. Much to her mother's delight, Saraswathy was whisked off to the manager's bungalow on an open cart drawn by the estate hands. She lived the life of a queen, except those few times when the British agents paid their customary visits — then she would be hastily hidden in the labour lines since a white manager was not allowed a "native" wife. Soon, war loomed large on the horizon and Mr Grant decided to leave Malaya. Saraswathi, with the children born to her in the meantime, was left behind on the estate. But Saraswathy and Mr Grant's tale did not end here — it was discovered a generation later, that the following year Mr Grant had returned to Malaya, this time with his Scottish wife and, unknown to Saraswathy, had settled to a new life of peaceful domesticity.

Again, there is Palaniammal, Muthammal's mother. She grew up on a farm in a remote village of India and was rushed into an unhappy marriage at the age of ten to protect the honour of the *Gounder* clan to which she belonged. A spirited woman from her childhood, Palaniammal flung away her *thali* [sacred thread of marriage] and escaped from her husband's home to return to her parents. Life took a dismal turn: saddled with a daughter who had fled her husband's home in dishonour, the family migrated to Malaya. In Perak she became the second wife to Palanisamy — a *kangani* on the estate, with a wife and two children. Her new husband was kind and provided her with a home and basic financial security but could never sanctify their marriage with the sacred *thali*. Consequently, Palaniammal lived on with her children on the peripheries of plantation society — her life a continuous scuffle with relatives as she eked out the boundaries of her existence. The bitterness lasted till the very end when after Palanisamy's death she was forbidden from performing his last rites and could only sit at a distance and weep.

Muthammal's family moved back to India some time before the Japanese occupation, but returned to Malaya in late-1947. By then the war was over, the INA had long been disbanded, the women from the Rani of Jhansi Regiment had returned to the safety of their homes. Amidst the disarray and despair, Muthammal carved out the path of her young life. With time education became more accessible to girls — the plantation workers got together to organize better estate schools. Muthammal herself joined the Anglo-Chinese School where she would spend some of the best years of her life and be recruited as a teacher in the years to come.[1]

BOSE AND THE WOMEN OF HIS LIFE

Subhas Chandra Bose, when he left on his last ill-destined journey in August 1945, first to Saigon and then Taiwan, was yet to turn forty-nine. In these turbulent years he had been exiled, imprisoned, maligned by colleagues, opposed by the Congress, led an armed combat against the British. Simultaneously, he had formed some deeply nuanced, emotional bonds which sustained him, at the most critical turns of life. There had been a number of women, perhaps more numerous than the men, with whom he shared loving ties. With some he shared a mother-son relationship, with others he was the trusted brother, or an ever-indulgent uncle or just a friend: a sounding board for exchanging ideas.

Perhaps he is most tender and defenseless in his relationship with his ladylove and wife, Emilie Schenkl. Bose met Emilie in 1934, while on exile in Europe. She assisted him in his writing of *An Indian Struggle* and subsequently their long-distance relationship blossomed in numerous letters. His letters to her are desperate in their love and longing. On 4 January 1939 he writes: "In a way, it will be good not to be President again. I shall then be more free and have more time to myself." And then adds in German, "Und wie gent es Thnen, meire Liebste? Ich denke immer an Sie bei Tag und bei Nacht" [And how are you, my dearest? I think of you all the time, by day and night].[2] He writes this at the time of maybe the worst political crisis of his life — the second Presidential election of the Congress. He unabashedly confesses that she is the *first woman* he has loved and that, "Not a single day passes that I do not think of you ... I cannot tell you how lonely I have been feeling all these months and how sorrowful."[3] At times he conveys to her his very human moral dilemma as he is torn between thoughts of a safe haven with the person he loves and the powerful call of his nationalist mission. After their final parting in 1943, Emilie would eventually hear of his death in distant Vienna, where she had continued to live with their infant daughter after Bose moved to Southeast Asia. He had written to her earlier, "If fate should thus separate us in this life — I shall long for you in my next life ... My angel! I thank you for loving me and for teaching me to love you."[4] The war would end with the Axis Powers disintegrating. Emilie's home in Vienna would fall under the Russian territory and Allied troops would soon arrive at her doorstep to intercept the last letters Bose had written to her from Southeast Asia.

Bose is equally uninhibited in his expression of love to the other women of his life and sensitive to their welfare. But simultaneously, there is open encouragement to look beyond the socially accepted roles of mother or wife and integrate themselves with the Indian nationalist struggle. The trend is noticeable from very early. He writes to his mother, Prabhabati Bose, when he himself was an adolescent and his reading of Swami Vivekananda

Janaki Athi Nahappan (nee Davar) in Rani of Jhansi uniform.
Source: Courtesy of Datin Janaki Athi Nahappan.

Janaki (second from the left) in traditional attire with her compatriots, standing at the Rani of Jhansi camp.
Source: Courtesy of Datin Janaki Athi Nahappan.

Janaki at the Rani of Jhansi camp in Singapore, standing in the front row, second from right.
Source: Courtesy of Datin Janaki Athi Nahappan.

Janaki leading a Guard of Honour in Burma.
Source: Courtesy of Datin Janaki Athi Nahappan.

Janaki (in uniform, facing the camera), leads the Guard of Honour for Aung San and his wife, Burma, 1944.
Source: Courtesy of Datin Janaki Athi Nahappan.

Rasammah Bhupalan (nee Navarednam) in the Rani of Jhansi uniform.
Source: Courtesy of Datuk Rasammah Bhupalan.

Rasammah, as the President of the Women Teachers' Union delivering a speech at the Union's Equal Pay Rally, Malaysia, 1963.
Source: Courtesy of Datuk Rasammah Bhupalan.

Rasammah (on extreme right) at the presentation of the Tun Fatimah Award of the National Council of Women's Organizations, Malaysia, 2003.
Source: Courtesy of Datuk Rasammah Bhupalan.

James Puthucheary in INA uniform.
Source: Courtesy of Dato' Dominic Puthucheary.

James with Goh Keng Swee, Singapore's Minister for Finance, after release from detention and appointment as head of the Singapore Industrial Board, 1959.
Source: Courtesy of Dato' Dominic Puthucheary.

John A. Thivy in INA uniform.
Source: Reproduced with permission from the National Archives of Singapore.

Mr and Mrs Thivy with Major General D. Dunlop, GOC Singapore District, at the American Consulate on the last evening to celebrate the American day of independence.
Source: Reproduced with permission from the Singapore Press Holdings Ltd.

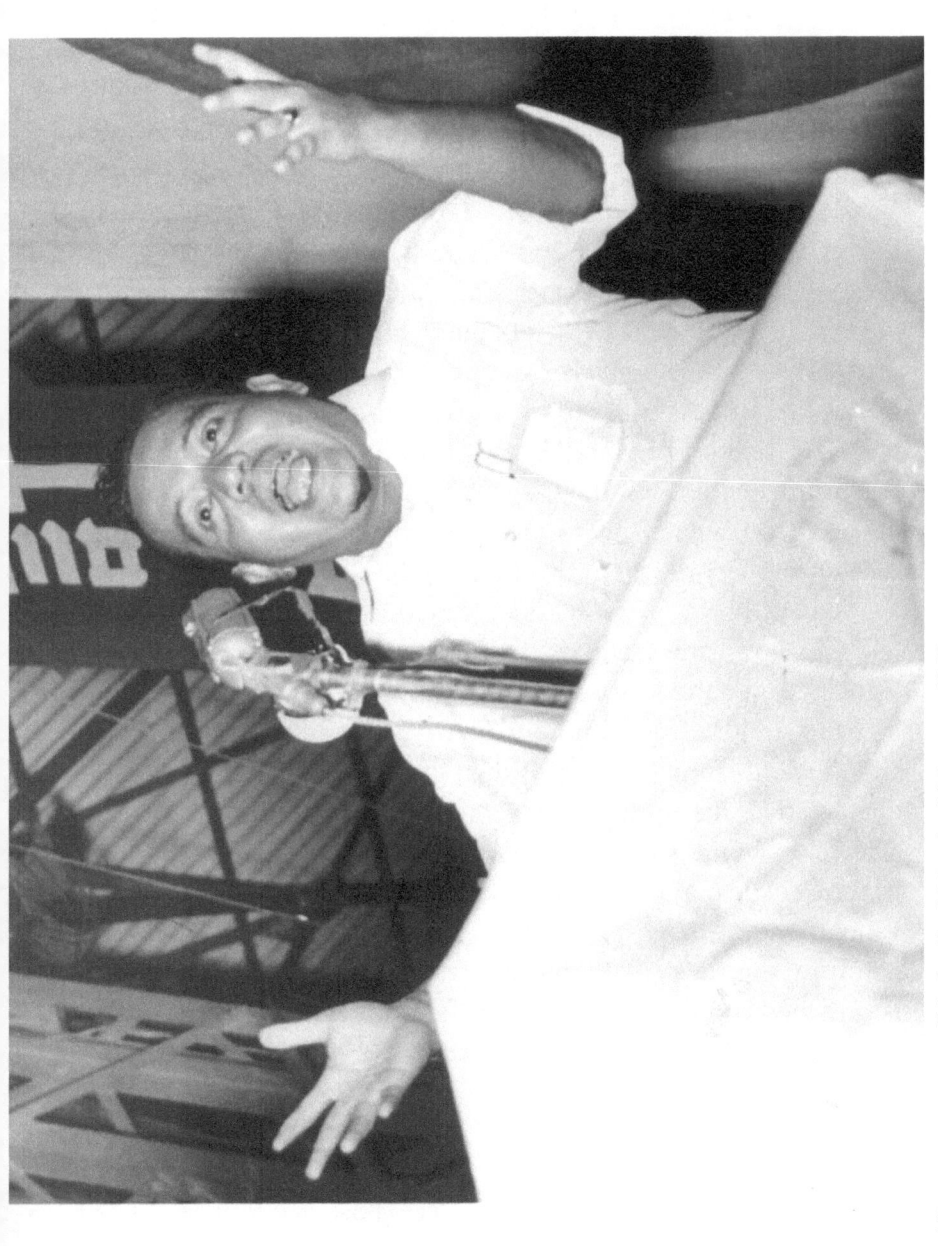

Ahmad Boestamam at a political rally, Malaysia, 30 January 1962.
Source: Reproduced with permission from the Singapore Press Holdings Ltd.

and Sri Aurobindo opened up new windows of longing to contribute to the cause of his country. In his letters the shadow of Mother India looms large. He sounds rather impatient that the nationalist ideal that motivates him, does not make his mother similarly restless: "You are a mother, but do you belong only to us? No, you are the mother of all Indians — if every Indian is a son to you, do not the sorrows of your sons make you cry out in agony? Can a mother be heartless?"[5] Bose shared close emotional ties also with Basanti Devi, his political guru, C. R. Das' wife. After Das' death, Bose was convinced she should take over his mantle. In a number of letters, written from Shillong in Eastern India, he tried to convince her to take on the leadership role that her country and the followers of C. R. Das expected of her. But Basanti Devi would opt to continue to support her husband's cause from beyond the proscenium arch.[6]

With Bivabati, Sarat Chandra Bose's wife, Bose shared a different relationship — she was more of a friend to him and maintained regular correspondence while Bose was imprisoned in Burma. But here too, amidst little humorous anecdotes about the resident cats and the flourishing vegetable garden of the prison, are his anxious queries about his family's involvement with the nationalist cause: "Please do let me know who amongst you are spinning [referring to the *charkha* popularized by Gandhi] and how you all are faring. Who is the most enthusiastic ... I hope your enthusiasm will go on increasing steadily."[7] The intention is clear: he desires his family members, including the ladies of the house, to imbue the nationalist culture and play a proactive role in its evolution.

BOSE'S BRAND OF FEMINISM: SITA VS. THE RANI

In the autograph book of a young niece, Bose had written: "The lives of women are no less valuable than the lives of men and the purpose of the lives of women do not merely consist in cooking and having children. Women can also have a life of fulfillment if they can accept an ideal and follow it. If you can do that, then I shall be happy and there will be full justification of your birth as a human being."[8] In Bose's eyes, women needed to emerge from the shadows of "mother", "wife", "sister" typecasts and immerse themselves in the nationalist struggle, if they wished to lead a more fulfilling existence. He also believed that for India to be free, the role of women as equal partisans in the nationalist struggle could not be over emphasized. In this he was heavily influenced by his own reading of Swami Vivekananda who had been vociferous in his support for the women's cause: the welfare of India could not be achieved if the lot of women was not improved because "It is not possible for a bird to fly on only one wing."[9] Bose's individual brand of feminism, like his *realpolitik* views, evolved from a pragmatic understanding of the real-life situation of Indian women. He felt the need for Indians to look beyond emulation of the West and instead look inward, at their own cultural heritage, to provide a model for addressing the issue of women's emancipation. Vivekananda had said that Indian women should, "… acquire the spirit of valour and heroism. In the present day it has become necessary for them also to learn self-defense. See, how grand was the Queen of Jhansi!"[10] In a conscious adoption of the Swami's thoughts, Bose would declare in his Presidential speech to the Maharashtra Provisional Congress in Poona in 1928: "I do not want the feminist movement of Europe and America to be reproduced in India. I have no love for bobbed hair and short skirts. On the other hand, I firmly believe that the women's movement in India will be inspired by our national ideals and traditions and will follow its own distinctive course."[11] Bose's thoughts on feminism took early shape in the women's cadre of the Bengal Volunteers (mentioned in Chapter 1), but found final fulfillment in the INA's Rani of Jhansi Regiment of Southeast Asia.

Bose's parents' beliefs and family traditions were also reflected in his feminist ideals. On one hand, there was his father, Janaki Nath, who was a follower of the eclectic *Brahmo Samaj*, a more evolved form of Hinduism. Janaki Nath was a child of the Bengal Renaissance which had brought to the fore various women-centric issues like child marriage, widow remarriage and sati. On the other hand, there was his mother, Prabhabati, an orthodox Hindu and a follower of the *Shakta* cult of worship which believed in the feminine form of divinity. During his lifetime, Bose himself would remain a believer in the Mother Goddess, a form of worship which coalesced with his devotion to Mother India.

Bose's views on women's role in the nationalist struggle, like his political philosophy, were very different from Gandhi's. Women's participation in the nationalist movement was largely initiated by Gandhi and, in the years 1919–25, a large number of Indian women had responded to his call of non-cooperation and taken up spinning, worn *khadi* and contributed their jewellery to the nationalist cause. In Calcutta, the veteran Congress leader, C. R. Das' wife, Basanti Devi, was arrested on charges of hawking *khadi* and encouraging people to join a strike. The effect of this arrest was electrifying and unleashed a great wave of patriotism in response. Reflecting on this phenomenon in Calcutta, Gandhi suggested that other women follow the example of their sisters in Bengal: women who illustrated the "silent and dignified suffering" which is the "badge" of the female sex.[12] And herein lay the fundamental difference in approach between the senior Congress leader and a then young, Cambridge-returned Bose.

The doctrinaire attitude of Gandhi, with Sita as his role model solely emphasized women's innate propensity for silent suffering. For Gandhi, women were the ideal *satyagrahis* [followers of Gandhi's form of civil resistance], useful in his campaign of picketing, boycott and Civil Disobedience. He would invoke the image of Sita and the other famous *Satis* of ancient Hindu tradition and consequently, Gandhian women personified the Hindu ideals of motherhood and the devoted wife — quiet, resilient, sacrificing and supportive. But what Bose envisaged was more radical — an equal and empowered participation. While ungrudging in his acknowledgement of Gandhi's contribution: "One of the miracles for which the Mahatma is responsible to a very large extent, is this awakening [of women]", Bose himself chose the militant Rani of Jhansi as mascot for his feminist movement in Asia.[13]

In the Rani there existed a powerful metaphor for resistance to colonial rule. She was reminiscent of India's first war of independence, which Bose connected to the Southeast Asian experience by calling it the last and final war of independence. On one hand, she invoked the glorious Indian past and was somebody to whom the traditional, home-bound Indian woman living on a plantation, would find it easy to pledge her loyalty. And yet, the image goes far beyond a mere sentimental invocation of past history: she is remembered as a mother, a proud protector of her infant son, a queen who fiercely fought for her own men and territory. She has remained a part of popular memory as a queen astride a horse with her child tied to her back as she heads the garrison of Indian soldiers of Jhansi. She springs from India's mythological past and yet is human in her mortality. She is reminiscent of the female deities worshipped by the *Shakta* school of Hinduism. Like Durga, she combines invincible fierceness with motherly compassion. She is a fitting Indian idol denoting strength and militancy, without breaking too many barriers of tradition. But unlike all the other timeless idols that preceded her, she is emphatically young. It is this youthfulness that Bose speaks of while addressing the women of the Rani of Jhansi Regiment: "When the Rani of Jhansi started her fight, her age was only twenty. You can easily imagine what it would have been for a girl of twenty, riding a horse, and wielding her sword in open battle."[14] She is a wife without being submissive, a powerful, effective leader of her people who can fight her own battles and can independently manoeuvre a war. In her valour she is at par with her male compatriots — the rebellious Tatya Tope or Rao Saheb. The final image of her is as she stands ready for battle on the hilly ground, at the crossroads between Kotah-ki-Serai and Gwalior. It is the final fight for survival and she stands alone, dressed in warrior's clothes, ready to take on the might of her enemy — a powerful testimony to Bose's ideal of equality between the sexes. She is emblematic of the new-age Indian woman — youthful, effective, empowered and yet careful of her country's proud heritage.

Back in India, it is this youthful, new age of liberation that the poets celebrated in the Rani of Jhansi.[15]

> Sinhasan hil uthey raajvanshon ney bhrukuti tani thi,
> Budhey Bharat mein aayee phir se nayi jawani thi,
>
> ... Jao Rani yaad rakhengey yeh krutagna Bharatwasi,
> yeh tera balidaan jagavega Swatantrata avinasi.
>
> ... Bundeley Harbolon key munh hamney suni kahani thi,
> Khoob ladi mardani woh to Jhansi wali Rani thi.

A rough adaptation would read:

> The throne was shaken as tensions rose
> among the dynasties of kings,
> India was awash with a new wave of youthfulness.
>
> ... We bid you farewell Rani though Indians will
> always be in your debt,
> Your mortal sacrifice will awaken the indestructible
> soul of liberty.

> ... We will hear the bards of Bundelkhand serenade you,
> They will sing of the gallant Rani of Jhansi who fought with
> the valour of a man.

THE RANI OF JHANSI REGIMENT (RJR)

During his long submarine journey from Kiel, Germany, Subhas Chandra Bose dictated a speech to his adjutant, Abid Hasan. Bose intended this speech for the yet-to-be-raised women's regiment and Hasan, in an interview transcript, reminiscences that even a torpedo attack did not warrant a faltering in the dictation. Once he reached Singapore, Bose set about transforming his long cherished dream of raising a women's army of battle-hardy soldiers to reality. When he first mentioned the Rani of Jhansi regiment in his momentous 5 July speech at the Singapore Padang, Captain Lakshmi Sahgal reminiscences: "there was absolute silence and there were looks of complete disbelief on the faces of all present except Sri Yellappa, the Singapore IIL President, and myself."[16] The women's army was again mentioned by Bose at the mass rallies of 6 and 9 July and was perhaps the most startling part of the speech: "Let the slogan of the three million Indians in East Asia be — 'Total Mobilization for a Total War'. Out of this total mobilization, I expect at least three hundred thousand soldiers ... I want also a unit of brave Indian women to form a 'Death-defying Regiment' who will wield the sword, which the brave Rani of Jhansi wielded in India's First War of Independence in 1857."[17]

Dr Lakshmi Sahgal (nee Swaminadhan), a young medical doctor who had come to Singapore from Madras in 1940, after initial discussions with Attavar Yellappa and John A. Thivy, took on the leadership role of the women's army. On 12 July 1943, Bose addressed the first twenty recruits of the Rani of Jhansi Regiment. Joyce Chapman Lebra writes: "On the morning of

12 July 1943, Indians in Singapore saw something they had never seen or imagined before: a woman's guard of honour parading in white saris and presenting arms to Netaji."[18]

Bose, thrilled at the sight of the smartly turned out women carrying heavy Enfield rifles, was equally rousing in his speech. In the initial part of his speech he acknowledged the traditional role of the woman as a mother but as he continued, he mentioned the need of the hour was to extend this role and take on a more proactive part in India's struggle for freedom. Mentioning the 5 July rally at the Padang, he said, "Not only myself but also the other friends and guests who were with me on the platform were exceedingly impressed by the brave manner in which you stood the rain and inclement weather ... I know that some of you had brought your babies also along with you." He then spoke of the work done by women revolutionaries in the past who had proven that "when the need arises they could, like their brothers, shoot very well." And in a continuation of the same glorious heritage, he exhorted them to take on their new roles in right earnest: "Sisters, the time has come for us to begin our final preparations for the final struggle ... No one can predict when the call may come ... As I said the other day there is but one thought in our minds, there is but one cry which rises from our lips — 'Onward to Delhi, Onward to Delhi!' "[19] Derisive of the cynics who thought the national struggle was a "man's affair", he spoke of his conviction that until Indian women play their due part, India can never hope to be free.

The Japanese needed some convincing to provide the women's regiment with the necessary weapons and infrastructure, but Captain Lakshmi and A. Yellappa helped overcome the objections and recruitment of the women began in earnest. The regiment eventually came to recruit around 1,000 women, a majority of whom were Tamils from Malaya and Burma. What was remarkable was, while women from educated upper-classes formed the officer-corps of the RJR, the larger proportion of the regiment was from simple tapper families living on the plantations of Malaya.

On the evening of 21 October 1943, the same day Bose proclaimed the creation of the Provisional Government of Azad Hind [Free India], he formally inaugurated the RJR training camp in Singapore. He mentioned the "156" women who were to start their training at the camp but hoped that the numbers would reach a 1,000 very soon. He also mentioned the training camps for women that had been initiated in Burma and Thailand, but the one in Syonan would be the "Central Camp".[20] The women of RJR spent the first six months of their training at this camp and then in January 1944, when the advance headquarters of the INA and the Provisional Government were shifted to Burma, a RJR camp was opened at Thingangyun, near Rangoon. In Burma, a large number of women from the Bengali community joined the RJR even as training was further intensified and they used live ammunition as a part of their arms exercise. In April 1944 the first unit of the RJR moved again — further north to the new headquarters of both the INA and the Provisional Government at Maymyo, while another large batch of RJR girls, commanded by Janaki Davar, arrived from Singapore to Rangoon.

Despite repeated requests from the women, the RJR did not fight at the actual battlefields spread across the Indo-Burmese border. They played a key role in nursing the war wounded even as the number of wounded INA soldiers soared at the hospitals of Mandalay and Rangoon. As the eventful 1944 ended and 1945 began, it was obvious to everybody that the coveted long march to Delhi was drawing to a close. On 23 April 1945, Bose announced that he would not leave Rangoon as long as transport had not been organized for the women of the Rani of Jhansi Regiment. The women who had been recruited in Burma had already been sent onward to their respective homes. Another batch of girls had also left by train from Rangoon in early December 1944. On the night of 24 April 1945, a group of around a 100 RJR women started on the historic retreat from Rangoon in war trucks given by the Japanese, with Bose at the head of the column. It was a long trek of twenty-six days during which they crossed the monsoon swollen rivers, Waw and Sittang. With most of their trucks destroyed by enemy bombing or stuck in the muddy terrain, they covered the last ten miles to the Sittang River on foot and arrived at Moulmein on 1 May. From here they boarded a goods train and after several stops and train changes, reached Bangkok on 7 May 1945. The unfortunate duo, Stella and Josephine, died in a guerilla shootout during the return train journey — the only fatalities of the RJR.

The Southeast Asian Experience

The forests of Burma were ablaze as the girls started on their journey home. That evening, for the girls of the Rani of Jhansi Regiment who started on the long retreat to the safe sanctuary of Thailand from the camp in Helpin Road, it was like moving through a wall of fire — trees and grass on either side of the road had been torched by the retreating Japanese Army. Deep crevices had opened up in the roads because of heavy bombardment ... It was a new moon night. There was little light in the dense jungles as they walked, holding onto each other's bayonets, so that they did not lose their way. In the death of night they crossed a fast moving river — the dark waters threatened to sweep them away as they moved with their guns held aloft their heads. On one such night, they came upon a tree on which was carved the names of two INA colleagues who had died during the retreat. They stopped for a while to pay their last homage.[21]

In another incident, the charismatic Captain of the Regiment, Lakshmi Sahgal, describes another fire that they encountered during the retreat. Ziawadi was the first halt on their journey from Maymyo. The Zamindar of Ziawadi had always been a crucial link in the support system that the INA discovered in Burma. Captain Lakshmi Sahgal and her team took shelter in the Zamindar's sugar factory. Other retreating units of the INA were also resting here before regrouping for further action. Soon after their arrival the factory was bombed by the British. Many of the factory workers were fatally burned. The few who were alive were in ineffable agony as the hot molasses stuck to their flesh and splintered bones. It was Captain Lakshmi and her team's task to nurse these miserable men. She calls it a scene from "Dante's Inferno".[22]

Hundreds of wounded INA soldiers had been brought to the Mingaladon Hospital from the battlefronts of Imphal, Kohima and Arakan. Nurses from the Rani of Jhansi Regiment were in charge of the hospital. The normal running of medical facilities became impossible when the hospital came under carpet-bombing by the enemy planes. The girls struggled on bravely as men with, "burnt skin, loose gaping flesh, eyes bulging out" turned to them for some relief.[23]

The Rani of Jhansi Regiment was no ordinary experience for the hundreds of women who joined its ranks from across Southeast Asia. It is true that despite Bose's repeated attempts with the Japanese, the girls did not actually fight at the battlefront but they did get the chance to discover life at its most perilous. Death was a mere hair-breadth away. When the 100 or so girls emerged in Bangkok, after the hazardous twenty-six-day trek through the rivers and forests of Burma, the psychological impact of the war and the ensuing retreat would have been immense. Janaki Davar mentions, it was like "being blessed with a new life" at the end of the journey.[24] Even apart from the retreat, it had not been an easy life for the girls. The camp in Singapore and the subsequent camps in Burma had been completely bereft of any physical comforts. The arms training which had started in Singapore had further intensified in Burma with the inclusion of guerilla warfare, sabotage missions, reconnoitering, ambush training and digging of trenches and had challenged their tenacity.[25] And yet, Captain Lakshmi, who would read some of the letters the girls wrote to their parents, noticed, none complained. Instead, they wrote, they felt more at home in their new surroundings than they had felt in their natal homes.[26] Janaki Davar too remembers her camp days with the same sense of *joie de vivre*. This was perhaps because the journey these women undertook went much deeper than the mere physical journey to Burma and back. Just as Alice, in *Alice's Adventures in Wonderland*, with her first step through the looking glass, started on a journey of self-discovery, for these women too, the RJR experience was a psychological journey during which their inner strength and fortitude were severely tested. But, it was also a fulfilling time when they were encouraged to be free, empowered to take independent decisions and were conscious of the nobility of their mission. Bose in an address to the Regiment had mentioned:

> ... you should bear in mind that ours is not a merely political movement. We are, on the other hand, engaged in the great task of regenerating our Nation. ... we are in fact witnessing the re-birth of India. And it is only in the fitness of things that there should be a stir of New Life among our womenfolk.[27]

What makes the Rani of Jhansi Regiment a remarkable movement is this "regeneration" of new life among the women, that it fosters. Through the nationalist message, it teaches the women new lessons in equality and empowerment and takes them on a journey of self-discovery.

One of the ways in which Subhas Chandra Bose achieved this no mean feat was by returning to these women, living as migrant communities across Asia, their sense of history. A major part of the RJR consisted of women immigrants who had migrated as dependents of the plantation labourers. Like the men, majority of them were South Indians with Tamil women being the most numerous, followed by Telegus, and Malayalees.[28] On the plantations, though they supplemented the family income, they were consistently paid at a lower rate than the men (it was only in 1953, that wage discrimination would be finally abolished).[29] Apart from these plantation women of Malaya, there were the wives and daughters of clerks at the British mercantile houses and a small number of lawyers, doctors and traders who formed the balance of the populace of Indian women in Burma and Malaya. They lived within their domestic boundaries with absolutely no interest outside their "homes and families". Captain Lakshmi writes "...the large Indian community was solely occupied with the task of earning and saving enough money to be able to settle comfortably in India on retirement."[30]

Among the women who enlisted with the RJR, there were many who were second or even third generation migrants and particularly among the poor and uneducated there had occurred an erosion of connection with their roots. Though they wore the traditional saree and celebrated the Indian festivals, psychologically they were the "minority" community living on the peripherals of mainstream society. Bose, from his first speeches, was careful in reminding them of their connection with the Indian past. Besides the iconic Rani of Jhansi, he extolled the greatness of Indian womanhood which had its roots in its Sanskrit culture, spoke of the inspiring examples of Ahalyabai of Maharashtra, Rani Bhawani of Bengal, Razya Begum and Noor Jehan from the more recent past, mentioned the role of Indian women in not only Gandhi's passive resistance but the active courage of women in revolutionary acts against the British and invited them to join the same proud tradition. This would help the women not only rediscover their lost identity but also feel a sense of national pride.

But even as he sought to reconnect these women with their glorious past, Bose actively sought a change in their physical appearance. This would make it easier for them to look beyond their traditional role and carve out a new identity for themselves. In his essay, "A Soldier Remembers", published in the *Oracle*, Abid Hasan writes that during the submarine voyage from Kiel, while they were discussing the RJR, he had expressed his skepticism about the women changing from the traditional Indian *sarees* and *shalwar-kameez* to don trousers and shirts. But Bose had been adamant about this being a necessity and confident of his ability to persuade the Indian women. As Bose had envisaged, the response to his call to join the nationalist struggle was incredible: women in their hundreds, "young and old, poor and rich, educated and uneducated, skilled and unskilled, mothers, daughters, and sisters thronged the Indian Independence League's offices for enlistment".[31] This coming forward had a physical connotation — it implied a veritable transformation of image for the women.

During Rashbehari Bose's leadership of the IIL (Indian Independence League), the women were restricted to a peripheral cheerleader's role: arousing patriotism among the Indians with their songs, recitations and dramatic shows, primarily by non-*purdah*-observing middle-class women.[32] But the mass mobilization that occurred under Bose meant scores of *purdah*-observing women came forward to don the army fatigues and handle the essentially male weapons of war. Unlike the Bengal Volunteers organized by Bose, who had paraded the streets of Calcutta in saris, these women cut their hair, wore khaki breeches and half caps of the Regiment. This dramatic physical transformation did not occur overnight: their initial shyness and awkwardness on the parade ground prompted a return to a type of seclusion and this area was fenced in. It was only after a few months that the girls were ready to march in public.[33] Bose, very consciously, fostered this change in the physical image of the Indian woman. Maya Banerjee narrates an incident when a performance was organized at the Rangoon City Hall. Bose was particularly keen about an item in which the girls come marching onto the stage in full army uniform, carrying rifles and singing "Delhi Chalo!" Such was his enthusiasm for the act that, at times, he would come to their camp even twice in a day to supervise the rehearsing. When on the final day the marching scene was executed perfectly, he was overjoyed and sent baskets of sweets to the girls.[34] Bose was aware that a change in the physical image of the women was necessary before any change of psychosis could be initiated.

This change in appearance of the women implied an equality of status with the men in uniform. In fact, right from its initiation, Bose was extremely vocal about the equal status of the Women's Regiment. This extended from minute details like the poker faced reminder he adds in a letter to Lieutenant M. Satyavati Thevar (distinct from Janaki Davar), who was in charge of the rear headquarters in Singapore, after Captain Lakshmi had moved to Rangoon: "Please tell all the girls of your Regiment that while greeting anyone they should simply say 'Jai Hind' and not 'Jai Hind Sahib'"; to much larger issues like the promotions of the Ranis.[35] In another letter to Lt. Thevar, he castigates her, in no uncertain terms, for her partiality in recommending promotions for Tamil speaking members of the Regiment and remarks: "I want to see the Rani of Jhansi Regiment Officers as efficient as the men Officers of the INA, so that nobody can have any justification for thinking that promotions in the Rani of Jhansi Regiment are easy."[36] The emphasis, throughout, was on military training and physical discipline which would help the girls achieve the necessary skill for equality of status. It is this equality of status and opportunities that the Provisional Government had proclaimed in 1943, "It guarantees ... equal rights and equal opportunities to its citizens. It declares its firm resolve to pursue the happiness and prosperity of the whole nation equally and transcending all the differences ..."[37]

What started as a movement of women hesitant to shed their *purdah* on the parading fields, soon metamorphosed into a regiment of women eager to do battle at the front. Right from the start Bose had encouraged the women to take independent decisions. Captain Janaki recalls an incident when she refused entry to the military commander and member of cabinet for the Provisional Government of Azad Hind, J. K. Bhosle, to the RJR camp at Singapore because as per the laid down rules, no males were allowed to enter. In another case, Rasammah Bhupalan recalls when she, along with some of her peers at the Helpin Road camp, refused to doff their caps to Japanese officers, irrespective of their rank, because the Japanese did not reciprocate by saluting the INA officers. In both cases Bose supported their judgment. In another incident, Manawati Arya, who was born in Meiktila in 1920, had had her schooling almost entirely in Burmese and English, narrates: she was the daughter of an official from the postal department and at the time of the INA's coming to Rangoon worked as a teacher in the Viswa Bharati Academy, Rangoon. Manawati submitted a petition to Bose for involving all classes of women in the Women's Section of the IIL. Bose readily agreed and asked her to implement her plan. She set to work, spending her days walking from village to village, trying to enlist civilian women for the cause and soon a full-fledged Women's Department was established with Arya as the Secretary.[38] It was partly because of this scheme that in the initial days, uneducated, *purdah*-observing women were brought under the aegis of the movement.

That the women had lost their traditional reticence and were restless to take on front-line roles is evident in another petition they submitted to Bose, this time signed with blood. The unit was ready to do battle and yet their first assignment was to nurse wounded INA soldiers at the Maymyo Hospital. The frustrated women wrote to Bose: "Our training has been satisfactory and complete. But we are now denied access to the front-line. We are reduced to a corps of nurses."[39] Their immersion in the male-dominated world of war was complete and in the final trial they were not found wanting.

A feminist movement, anywhere in the world, is hinged on equality between the two sexes. It implies a change in women's social, economic and political status. That the Rani of Jhansi movement was started with a much wider mission than its political-nationalist one is nowhere more obvious than in this initial conversation between Bose and Captain Lakshmi. The latter had been called in for her first personal meeting with Bose and he spoke at length of women's contribution in the independence movement down the ages:

> I know women in our country are suffering from very grave social and economic disabilities ... but even after freedom, women will have to fight for their rights and their proper place in our society, because men won't give it to them that easily, they've had their own way all these centuries ... it's so ingrained in them. So this will be an opportunity for women to fight for their own rights.[40]

Thus, in the Rani of Jhansi movement, Subhas Chandra Bose gave the migrant Indian woman an opportunity to rediscover her identity by evoking her proud past and yet compelled her to enrich her own traditional role with a gratifying experience, founded on equality and empowerment.

The Homecoming of the Ranis

At the end of the war the women of Rani of Jhansi Regiment found themselves truly on their own. Their leader, Captain Lakshmi, had chosen to remain back at Burma: she wished to use her medical training and volunteered to continue work at the new hospital which was being set up at Kalaw, in the Shan states of Burma. From here onwards her life would follow a different trajectory and she would subsequently return to India. Subhas Chandra Bose, who had been much more than just a military leader for the women and had treated them with paternal affection, escorted them back to safety till Moulmein on 1 May 1945. Thereafter, he would return to Singapore only for a brief while. With the bombings at Hiroshima and Nagasaki, the war would grind to a sudden halt and he would be compelled to leave for first Bangkok and then Saigon on 16 August 1945. The women would be aghast at the news of his plane crash and death at Taipei soon after. This was a period of turmoil at Singapore and Malaya with the British Military Administration (BMA) taking over control for the interregnum and this was also the time for the women of RJR to prove their mettle.

Lakshmi Sahgal recounts that the British Intelligence Officers of Malaya had their "biggest shock" when after dealing with the ex-soldiers of the Indian Army and the male civilian troops, they turned their attention to the women of RJR. Men and women alike were segregated into white, black or grey groups depending on the culpability of their motives. When called for interrogation by the British Officers, women of the Rani of Jhansi Regiment turned up in their uniforms which they had washed, starched and ironed. On entering the room of interrogation they saluted smartly and refusing all friendly overtures of tea or light refreshments, declared they had joined the Regiment "voluntarily" and had no regrets apart from "failing in defeating the British".[41]

Janaki Athi Nahappan (nee Davar) recalls the interrogations with the British officers. On her return to her home at Rifle Range, Kuala Lumpur, she was put on house arrest for six months. During this time, she and her sister, Papathi, who had also joined the RJR, would be repeatedly called to the intelligence offices. She would ride with the British Officers in their jeep and insisted on being dressed in trousers and a shirt, much to the surprise of her neighbours. Incidentally, other veterans of the INA too recall the censorious looks the RJR women had to encounter for appearing in male attire in public. Bala A. Chandran, who joined the *Balak Sena*, reminiscences of the two RJR girls who would return home on Sundays during their training at the Singapore camp. Older neighbours, particularly the women living at the *kampong* in Bukit Timah, did not hesitate to express their cynicism at their attire.[42]

To return to Janaki's story, she and her sister would be repeatedly asked why they had joined the RJR and when the girls replied they had joined to fight for the freedom of their country, they would be asked why, when Malaya was their homeland and not India, they had decided to fight for a strange country.[43] Rasammah Bhupalan (nee Navarednam) also recalls her sister, Ponnamah and her interrogation by officers at the British Headquarters, near Brown Road at Penang. She would be asked if now that the INA had been defeated, would she be joining any other "movement in Malaya against the British?"[44] According to Janaki, the interrogations would stop only with Nehru's visit to Malaya in April 1946.

Even apart from the British interrogations faced by a few of the Rani of Jhansi soldiers, life would be at its most difficult for the majority of the women who had joined from the plantations. In the aftermath of war, a lot of them would return to the plantations to find their husbands and fathers without jobs, their household incomes greatly depleted, and would decide to take on work or business occupations. Ahilangdam, who was born of a Chinese mother and Indian father and had joined the regiment from Rifle Range in the wake of Janaki Davar, would take to door-to-door selling of vegetables on a cycle. Anjalai Ponnusamy was born and raised in the Senthul district of Kuala Lumpur where her father worked in the health department as an anti-malaria supervisor. She had trained at the Singapore camp and then travelled to Burma in the same group as Josephine and Stella. During training, she had learnt to shoot fifteen rounds at a time and to manoeuvre a tommy gun and a sten gun.[45] She returned to find her father had moved to town to set up a business of selling mutton. Anjalai would decide to join the business to supplement family income and later emerge as a community leader. All along her difficult life, Anjalai would preserve her RJR cap.

Yet another Tamil woman to join from the rubber estates was Meenachi Perumal. Born in 1925 on Bukit Kemming Estate in Selangor, she was already married when at sixteen she signed up for the RJR. She had also volunteered for the *Jan Baz* "suicide unit" in response to Bose's call. She remembered Subhas Chandra Bose's last words: "Promise not to go back and hide in the kitchen. Bring up your children to be strong and brave and fight for freedom."[46] Life for the women of RJR, subsequent to the war, followed different trajectories. For some of those who were educated and came from the upper strata of society, a prominent life of purpose beckoned; while for the less fortunate, it meant a return to the rigours of raising a family. But whatever the future life, the RJR experience remained with them and helped them to return to confront life with renewed faith in themselves.

RANIS IN MALAYSIA

Malaysia is home to two of the most remarkable RJR veterans — Janaki Athi Nahappan (nee Davar) and Rasammah Bhupalan (nee Navarednam). For both of them their life's journeys took a new turn with hearing Bose speak at a mass rally in Malaya.

Janaki Athi Nahappan — A Rani on Horseback

Janaki's father, Rengasamy Davar, had migrated from South India to work as manager of a tea plantation in Malaya: a part of the large force of Indian administrative staff to be found at British colonies across Asia. Later, he was to start his independent enterprise — a dairy farm at Rifle Range, Kuala Lumpur and rose to become one of the prominent members of the Indian community. Janaki was eighteen when one afternoon, in July 1943, she stole to the Selangor Padang to hear Subhas Chandra Bose. It was a large gathering of mostly Indians — plantation workers squatted on the floor in front, while the women stood at a diffident distance. Subhas Chandra Bose arrived in an open car with two outriders at the front and spoke in Hindustani which was largely incomprehensible to Janaki, though she eagerly heard the Tamil interpretation of the speech by Chidambram, a senior League member. A second generation migrant to Malaya, Janaki had never seen India (and would not visit India till November 2000, when she would come to collect the *Padma Shri* conferred on her by the Indian President) and yet the country came alive in the word-pictures so deftly drawn by Bose. Emotionally moved, Janaki raised her fist to the cries of, "Bharat mata ki jai!" [victory to Mother India] and went up to the raised platform where Bose and Captain Lakshmi were seated and donated her earrings and necklace to the cause.[47] As it transpired, she was the first woman to respond to the INA's call and next morning's papers carried pictures of her handing over her jewellery to Bose. Captain Lakshmi would come to their house that day and convince her parents to allow Janaki and her sister Papathi to join the Regiment. Janaki seemed to have unwittingly pioneered a trend: other women signed up thereafter — Buddhist Josephine and Christian Stella who came from Rifle Range and would die an early death during the retreat; Anjalai who joined from Senthul district and Ahilandam who sent her ten-year-old daughter away to caregivers in Madurai, before being recruited as a Rani.

Shortly afterwards, Janaki and her sister Papathi moved to the Rani of Jhansi camp on Waterloo Street in Singapore, much to the dismay of their family. They spent the next six months here in intensive military training, preparing for the onward march to the Indo-Burma border battlefront. Camp life for these girls, brought up in relative luxury in an upper-middle class household, was not easy. They lived in *attap* sheds, slept on narrow wooden planks and had no blanket or pillow till an uncle living in Singapore brought them these little amenities. Breakfast was an unappetizing helping of ragi while the *langaar* [kitchen] commanders dished up something equally unappealing for the other meals of the day. Every afternoon, the girls travelled in open trucks to the Bidadari Camp for their military training and would return only in the evening. Yet, despite the obvious discomforts, they did not take long to get accustomed to camp life. At night they would get together to sing patriotic songs and soon forged new ties of friendship with the other girls.

Under orders of Bose, no male was allowed entry into their camp — the sentries at the front gate were female and so were the visiting doctors. Female tailors came in the initial days to fit out the girls in their new uniforms. Each camp resident received two sets — one was full-length for formal occasions while the other set consisted of shorts and half-sleeved shirts.

The uniforms in the beginning were a plain khaki and the INA tricolour bands were added only later. Janaki recalls the initial hesitation of her camp colleagues to wear the uniform and walk the streets of Singapore for their route marches. It was Bose's words of encouragement which helped them persist, despite the jeering crowds.

In June 1944, Janaki travelled with the first large batch of women to Rangoon and remained in charge there, while Captain Lakshmi moved with a smaller group northward, to Maymyo. By the time she reached Rangoon and the camp at Helpin Road, Janaki was the Camp Commandant with two pips on her shoulder.[48] She recalls being trained by two INA officers — Major P. S. Raturi who was from Garhwal and Mahboob Ahmad. They were taught to use hand grenades and live artillery. Janaki was in charge of the RJR girls working as nurses at the Mingaladon hospital. She would ride on horseback from the RJR camp at Helpin Road to the army hospital at Mingaladon, more than fifteen miles away and reminiscences: one day Bose stopped her en route, and said, "Ms Davar, let me show you a few things about good horsemanship." On some nights the girls would feel homesick and looking at the moon in the Burmese sky, conjecture about their parents, back in Malaya.

Janaki recalls the bombing of the army hospital at Myang, outside Rangoon, on 10 February 1945. Bombs dropped from American aircrafts completely razed the hospital to the ground. There were many casualties and some of the soldiers whom Janaki had come to consider her friends, died. They had often passed cheeky comments at the nurses, much to the amusement of Janaki. With some of the others who survived, she would maintain contact for many years after the war had ended.

Janaki was in command of the unit of around a hundred women from the RJR who retreated from Rangoon in the company of Bose. The women started their journey from the Helpin Road camp on 24 April 1945 on a "ramshackle convoy of trucks" but when the trucks broke down, were forced to continue on foot. They would march by night with constant fear of guerrilla forces in the jungles that surrounded them and the British-American warplanes hovering overhead. She remembers an encounter with the Chinese communists during the retreat. One day, during the long retreat, Janaki noticed Bose take off his heavy military boots and socks. She was shocked to see his feet were a mass of blisters: "His car was following us, but he never thought of using it."[49] That night they marched another fifteen miles with Bose at the head of the column. The battalion reached Bangkok on 7 May 1945. Once in the Bangkok camps, the prospect of prison loomed large for the girls. Yet they were undaunted: "To live after failure with the burning hope that this was not the end, we were not bereft of the desire to continue to live, fight and die for India's freedom."[50]

Janaki led her platoon of girls to safety from Bangkok onwards and ensured they reached their homes in the various districts of Malaya. By the time she reached back Singapore, on 12 August 1945, the Japanese had surrendered and Subhas Chandra Bose was preparing to leave on yet another undisclosed journey. Janaki recalls: "He gave me a signed copy of his photograph and said, 'Don't worry, Janaki. The British will never get me — dead or alive.'" That was the last time she saw him.

Janaki was just a girl of twenty-one when the war ended and she was placed under house arrest for six months by the returning British forces. Afterwards, she carried her sense of mission to the plantations of Malaya. She would cross the Langat River to travel to Carey Island everyday to serve the Indian plantation workers whose lives were completely devastated by war. The advanced training as a nurse she had received while working with the

Regiment served her well. She joined as a nurse in the Indian Medical Mission and British Medical Mission from 1945–46 and also worked closely with the Indian Relief Committee in Malaya when she was appointed by Nehru as a member of the Committee. In 1947, she would join the Mahatma Gandhi High School as a teacher with students from the Malay, Indian and Chinese communities.[51] In another highlight of her political career, she was one of the founding members, along with John Thivy, to have established the Malayan Indian Congress (MIC) and remained actively involved with the party for a major part of her life. In her political life she was joined by her husband, Athi Nahappan, again an INA veteran, who worked closely with the Indian community of Malaysia, was the Deputy President of MIC and a Cabinet Minister of Malaysia. Janaki herself was a senator of the Malaysian Parliament. Besides her active involvement with the Girl Guides of Malaya, Janaki has served on numerous committees like the Royal Commission of Marriages and Divorce for Non-Muslims, National Council of Integration of Women in Development Malaysia, National Woman Leader of MIC. She was awarded the Swift Medal which is the highest honour in the Girl Guides and was the first recipient of the Netaji Award, instituted by the Government of West Bengal. In 2000, she was awarded the *Padma Shri* by the President of India and lives on in a happy fusion of her two selves: an ardent worker for the women's cause in Malaysia and her familial roles as wife and mother.[52]

Rasammah Bhupalan — A Life Less Ordinary

Rasammah Bhupalan, inspired by Bose's speech at Ipoh, had enlisted with RJR, travelled to Singapore and then to the Kamayut camp at Burma. Rasammah recounts her last encounter with Bose. On that last day Bose had written on Rasammah's sister's autograph book: "Live for others — if you want to live."⁵³ Rasammah took this on as a motto and since then, has led her life on an elevated plain. As she concedes herself: "My life changed forever. I forgot privilege and class-consciousness. The regiment gave me the strength, discipline and commitment with which I have served Malaysia and her people ever since. We felt different after our stint with the RJR — stronger, empowered to make a difference."⁵⁴ With this changed world-view, Rasammah went back to her studies after the RJR experience, first in Malaysia and then in Singapore and London. Since then, for long thirty-five years, she has been a teacher at various schools in Malaya: the Methodist Girls' School, Penang, St Marks Anglo Chinese Boys' School in Butterworth, Senior Methodist Girls' School at Klang and then Kuala Lumpur and as founder-principal of the Methodist College in Kuala Lumpur.

During her lifetime Rasammah has espoused various feminist causes. As the Founder-President of the Women Teachers' Union, she fought a long battle with the Malaysian bureaucracy to demand equal pay for both genders. They were the first all-women's union in the country and were able to unite teachers from English, Chinese, Malay and Tamil medium schools. During her work with YWCA, she was one of the key persons in the formation of the National Council of Women's Organization (NCWO) — a vital, non-political organization which has been fighting for legal, social and financial rights of women. Later she was unanimously elected NCWO's Secretary General and Deputy President. Her active involvement with YWCA, Malaysia and Kuala Lumpur continues. She is the founding Chairperson of the Vocational Training Opportunities Centre of YWCA which provides skills training to girls from marginalized families. On retirement, she continues to serve on the board of YWCA as its oldest member and for her long years of service has been honoured by the World Council, YWCA. Even today, she is involved with various NGOs, working at the grass root level with women and her human rights.

Rasammah is unstinted in her praise of Subhas Chandra Bose and accedes the value of her training with the Rani of Jhansi Regiment: "I have, however, made strenuous efforts to stand up for unity, justice, ... equality and equal opportunities and the real meaningful partnership for women with men for Malaysia's progress and development."[55] It is rather intriguing that these young girls took up various social issues as their mission in later life. It was their way of disseminating the awakening they had witnessed as a part of the Rani of Jhansi Regiment. Bose himself had had a lifelong fetish for social work — right from his student days he had led famine and flood relief work in India. Later, this had taken a more structured form in his work with the Calcutta Municipal Corporation and on an even wider-scale with the Provisional Government of Azad Hind's social welfare drive in Southeast Asia. For these remarkable women and for many others of the same generation it was a perpetuation of the same ethos.

WOMEN IN PRE-WAR AND POST-WAR SCENARIOS

Indian Community

In the pre-war scenario and as a part of a migrant community with little or no political standing, the Indian women played no role in political or social groups of Malaya. One organization, for the religious rights of the Sikh women called the Isteri Sat Sangha Sabha Sentul was formed around 1933, but remained very limited in its appeal. Though the Central Indian Association of Malaya (CIAM) was established in 1937, the focus was on promoting the status of the Indian community in Malaya. Labour related issues were taken up and an Indian nationalist opinion of sorts was fostered. Control of the CIAM was held by a President and ten leading members — none of whom were women.[56] After this came the war and the Japanese occupation. The Rani of Jhansi movement elicited a remarkable response from the women of Malaya. It was a common sight at Bose's rallies to have women stripping themselves of their gold jewellery, including the sacred *thali*, and donating them for the nationalist cause. Young girls would come and later convince their parents to join in, mothers would come with their infant children. And more surprisingly, this proved to be not a temporary phenomenon. As Captain Lakshmi remarks, "As the days and weeks passed the number of volunteers steadily increased" and later when military training started, "... except for those whom we had to reject on medical grounds, not a single volunteer to the Rani of Jhansi Regiment requested to be relieved."[57]

In the aftermath of war, the nationalist fervour awakened in the Indian women would be expressed through a number of associations. Some of these would have a socio-cultural message while others, a political one but in most of them women would play an active role. The pre-war Sikh women's groups would re-emerge — pushing for the education of Punjabi girls. Indian Women's Associations sprouted — one in Negri Sembilan and the other in Selangor. Mrs S. M. Thevar, the President of the Association would urge the Indian woman to take up a more visible role in political, social and military affairs.[58] But perhaps in the most significant step forward, the Malayan Indian Congress would be formed in 1946 with Janaki Athi Nahappan from Malaya and Mrs Lobo from Singapore playing key roles. The first President of MIC, John A. Thivy would actively encourage women to participate and the MIC would have women serving on the local and state executive committees of the party.[59] First attempts to create a separate women's section in the party would occur in 1955, in Selangor. It would be a joint effort between Devaki Krishnan, the first woman candidate elected in Malaya, and the Selangor MIC Regional Committee. Devaki would be appointed President of the section and the same year would see eleven branches spring up in different parts of Kuala Lumpur. The MIC would remain a crucial Indian platform and later form a part of the tripartite Alliance, along with MCA and UMNO.

Other Communities

In the other communities of Malaya as well, the post-war period saw a feminist awakening of sorts. Among the Chinese women it primarily took the form of anti-Japanese resistance during the war, as some women were formally indoctrinated by the Malayan Communist Party (MCP). By 1946, the Women's Federation came together under the leading light of Lee Kiu. The Federation had distinct communist leanings and would be the worst hit by the ban during communist insurgency with mass deportations of the women to Kuomintang China. By 1951, women would again surface as active workers with encouragement from the first President of the more conservative, MCA, Tan Cheng-lock.

Like the Indian and Chinese communities, the women from the Malay community did not play any dominant role in the society during the pre-war years. And yet the returning British encountered a change. Captain L. D. Gammons and Sir Theodore Adams, two parliamentary representatives who had been sent down to gauge the extent of opposition to the Malayan Union (MU) proposals, noted:

> In the towns there were demonstrations with 5,000 to 10,000 people standing in front of us. But the most remarkable thing of

all was the part the women were playing in this great national movement. In the 14 years I lived in Malaya I scarcely ever spoke to a Malay woman. But today they go up on political platforms and make speeches; unmarried girls make speeches through micro-phones that would not have disgraced anybody in this community.[60]

At this time, Malay women came together to form two critical socio-political bodies — the *Angkatan Wanita Sedar* (AWAS) affiliated to the radical Malay Nationalist Party (MNP) and the *Kaum Ibu Umno* (KI UMNO) the women's section of UMNO. These movements brought to the forefront some remarkable Malay women like Aishah Ghani, Sakinah Junid, Shamsiah Fakeh and Khatijah Sidek who would contribute to not only the nationalist cause but also play a role in independent Malaya.

In Malaya, the feminist movement was coloured by a nationalist fervour in the tumultuous years that followed the war. Nationalist movements against foreign domination straddled debates about women's role in the workplace, their right to education and their participation in political organizations. At these initial times, women articulating their demands were divided on the lines of ethnic communities. It was only in 1963, six years after Malaya's independence that a multi-racial women's organization of any significance, in the form of the NCWO (National Council for Women's Organization), would emerge.[61] International bodies like YWCA contributed significantly towards its formation. The NCWO, of which Rasammah Bhupalan was the Chairperson, had a leadership structure which mirrored the multi-ethnic culture of Malaya. Perhaps it was foreshadowed in the INA which evolved on a secular understanding of religious and communal beliefs, what Rasammah herself calls "an expansive understanding".[62]

CONCLUSION

Subhas Bose was a prolific letter-writer. During his lifetime he wrote numerous letters — in some he poured out adolescent angst, in some he clinically dissected philosophy, in others he spoke of love. He wrote replies to newspapers, which were in the habit of regularly incriminated him, to the odd adulating fan, to contemporary political activists. In one letter, no more than an office memo, addressed to Lt. M. Satyavati Thevar, in charge of the rear headquarters in Singapore after Captain Lakshmi's move to Rangoon, he had written: "I do not like the volunteers to waste their time unnecessarily in cooking and other domestic duties. These duties 'they have done enough at home'. In the Camp they should concentrate on the task that lies ahead of them."[63] This proved to be a precursor to what was to come. Two widely divergent worlds conflated in the Rani of Jhansi Regiment. On one hand was Bose — progressive in his feminist ideas, someone who had been working with women's issues at the grass root level, a legatee of the Indian Renaissance and its rich inheritance from the previous century. On the other hand, were the Indian women of Southeast Asia — a large majority of whom were tradition bound, marginally educated, accustomed to living as an oppressed minority. They subsisted behind the *purdah* and were trained to be subservient wives and mothers. For the migrant community, placed outside the confines of the Indian society and its joint-family system, the institute of marriage had diluted in its sanctity. While divorce remained an easy prerogative for the man, it was the woman's charge to perpetuate monogamy in marriages. Any political or social role of significance was restricted to the educated elite. Rounaq places the blame squarely on the, "norms of *purdah* — gender separation and limiting women's physical mobility", prevalent widely amongst all communities and classes in South Asia, "making it difficult for women to seek critical routes to leadership".⁶⁴ With the physical transformation that enlisting with the RJR involved, it is this veiled image of the Indian woman that Bose set about to decimate.

What makes the Rani of Jhansi movement even more remarkable, the collision of these two opposing worlds happened against the background of war and the Japanese occupation. It was a time when women from across Taiwan, the Philippines, Indonesia, Malaya, Singapore, Burma, Borneo were being herded together as Comfort Women. Considered by the Japanese military psychologists as essential elements for boosting the morale of the Japanese soldier, these women were victims of enforced sexual slavery. This was considered an accepted facet of the Japanese way of war and the estimated number of women involved was as large as 80,000 to 100,000.⁶⁵ Schools were converted to geisha houses and women who had not been taken, lived in constant fear of forced victimization. There are quite a few references to these women in the memoirs of the Rani of Jhansi war veterans. With a conscious display of their military manoeuvres, the girls had to convince the top brass of the Japanese and Burmese military of the seriousness of their training and intention.⁶⁶

Indian women from all over Southeast Asia, most of whom had never seen India or understood English or Hindustani — Bose's chosen mediums of communication, joined the ranks-and-files of the Regiment. The Rani of Jhansi Regiment nurtured a new image of the Indian woman which was evocative of the rich traditions of the country and yet looked beyond the accepted female stereotype. The Regiment proved to be a convergence of historical consciousness, feminist initiative and nationalist fervour. It brought to the forefront a number of politically inclined women who were driven by a new sense of mission. After the experience at the war-front they continued to impugn systemic flaws, representing causes of their own choice.

The post-war period in Southeast Asia saw an entire generation of women coming to the foreground who refused to conform to traditional roles. The women's movements that sprang up initially had an overtly nationalist message, with feminist issues nesting somewhere within. Women's groups across the region formed powerful networks of intelligence and guerilla resistance. Later, with an end of the anti-colonial struggle, women from diverse communities would coalesce to articulate the need of economic or social equality. At the individual level, some of these women like Janaki and Rasammah, could achieve a harmonious blend of their public and private personas. Others, like Khatijah Sidek, rocked the boat all too early, ruffled too many irate feathers and had to encounter collective male (and female too) indignation. She agitated against gender disparities from the initial days and was finally expelled from UMNO. The Rani of Jhansi Regiment provided an early role model of possibilities for the female potential and set aside political space for women to work in. With the symbolical donning of military fatigues by the Ranis, feminism took a step forward in its multi-layered and at times confounding journey of self-discovery.

Notes

1. From references spread across Muthammal Palanisamy, *From Shore to Shore: The Trials and Tribulations of an Indian Indentured Labor Migrant Family in Malaysia* (Malaysia: VGV Management Consultant, 2002).
2. Sisir Kumar Bose and Sugata Bose, eds., *Letters to Emilie Schenkl (1934–1942)*, Netaji Collected Works, vol. VII (Calcutta/New Delhi: Netaji Research Bureau/Permanent Black, 1994), p. 207.

3. Ibid., letter from Bose to Emilie, September 1937, plate 10.
4. Sisir Kumar Bose and Sugata Bose, ed., *The Essential Writings of Netaji Subhas Chandra Bose* (Calcutta/New Delhi: Netaji Research Bureau/Oxford University Press, 1997), p. 161.
5. Sisir K. Bose and Sugata Bose, ed., *The Indian Pilgrim: An Unfinished Biography*, Subhas Chandra Bose, Netaji Collected Works, vol. I (Calcutta/New Delhi: Netaji Research Bureau/Oxford University Press, 1997), pp. 141–42.
6. Gordon mentions: "It took her a long time to convince Subhas that this was what she wanted. He wanted the mother of the youth to emerge as an activist Goddess." Leonard A. Gordon, *Brothers Against the Raj: A Biography of Indian Nationalists*, p. 135. For Bose's letters: Sisir Kumar Bose and Sugata Bose, eds., *The Essential Writings of Netaji Subhas Chandra Bose* (Calcutta/New Delhi: Netaji Research Bureau/Oxford University Press, 1997), pp. 77–81.
7. Letter written by Subhas Chandra Bose to Bivabati Bose, Sisir K. Bose, eds., *In Burmese Prisons, Correspondence May 1923–July 1926*, Netaji Collected Works, vol. III (Calcutta/New Delhi: Netaji Research Bureau/Permanent Black, 2009), pp. 168–69.
8. From the autograph book of Gita Bose, quoted in Gordon, p. 161.
9. *Thus Spake Vivekananda* (Calcutta: Ramakrishna Mission), p. 47.
10. *Swami Vivekanada, Collected Works*, vol. V (Calcutta: Ramakrishna Mission), p. 342.
11. *Ananda Bazar Patrika*, Calcutta, 3 and 4 May 1928.
12. Geraldine H. Forbes, "The Women Revolutionaries of Bengal", *The Oracle*, vol. II, no. 2 (April 1980): 2–3.
13. Sisir Kumar Bose and Sugata Bose, eds., *The Indian Struggle: 1920–1942*, Subhas Chandra Bose, Netaji Collected Works, vol. II (Calcutta/New Delhi: Netaji Research Bureau/Oxford University Press, 1997), p. 329.
14. Speech delivered to the Rani of Jhansi Regiment on 22 October 1943 at Singapore: Sisir K. Bose and Sugata Bose, eds., *Chalo Delhi*,

1943–1945, Netaji Collected Works, vol. XII (Calcutta/New Delhi: Netaji Research Bureau/Permanent Black, 2007), p. 126.
15. Poem written in the 1930s by Subhadra Kumari Chauhan, a part of the popular culture of India.
16. Lakshmi Sahgal, "The Rani of Jhansi Regiment", *The Oracle*, vol. II, no. 2 (1980): 61, cited in Joyce Chapman Lebra, *Women Against the Raj: The Rani of Jhansi Regiment* (Singapore: Institute of Southeast Asian Studies, 2008), p. 72.
17. *Chalo Delhi*, p. 54.
18. Joyce Chapman Lebra, *Women Against the Raj: The Rani of Jhansi Regiment*, p. 72.
19. *Chalo Delhi*, pp. 55–58.
20. Ibid., p. 127.
21. Shanti Majumdar, "Netaji's Rani of Jhansi Regiment", *The Oracle*, vol. II, no. 3 (July 1980): 24.
22. Lakshmi Sahgal, "The Rani of Jhansi Regiment", *The Oracle*, vol. I, no. 2 (April 1979): 18.
23. Janaki Athinahappan, "The Rani of Jhansi Regiment", *The Oracle*, vol. II, no. 1 (January 1980): 31.
24. Interview with Janaki Athi Nahappan by author, Kuala Lumpur, 23/24 September 2011.
25. Joyce Chapman Lebra, *Women Against the Raj: The Rani of Jhansi Regiment*, p. 88.
26. Ibid., p. 85.
27. Speech delivered on 22 October 1943: *Chalo Delhi*, p. 124.
28. J. E. Nathan, *The Census of British Malaya: The Straits Settlements, Federated Malay states and protected states of Johore, Kedah, Perlis, Kelantan, Trengganu, and Brunei, 1921* (London: Waterlow, 1922), p. 190.
29. Virginia H. Dancz, *Women and Party Politics in Peninsular Malaysia* (Singapore: Oxford University Press, 1987), p. 65.
30. Lakshmi Sahgal, "The Rani of Jhansi Regiment", *The Oracle*, vol. I, no. 2 (April 1979): 15.

31. Janaki Athinahappan, "The Rani of Jhansi Regiment", in *Netaji Subhas Chandra Bose: A Malaysian Perspective* (Kuala Lumpur: Netaji Centre, 1992), p. 42.
32. Manawati Arya, "Rani of Jhansi Regiment in Burma", *The Oracle*, vol. II, no. 2 (April 1980): 18.
33. Geraldine Forbes, *Mothers and Sisters: Feminism and Nationalism in the Thought of Subhas Chandra Bose*, Asian Studies 2, Cambridge [U.K.]; New York, NY, Cambridge University Press, p. 30.
34. Maya Banerjee, "My Life with the Rani of Jhansi Regiment", *The Oracle*, vol. II, no. 2 (April 1980): 22.
35. Letter written to Lt. M. Satiavati Thevar, Commandant, Rani of Jhansi Training Camp, 18 June 1944, *Chalo Delhi*, p. 423.
36. Ibid., p. 431.
37. S. A. Ayer, *Unto Him a Witness: The Story of Netaji Subhas Chandra Bose in East Asia* (Bombay: Thacker, 1951), pp. 163–64.
38. Manawati Arya, "Rani of Jhansi Regiment in Burma", *The Oracle*, vol. II, no. 2 (April 1980): 19.
39. *Jai Hind: The Diary of a Rebel Daughter of India with the Rani of Jhansi Regiment* (Bombay: Janmabhoomi Prakashan Mandir, 1945), p. 82. Reference to the incident is also found in *The Glory that is INA*, P. B. Roy, p. 37.
40. Lakshmi Sahgal, *A Revolutionary Life: Memoirs of a Political Activist* (New Delhi: Paul's Press, 1997), p. 166.
41. Lakshmi Sahgal, "The Rani of Jhansi Regiment", *The Oracle*, vol. I, no. 2 (April 1979): 19.
42. Interview with Bala A. Chandran by author, Singapore, 16 September 2011.
43. Interview with Janaki Athi Nahappan by author, Kuala Lumpur, 23/24 September 2011.
44. Aruna Gopinath, *Footprints on the Sands of Time: Rasammah Bhupalan — A Life of Purpose* (Malaysia: Arkib Negara, 2007), pp. 94–95.
45. Joyce Chapman Lebra, *Women Against the Raj: The Rani of Jhansi Regiment*, p. 66.

46. Ibid., p. 64.
47. Interview with Janaki Athi Nahappan by author, Kuala Lumpur, 23/24 September 2011.
48. Descriptions of Janaki's early life from an interview with her son Ishwar Nahappan, Singapore, 12 May 2011 and with Janaki Athi Nahappan by author, Kuala Lumpur, 23/24 September 2011.
49. Shah Nawaz Khan, *My Memories of INA and Its Netaji* (Delhi: Rajkamal Publications, 1946), pp. 206–7.
50. Janaki Athinahappan, "The Rani of Jhansi Regiment", in *Netaji Subhas Chandra Bose: A Malaysian Perspective*, p. 46.
51. Interview with Ishwar Nahappan by author, Singapore, 12 May 2011.
52. Parts of this section have appeared in *Netaji Subhas Chandra Bose: The Singapore Saga* (Singapore: Nalanda-Sriwijaya Centre, Institute of Southeast Asian Studies, 2011).
53. Aruna Gopinath, *Footprints on the Sands of Time: Rasammah Bhupalan — A Life of Purpose*, p. 91.
54. Nilanjana Sengupta, *Life at the Frontlines: Interview of Rasammah Bhupalan* published in Hindustan Times, Bombay, 27 February 2011.
55. Aruna Gopinath, *Footprints on the Sands of Time: Rasammah Bhupalan — A Life of Purpose*, p. 104.
56. Virginia H. Dancz, *Women and Party Politics in Peninsular Malaysia*, p. 70.
57. Lakshmi Sahgal, "The Rani of Jhansi Regiment", *The Oracle*, vol. I, no. 2 (April 1979): 17.
58. *Malaya Tribune*, Malaya, 29 April 1946.
59. Virginia H. Dancz, *Women and Party Politics in Peninsular Malaysia*, p. 104.
60. Captain L. D. Gammons and Sir Theodore Adams, "British Malaya", *London Association of British Malaya*, vol. 21 (August 1946): 53.
61. Cecilia Ng, Maznah Mohamad and Tan Beng Hui, *Feminism and the Women's Movement in Malaysia: An Unsung (R)evolution* (Milton Park, Abingdon, Oxon; New York: Routledge, 2007), p. 19.

62. Aruna Gopinath, *Footprints on the Sands of Time: Rasammah Bhupalan — A Life of Purpose*, p. 95.
63. Letter to Lieutenant M. Satiavati Thevar, 14 May 1944, *Chalo Delhi*, p. 419.
64. Rounaq Jahan, *Women in South Asian Politics* (Third World Foundation, 1987), p. 854.
65. *Forgotten Armies*, p. 409.
66. Aruna Gopinath, *Footprints on the Sands of Time: Rasammah Bhupalan — A Life of Purpose*, p. 73.

BIBLIOGRAPHY

Allen, Louis. *End of the War in Asia*. London: Hart-Davis MacGibbon, 1976.

Ampalavanar, Rajeswary. *The Indian Minority and Political Change in Malaya, 1945–1957*. Kuala Lumpur: Oxford University Press, 1981.

Arasaratnam, S. *South Indians in Malaysia and Singapore*. London: Oxford University Press, 1970.

Arya, Manawati. "Rani of Jhansi Regiment in Burma". *The Oracle*, vol. II, no. 2 (April 1980).

Asma, Paul and Abdullah Pedersen. *Understanding Multi-cultural Malaysia*. Malaysia: Pearson/Prentice Hall, 2003.

Athinahappan, Janaki. "The Rani of Jhansi Regiment". *The Oracle*, vol. II, no. 1 (January 1980).

Ayer, S. A. *Story of the INA*. New Delhi: National Book Trust, 1997.

———. *Unto Him a Witness: The Story of Netaji Subhas Chandra Bose in East Asia*. Bombay: Thacker & Co., 1951.

Bakshi, Akhil. *The Road to Freedom: Travels through Singapore, Malaysia, Burma, and India in the Footsteps of the Indian National Army*. New Delhi: Odyssey Books, 1998.

Banerjee, Maya. "My Life with the Rani of Jhansi Regiment". *The Oracle*, vol. II, no. 2 (April 1980).

Barua, P. *Gentlemen of the Raj: The Indian Army Officer's Corps, 1817–1949*. London: Conn. Praeger, 2003.

Bayly, Christopher A. and Timothy N. Harper. *Forgotten Armies: Britain's Asian Empire and the War with Japan*. London: Penguin Books, 2005.

———. *Forgotten Wars: The End of Britain's Asian Empire*. London: Penguin Books, 2008.

Becka, Jan. "Subhas Chandra Bose and the Burmese Freedom Movement". In *Netaji and India's Freedom*, edited by Sisir Kr Bose. Calcutta: Netaji Research Bureau, 1975.

Bhargava, Moti Lal Dr. *Netaji Subhas Chandra Bose in Southeast Asia and India's Liberation War (1943–45)*. Kerala and New Delhi: Vishwavidya Publishers, 1962.

Bhattacharya, S. N. *Netaji Subhas Bose in Self Exile*. New Delhi: Metropolitan Book Company Pvt. Ltd., 1975.

Boestamam, Ahmad. *Carving the Path to the Summit*. Athens: Ohio University Press, 1979.

Boothe Anne. *Colonial Legacies: Economic and Social Development in East and Southeast Asia*. Honululu: University of Hawaii Press, 2007.

Bose, Krishna. *Charan Rekha Taba*. Calcutta: Ananda Publishers Pvt. Limited, 1996.

Bose, Mihir. *The Last Hero*. London and New York: Quartet Books, 1982.

Bose, Romen. *A Will for Freedom: Netaji and the Indian Independence Movement in Singapore and Southeast Asia 1942–1945*. Singapore: VJ Times, 1993.

Bose, Subhas Chandra. *Crossroads: 1938–1940*. New Delhi: Oxford University Press, 1997.

Bose, Sisir and Sugata Bose, eds. *Essential Writings of Netaji Subhas Chandra Bose*. Calcutta/New Delhi: Netaji Research Bureau/Oxford University Press, 1997.

———. *Netaji Collected Works*. 12 volumes. Calcutta/New Delhi: Netaji Research Bureau/Permanent Black, 1995–2007.

Bose, Subhas Chandra. *Selected Speeches of Subhas Chandra Bose*. New Delhi: Government of India Publication Division, 1962.

———. *The Mission of Life*. Calcutta: Thacker Spink, 1953.

Bose, Sugata. *A Hundred Horizons: The Indian Ocean in the Age of Global Empire*. Cambridge, Massachusetts: Harvard University Press, 2006.

———. *His Majesty's Opponent: Subhas Chandra Bose and India's Struggle Against Empire*. Cambridge, Massachusetts and London, England: The Belknap Press of Harvard University, 2011.

———. *Modern South Asia: History, Culture, Political Economy*. London and New York: Routledge, 2004.

Chakravarty, S. R. and Madan C. Paul. *Netaji Subhas Chandra Bose: Relevance to Contemporary World*. New Delhi: Har-Anand Publication, 2000.

Chandler, Malcolm and John Wright. *Modern World History*. 2nd Review Edition. London: Heinemann Educational Books, 2001.

Chatterjee, Kumar Suniti. "Netaji, National Unity, the Language Question and the Roman Script". *The Oracle*, vol. I, no. 1 (January 1979).

Chatterji, A. C. Major General. *India's Struggle for Freedom*. Calcutta: Chuckervertty Chatterjee, 1947.

Christie, J. Clive. *South East Asia in the Twentieth Century*. London: Tauris, 1998.

Corr, Gerard H. *The War of the Springing Tigers*. London: Osprey, 1975.

Dancz, H. Virginia. *Women and Party Politics in Peninsular Malaysia*. Singapore: Oxford University Press, 1987.

Daniel, E. Valentine, Henry Bernstein and Tom Brass, eds. *Plantations, Proletarians and Peasants in Colonial Asia*. London: Frank Cass, 1992.

Das, Hari Hara. *Netaji Subhas Chandra Bose: The Great War for Political Emancipation*. Jaipur: National Publishing House, 2000.

Das, Khosla and Madan Gopal. *Last Days of Netaji*. Delhi: Thomson Press, 1974.

Das, S. A. and K. B. Subbaiah. *Chalo Delhi: An Historical Account of the Indian Independence Movement in East Asia*. India: 1974.

Dasgupta, K. R. "Subhas Chandra as a Writer". *The Oracle*, vol. VI, no. 1 (January 1984).

Dhillon, G. S. Col. "The Nehru Holds the Irrawaddy". *The Oracle*, vol. VI, no. 1 (January 1984).

———. "The Indo-Burman Relations during World War II". *The Oracle*, vol. VII, no. 3 (July 1985).

———. *From My Bones: Memoirs of Col G S Dhillon*. Delhi: Aryan Books International, 1998.

Fakeh, Shamsiah. *The Memoirs of Shamsiah Fakeh: From AWAS to*

10th Regiment. Petaling Jaya: Strategic Information and Research Development Center, 2009.

Fay, Ward Peter. *The Forgotten Army: India's Armed Struggle for Independence, 1942–1945*. USA: University of Michigan Press, 1993.

Forbes, Geraldine. "The Women Revolutionaries of Bengal". *The Oracle*, vol. II, no. 2 (April 1980).

Fujiwara, Lieutenant General Iwaichi. *F Kikan: Japanese Army Intelligence Operations in Southeast Asia during World War II*. London: Heinemann Educational Books, 1983.

Gamba, Charles. *The National Union of Plantation Workers: The History of the Plantation Workers of Malaya, 1946–1958*. Singapore: Eastern Universities Press, 1962.

———. *The Origins of Trade Unionism in Malaya*. Singapore: Eastern Universities Press, 1962.

Gandhi, M. K. *The Collected Works of Mahatma Gandhi*. New Delhi: Government of India, Publications Divisions, 1958–1982.

Ghosh, K. K. *The Indian National Army: Second Front of the Indian Independence Movement*. Meerut: Meenakshi Prakashan, 1969.

Ghosh, Lipi. "Indian Revolutionaries and Subhas Chandra Bose in Thailand: The Era of Plaek Pibulsongkram". In *Netaji and India's Freedom*, edited by Sisir Kr Bose. Calcutta: Netaji Research Bureau, 1975.

Gopal, Madan. *Life and Times of Subhas Chandra Bose as told in his Own Words*. New Delhi: Vikas, 1978.

Gopinath, Aruna. *Footprints on the Sands of Time: Rasammah Bhupalan, A Life of Purpose*. Malaysia: Arkib Negara, 2007.

Gordon, Leonard A. *Brothers Against the Raj: A Biography of Indian Nationalists, Sarat and Subhas Chandra Bose*. New York: Columbia University Press, 1990.

Gravers, Mikael. *Nationalism as Political Paranoia in Burma*. Great Britain: Curzon Press, 1999.

Hasan, Abid. "A Soldier Remembers". *The Oracle*, vol. VI, no. 1 (January 1984).

———. "Netaji and the Indian Communal Question". *The Oracle*, vol. I, no. 1 (January 1979).

Hoong, Khong Kim. *Merdeka! British Rule and the Struggle for Independence in Malaysia, 1945–1957*. Petaling Jaya: Strategic Information and Research Development Center, 1984.

Hussain, Abid Safrani. *The Men from Imphal*. Calcutta: Netaji Research Bureau, 1971.

Hussain, Mustapha. *Malay Nationalism before UMNO: The Memoirs of Mustapha Hussain*. Kuala Lumpur: Utusan Publications & Distributors Sdn. Bhd., 2005.

Jain, Ravindra K., ed. *South Indians on the Plantation Frontier in Malaysia*. New Haven, CT: Yale University Press, 1970.

Jog, N. C. *In Freedom's Quest: A Biography of Subhas Chandra Bose*. Bombay: Orient Longmans, 1968.

Kesavapany, K., A. Mani and P. Ramasamy, eds. *Rising India and Indian Communities in East Asia*. Singapore: Institute of Southeast Asian Studies, 2008.

Khan, Shah Nawaz Maj. Gen. *My Memories of INA and Its Netaji*. Delhi: Rajkamal Publication, 1946.

———. *The INA Heroes: Autobiographies of Maj. Gen. Shah Nawaz, Col. Prem K Sahgal and Col. G S Dhillon of the Azad Hind Fauj*. Lahore: Hero Publications, 1946.

Kheng, Boon Cheah. *Red Star over Malaya: Resistance and Social Conflict during and after the Japanese Occupation of Malaya, 1941–1946*. Singapore: Singapore University Press, 2003.

Khoo, Agnes. *Life as the River Flows: Women in Malayan Anti-Colonial Struggle* (An Oral History of Women from Thailand, Malaysia, Singapore). Petaling Jaya: Strategic Information and Research Development Center, 2004.

Kiani, Mohammad Zaman Maj. Gen. *India's Freedom Struggle and the Great INA*. New Delhi: Reliance Publishing House, 1994.

Kyi, Aung San Suu. *Aung San*. Australia: University of Queensland Press, Lawrence, Mass., USA; Distributed in the USA and Canada by Technical Impex Corp., 1984.

Latif, Asad-ul Iqbal. *India in the Making of Singapore*. Singapore: Singapore Indian Association, 2008.

Lebra, Joyce Chapman. *Japanese Trained Armies in Southeast Asia*. Singapore: Institute of Southeast Asian Studies, 2010.

———. *The Indian National Army and Japan*. Singapore: Institute of Southeast Asian Studies, 2008.

———. *Women against the Raj: The Rani of Jhansi Regiment*. Singapore: Institute of Southeast Asian Studies, 2008.

———, ed. *Japan's Greater East Asia Co-Prosperity Sphere in World War II*. Kuala Lumpur: Oxford University Press, 1975.

MacMunn, George. *The Martial Races of India*. London: Sampson Low, Marston and Co., 1933.

Mahajani, Usha. *The Role of Indian Minorities in Burma and Malaya*. Bombay: Vora & Co., Ltd. for the Institute of Pacific Relations, 1960.

Majumdar, R.C. *Three Phases of India's Struggle for Freedom*. Bombay: Bharatiya Vidya Bhavan, 1967.

Majumdar, Shanti. "Netaji's Rani of Jhansi Regiment". *The Oracle*, vol. II, no. 3 (July 1980).

Maw, Ba. "The Great Asian Dreamer". *The Oracle*, vol. II, no. 1 (January 1980).

———. *Breakthrough in Burma: Memoirs of a Revolution, 1939–1946*. New Haven: Yale University Press, 1968.

Michael, Edwardes. *The Last Years of British India*. Cleveland: World Pub. Company, 1964.

Mookerjee, Girija K. *Subhas Chandra Bose*. Government of India: Ministry of Information and Broadcasting, Publications Divisions, 1975.

Mookherjee, Nanda. *Vivekananda's Influence on Subhas*. Calcutta: Jayashree Prakasan, 1977.

Muang, Muang U, ed. *Aung San of Burma*. Yale University: The Hague, M. Nijhoff, 1962.

———. *A Trial in Burma: The Assassination of Aung San*. Yale University: The Hague, M. Nijhoff, 1962.

Muggeridge, Malcolm, ed. *Ciano's Diary, 1939–1943*. London: William Heinemann, 1947.

Nathan, J. E. *The Census of British Malaya: The Straits Settlements, Federated Malay states and protected states of Johore, Kedah, Perlis, Kelantan, Trengganu, and Brunei, 1921*. London: Waterlow, 1922.

Nathan, S. R. *An Unexpected Journey: Path to the Presidency.* Singapore: EDM, 2011.

———. *Winning Against the Odds: The Labour Research Unit in NTUC's Founding.* Singapore: Straits Times Press, 2011.

Naw, Angelene. *Aung San and the Struggle for Burmese Independence.* Thailand: Silkworm Books, 2001.

Netaji Subhas Chandra Bose: A Malaysian Perspective. Kuala Lumpur: Netaji Centre, 1992.

Ng,Cecilia, Maznah Mohamad and tan beng hui. *Feminism and the Women's Movement in Malaysia: An Unsung (R)evolution.* Milton Park, Abingdon, Oxon; New York: Routledge, 2007.

Palanisamy, Muthammal. *From Shore to Shore: The Trials and Tribulations of an Indian Indentured Labour Migrant Family in Malaysia.* Malaysia: VGV Management Consultant, 2002.

Pandit, H. N. *The Last Days of Netaji.* Delhi: Dariagunje, April 1993.

Parmer, J. N. *Colonial Labour Policy and Administration: A History of Labour in the Rubber Plantation Industry in Malaya (1910–1941).* New York: J. J. Augustin Publisher, 1960.

Puthucheary, Dominic and K. S. Jomo, eds. *No Cowardly Past: James J Puthucheary — Writings, Poems, Commentaries.* 2nd ed. Petaling Jaya: Strategic Information and Research Development Center, 2010.

Rahman, Abdul Tunku. *As a Matter of Interest.* Kuala Lumpur and Singapore: Heinemann Asia, 1981.

Ram, S. and R. Kumar. *Role of INA and Indian Navy.* New Delhi: Commonwealth Publishers, 2008.

Rounaq, Jahan. *Women in South Asian Politics.* Third World Foundation, 1987.

Roy, Kumar Dilip. *Netaji: The Man, Reminiscences.* Bombay: Bharatiya Vidya Bhavan, 1966.

———. *The Subhas I Knew.* Bombay: Nalanda Publications, 1946.

Sahgal, Lakshmi. "The Rani of Jhansi Regiment". *The Oracle,* vol. I, no. 2 (April 1979).

———. Sahgal, Lakshmi. "The Rani of Jhansi Regiment". *The Oracle,* vol. II, no. 2 (1980).

―――. *A Revolutionary Life: Memoirs of a Political Activist*. New Delhi: Paul's Press, 1997.

Sahgal, P. K. Colonel. "Principles of Netaji's Strategy". *The Oracle*, vol. 1, no. 1 (January 1979).

Sandhu, Kernial Singh. *Indians in Malaya: Immigration and Settlement (1786–1957)*. Great Britain: Cambridge University Press, 1969.

Sandhu, S. K. and A. Mani, eds. *Indian Communities in Southeast Asia*. Singapore: Institute of Southeast Asian Studies, 2006.

Seth, Amritlal. *Jai Hind: The Diary of a Rebel Daughter of India with the Rani of Jhansi Regiment*. Bombay: Janmabhoomi Prakasan Mandir, 1945.

Silverstein, Josef, ed. *The Political Legacy of Aung San*. New York: Southeast Asia Program Publications, 1993.

Singh, Prasad Surendra. *Growth of Nationalism in Burma, 1900–1942*. Calcutta: Firma KLM Pvt. Ltd., 1980.

Sivaram, M. *The Road to Delhi*. Vermont and Tokyo: Rutland, 1967.

Som, Reba. *Gandhi, Bose Nehru and the Making of the Modern Indian Mind*. India: Penguin Viking, 2004.

Stenson, R. Michael. *Industrial Conflict in Malaya: Prelude to the Communist Revolt of 1948*. Great Britain: Oxford University Press, 1970.

―――. *Class, Race and Colonialism in West Malaysia: The Indian Case*. Australia: University of Queensland Press, 1980.

Tendulkar, D. G. *Mahatma: Life of Mohandas Karamchand Gandhi*. New Delhi: Publications Divisions, Ministry of Information and Broadcasting, Government of India, 1963.

Thivy, John A. *The Struggle in East Asia*. Calcutta: Netaji Research Bureau, 1971.

Tinker, Hugh. *Men who Overturned Empires, Fighters, Dreamers and Schemers*. Great Britain: Macmillan Press, 1987.

Toye, Hugh. *Subhas Chandra Bose, The Springing Tiger: A Study of a Revolution*. Bombay: Jaico, 1959.

Weizsacke, Ernst r von. *Memoirs of Ernst von Weizsacker*. London: Victor Gollancz, 1951.

Yong, C. F. *The Origins of Malayan Communism*. Singapore: South Sea Society, 1997.

INDEX

A

Abdullah Sani bib Raja Kechil, 141
  see also Ahmad Boestamam
Abdul Samad, 138
Abdul Zainuddin, 64
ABIC (All Burma Indian Congress), 137–38
Abid Hasan, 1, 3, 7, 31, 97–98, 109, 204, 211
absolute monarchy, 55–56
ACCC (Associated Chinese Chamber of Commerce), 154
Adams, Theodore, 226
AFPFL (Anti-Fascist People's Freedom League), 121, 128–31, 134–36
Ahmad Boestamam, 138, 140, 157
  API (Generation of Aware Youth), and, 141–45
Aishah Ghani, 227
AITUC (All India Trade Union Congress), 167, 169–70

All Bengal Railway Indian Employees Association, 167
All Burma Congress, 133
All Burma Indian Congress, *see* ABIC
Allied forces, 66–67
Allied POWs, 84
All India Radio, 106–07
All India Trade Union Congress, *see* AITUC
All Malaya Indian Political Conference, 150
All Malayan Hindustani Conference, 150
AMCJA (All Malayan Council of Joint Action), 147, 154
AMCJA-*Putera* alliance, 141, 147, 151, 154–55
Andaman and Nicobar islands, return of, 46, 72
Angkatan Wanita Sedar (AWAS), 227
Anglo-American war efforts, 106
Anglo-Japanese relations, 68
Anglo-Mysore War, Fourth, 33

Anti-British League, 185
anti-British sentiments, 11, 30
Anti-Compromise Conference, 123
Anti-Fascist People's Freedom League, *see* AFPFL
anti-India Radio, 106
anti-Japanese sentiments, 119, 121
Anuman Rachodhon, 59
Anushilan Samiti, revolutionary organization, 19, 35
API (*Angkatan Pemuda Insaf*), 185
  Ahmad Boestamam and, 141–45
Arya, Manawati, 213
Asaf Ali, 77
A. Samad Ismail, 142
Asian "superpower", 56
Associated Chinese Chamber of Commerce, *see* ACCC
Ataturk, Mustafa Kemal, 96, 138
Atma Sakti, daily, 108
Auchinleck, Claude, 78, 80
August Revolution, 17
Aung San, 51, 85, 118, 121, 129–36, 157
  Bogyoke, 124, 127–28
  Subhas Chandra Bose, and, 122–28
Aung San-Atlee Agreement, 134–35
Aung San Suu Kyi, 131
Aurobindo, Sri, 4, 12, 19, 24, 35, 100, 198

AWAS (Angkatan Wanita Sedar), 227
Axis Powers, 5, 8–9, 32, 46, 66–68, 131, 198
Ayer, S.A., 105, 108
Azad Brigade, 46–47, 184
Azad Guerilla Regiment, 27
"Azad Hind Dal", 75
Azad Hind Day, 151
Azad Hind Fauj [Free India Army], 6, 18, 81, 110, 125
Azad Hind [Free India] Broadcasting Station, 105
Azad Hind [Free India], newspaper, 42, 105
Azad Hind Radio, 107, 113–14
Azad, Maulana, 123
Azad Muslim Radio, 114
Azad School, 49
Aziz Ahmad, 107

B

BAA (Burma Area Army), 73, 74
Bahadur Group, 47
Baisakhi, festival, 11
Bajaj, Darshan Singh, 58
Balak Sena, youth wing, 102, 175, 216
Ba Maw, 50, 53–54, 70, 126
  Subhas Chandra Bose, and, 118–22
Banerjee, Maya, 212
Banglar Katha, daily, 108
Bangkok Conference, 58, 88, 99–100

Barisan Sosialis, 184
Battle of Beiping-Tianjin, 71
Battle of Shanghai, 71
Batu Arang Collieries, 176
Bayly, Christopher, 124
BBC, 106
Bengal Pact, 22, 101
Bengal famine, 41–42
Bengal Oil and Petrol Workers' Union, 167
Bengal partition, 21
Bengal Provincial Congress, 22
Bengal Renaissance, 201
Bengal Volunteers, 23–24, 200, 211
Berita Malai, 142
"Berita Minggu", 144
Bernard Free Library, 130
"Bertram Mills circus", 20
Bhonsle, J.K., 48, 213
Bhupalan, Rasammah, 28, 29, 213, 216, 222–24, 227, 230
BIA (Burma Independence Army), 51, 53, 120–21, 126–27, 139
"Big Six" trade unionists, 184
Birkenhead, Lord, 14
"Black Hole" of Calcutta, 101, 159
  see also Holwell Monument
BMA (British Military Administration), 147, 178, 215
Bogyoke, and Aung San, 124, 127–28
Bo Let Ya, 122

Bo Min Yaung, 157
bonded labour, 60
Bose, Acharya Jagadish Chandra, 4
Bose, Anita, 3, 32
Bose, Krishna, 76, 78, 93
Bose, Prabhabati, 198
Bose, Rashbehari, 8, 9, 39, 44, 58, 68, 99–100, 102, 110, 172, 211
Bose, Sarat Chandra, 2, 32, 135–36, 199
Bose, Subhas Chandra
  adulation, 26–27
  Aung San, and, 122–28
  Ba Maw, and, 118–22
  Burma, in, 2–3, 28, 30, 47–50, 53–54, 116–38
  Cambridge, in, 4–5, 19, 23, 112
  death, 49, 59, 94, 135
  feminism, and, 199–204, 210–11, 228–30
  Formosa, in, 93–94
  image of, 18
  Indian community in Malaya, political legacy for, 145–58
  Japanese alliance, and, 66–76, 108–09
  letters, 50, 228
  Malaya, political legacy in, 138–45
  military, and, 19–20
  "Netaji", as, 6, 18, 78, 110, 124, 136
  philosophy and beliefs, 10–12

political prisoner, 2
Singapore, in, 8, 10, 44, 111
Southeast Asia, in, 43–49, 65
speeches, 12, 25, 29, 30, 34–36, 44–45, 80–81, 111–12, 143, 200, 205
submarine journey, 1–2, 7, 43, 97, 204
Thailand, in, 55–59
trade unions, and, 167–70
Turkey, in, 96
women, and, 197–99, 225
Boycott of British Goods, book, 168
Brahmo Samaj, 201
British Army, 128
British Asian Empire, 38
British imperialism, 10
British Indian Army, 11, 17, 23, 30, 44, 65, 79, 81, 83, 102, 107
British Malaya, 176
British Medical Mission, 222
British Military Administration, *see* BMA
British Occupation Force, 76
British propaganda, 99, 106–07
British Raj, 2, 79, 82
British Special Operations Executive, *see* SOE
Buddhism, 39, 50, 132–33
Buddhist-Muslim riots, 52
Burhanuddin Al-Helmi, 140–41, 143–44

Burma
communism in, 117
Indian community in, 51–55, 136–38
Japanese invasion, 51–52, 133
minority groups, equal rights for, 133–35
Subhas Chandra Bose in, 2–3, 28, 30, 47–50, 53–54, 116–38
Burma Area Army, *see* BAA
Burma Army, 128
Burma Independence Army, *see* BIA
Burma-Siam railway, 147
see also "Death Railway"
Burmese-Japanese alliance, 127
Burmese nationalist movement, 50–51
Burmese Press, 120

C

Calcutta, "Black Hole" of, 101, 159
Calcutta Congress, 15, 20, 23–24
Calcutta Corporation, 167
Calcutta Municipal Corporation, 22, 224
Calcutta University Journal, 96
Cambridge, Subhas Chandra Bose in, 4–5, 19, 23, 112
Carving the Path to the Summit, book, 144
caste system, 151
Castle Barracks, 80

Central Indian Association of
    Malaya, *see* CIAM
Ceylonese community, 104
censorship, 43, 86, 113–14
"Chalo Delhi", 109, 212
Chandran, Bala A., 216
Charana Rekha Taba, book, 93
charkha, emblem, 13, 33
"charter of liberty", 70, 75
Chatterjee, Suniti Kumar, 95–96
Chaudhuri, Nirad C., 77
Chettyar
    community, 98, 148
    moneylenders, 62
"Chhattri Sangha", 24
Chiang Kai Shek, 71–72
"China Incident", 131
China Relief Fund, 173
Chinese Communist Party, 131
Chinese nationalism, 177
Choudhury, H.K., 179
Chulalongkorn University, 55, 58
Churchill, Winston, 9, 112
CIAM (Central Indian
    Association of Malaya), 63,
    148–49, 152, 155, 170–75,
    224–25
Ciano, Count, 8, 33
Civil Disobedience movement,
    12–13, 15–16, 34, 105, 109,
    116–17, 201
colonialism, 27, 39, 72, 130, 155
Comfort Women, 229

communalism, 186
communal riots, 84
communism, 117, 130–31, 146,
    169, 175
Communist Party of Burma, 117
constitutional monarchy, 56
convict labour, 62
Corr, Gerard H., 11
Council of Races, 154
Cripps Mission, 41

D

DAA (Dobama Asi-Ayon),
    116–18, 123–26
Dadachanji, 137
Dandi March, 15, 104
Das, Chittaranjan, 5, 12, 167
Das, C. R., 13–14, 22, 108,
    167–68, 199, 201
Das, Kalyani, 24
Davar, Janaki, 206, 208–09, 213,
    216–22, 225, 230
Davar, Rengasamy, 218
Death Curse, poem, 27–28, 36
"Death Railway", 173
de Cruz, Gerald, 114
"Deepali Sangha", 24
Defence of India Act, 32
"Defense of Burma", 134
Democratic Youth League, 151
Desai, Bhulabhai, 77
Deshpande, S.V., 169
Devaser, K.L., 156
Devi, Basanti, 199, 201

Dhillon, Gurbaksh Singh, 48, 54, 77, 120
Dobama Asi-Ayon, *see* DAA
Dominion Constitution for India, 14
Dublin Estate strikes, 180–83
Dugal, R.S., 137
Dutch East Indies, 39, 68–69
Dyer, Brigadier General, 11

E

East India Company, 81
Emergency, the, 145–46, 151, 155, 181, 183, 188–89
ESI (English speaking intelligentsia), 184

F

Fabian Society, 29
Faiz, Faiz Ahmad, 84
fascism, 130–31
Federation of Malaya Constitution, 155
Federation of Trade Unions, *see* FTUs
First World War, *see* World War I
Fourth Anglo-Mysore War, 33
Forbes, Geraldine, 24
Formosa, Subhas Chandra Bose in, 93–94
Fort William, 19
Forward Bloc, 17, 41, 68, 117, 123, 126
Forward, daily, 108

Freedom Bloc, 126–27
Free India Army, *see* Azad Hind Fauj
Free India Centre, 8, 108
Free India, publication, 175
Free India Radio Station, 114
"free labour" system, 60
French Indo-China, 39, 56, 68–69, 83, 140
FTUs (Federation of Trade Unions), 151, 181–82
Fundamental Rights Resolution, 25

G

Gammons, L.D., 226
Ganapathy, S.A., 181–82, 190
Gandhi Brigade, 46–47, 95
Gandhi, Mohandas Karamchand, 11–13, 34, 72, 96, 101, 104, 109, 111, 116, 123, 130, 138, 201–02, 211
  "sincere pacifist", as, 20
"Gandhi of Malaya", 140
Garewal, B.J.S., 95
General Labour Unions, *see* GLUs
Generation of Aware Youth, *see* API
Gent, Edward, 146
German Foreign Office, 6
Ghadr Conspiracy, 57
Ghadr Party, 88
Ghosh, Aurobindo, 35
  see also Aurobindo, Sri
Ghosh, Latika, 24

Gill, N.S., 99
GLUs (General Labour Unions), 155, 179, 181, 189
Goho, S.C., 172
Government of Burma Act, 124
Government of India Act, 123
Great Depression, 61, 177
"Greater Asianism", 40
Greater East Asia Conference, 30, 46, 54, 70–71, 75, 118, 157
Greater East Asia Co-Prosperity Sphere, 41, 69–70
"Greater Indonesia", 65, 139
  see also "Indonesia Raya"

H

Habibur Rahman, 18, 31, 49, 94, 101
Hachiro, Arita, 70
Harvard Estate Labour Union, 181
Hatta, 83, 139
Havildar, 94
Hikari Kikan, 32, 115
Hindu-Muslim rift, 21
Hindustan, ship, 81
Hindustan Standard, 3, 32
Hiroshima, 49, 145, 177, 215
Hitler, Adolf, 7–9, 33, 67
Holwell Monument, 32, 101, 159
  see also "Black Hole of Calcutta"
Ho See Beng, 190

I

IAC (Indian Armoured Corps), 82
Ibrahim Yaacob, 64–65, 138–39, 143
ICS (Indian Civil Service), 4, 6, 122, 125
Idris Hakim, 138
IGHQ (Imperial General Headquarters), 73
IIL (Indian Independence League), 8, 40, 44–45, 57–58, 65, 88, 100, 102–03, 105–06, 108, 111, 134, 137, 142, 156, 166, 172–75, 179, 188, 204, 211, 213
imperialism, 68, 71, 75, 131, 143, 176, 188
IMP (Independence of Malaya Party), 156
INA Defense Committee, 77
INA (Indian National Army), 8–10, 20, 23, 26, 29–31, 33, 38–40, 42, 44, 46–48, 54, 73–80, 82–83, 85, 94, 101, 119–21, 126, 134, 139, 141, 143–44, 149, 151, 155, 157, 166, 174–75, 178–85, 187–88, 190, 206–08, 212–14, 216, 218, 220, 222, 227
  communication tool, 96–97
  disbanded, 136, 197
  formation of, 58, 65–66
  Japanese, and, 72–75
  mass mobilization of, 102–05
  mercenary, as, 95
  print media, and, 113

propaganda against, 43, 86
radio, and, 113–16
religious unity, and, 98–99, 132
strength of, 45
war propaganda, 105–10
INA War Memorial, 178
INC (Indian National Congress), 5, 50, 63, 71, 77, 83, 116–17, 123, 128, 137, 150, 172, 182
indentured labour force, 57
Independence of Malaya Party, see IMP
India
   first war of independence, 101, 204
   rice supply, and, 42
Indian Armoured Corps, see IAC
Indian Army Officer Corps, 81
Indian Civil Service, see ICS
Indian Communist Party, 130
Indian Defence Force, 19
Indian diaspora, 1, 8
Indian Freedom Movement, 43
Indian Immigration Committee, 61
Indian Independence League, see IIL
Indian labour
   post-war scenario, 176–80
   pre-war scenario, 170–72
Indian Legion, 7
Indian Medical Mission, 222
Indian Muslim League, 148
Indian National Army, see INA

Indian National Congress, see INC
Indian National Council, 58
Indian National Navy, see INN
Indian National School, 49
"Indian Pilgrim, The", autobiography, 4, 19
Indian Relief Committee, 149, 222
Indian Renaissance, 228
   see also Bengal Renaissance
Indian Struggle, The, book, 11, 13, 112, 198
Indian Women's Association, 225
Indo-Burmese relation, 54, 116, 136
Indo-Malayan Association, 152
"Indonesia Raya", 139, 141
   see also "Greater Indonesia"
INN (Indian National Navy), 79
Interim Report on Prices and Wages, 187
Irish independence struggle, 115
   see also Sinn Fein movement
Irish Republican Army, 50
Irwin, Lord, 15
Ishak Haji Muhammad, 138, 140
Isoda, Lieutenant General, 32
Isteri Sat Sangha Sabha Sentul, 224
Ittefaq (unity), 20
Iwaichi, Fujiwara, 44, 58, 65

J

Jallianwala Bagh Massacre, 11, 13, 34
Jamshedpur Labour Association, 167

Index

Jan Baz (suicide unit), 217
"*Jana mana gana*", 6, 19
Japan
    Anglo-Japanese relations, 68
    INA, and, 72–75
    joining Allied powers, 67
    leadership role in Asia, 69
    return of Andaman and
        Nicobar islands, 46, 72
    surrender, 77, 94, 140
    tripartite agreement, 69
    war declaration, 68
Japanese Imperial Army, 9
Japanese Renaissance, 131
Japanese war propaganda, 10
Jugantar Samiti, revolutionary
    organization, 19, 35

K

Kailasam, Brahmachari, 149
Kandy Agreement, 128
kangani, 60–61, 174
Karachi Congress, 25
Kawabe, General, 74
Kedah Indian Labour Union, 180
Kesatuan Rakyat Indonesia
    Semenanjung, *see* KRIS
Kesatuan Melayu Muda, *see*
    KMM
Khan, Shah Nawaz, 46, 48,
    77–78, 101
Khatijah Sidek, 227, 230
Kiani, Inayat Jan, 47
Kiani, Mohammad Zaman, 46,
    48, 78, 99, 101

KI UMNO (Kaum Ibu Umno),
    227
Klang District Planting
    Associations, 171
KMM (Kesatuan Melayu Muda),
    64–65, 138–40, 142–43
Kohima-Imphal campaign, 40,
    47
Konoe, Fumimaro, 69
Krishnan, Devaki, 226
KRIS (Kesatuan Rakyat Indonesia
    Semenanjung), 65, 85, 139,
    141

L

Labor Code of 1923, 61
Labour Party, 14, 146
labour strikes, 189
Lal, Shankar Lal, 68
Lebra, Joyce Chapman, 204
Lee Kiu, 226
Left Book Club, 138
"line houses", 61
Linlithgow, Viceroy, 16–17, 106
Loganathan, A.D., 76, 107
Lukshumeyah, M.K., 147

M

"Mad Ridley", 59
Maharashtra Provisional
    Congress, 200
Macmunn, George, 19
Mahila Samities, 23
"Majlis", 143
"Majlis" at Cambridge, 112

Malay nationalism, 64–66
Malay Nationalist Party, *see* MNP
Malay Special Branch, 140
Malay Volunteer Force (Malai Giyu Gun), 139
Malaya, *see* Malaysia
Malayan Communist Party, *see* MCP
Malayan Democratic Union, *see* MDU
Malayan Emergency, *see* Emergency
Malayan General Labour Union, *see* MGLU
Malayan Indian Association, 148
Malayan/Malaysian Indian Congress, *see* MIC
Malayan People's Anti-Japanese Army, *see* MPAJA
Malayan People's Anti-Japanese Union, *see* MPAJU
Malayan Student's Party, 185
Malayan Union, 141, 145–47, 226
  Indian reaction to, 147–48, 150
  MIC response to, 151–56
Malaysia
  coffee crop, 59
  Indian labourers in, 60–63
  Indian nationalism in, 66
  Japanese invasion, 138–39, 176
  political legacy of Subhas Chandra Bose for Indian community in, 145–56
  rice bowl of, 139

rubber production, 59, 60–61, 173
Malaysian Chinese Association, *see* MCA
Manchester Guardian, 112
Manchu dynasty, 71
Manto, 84
Marco Polo bridge incident, 70–71
Martial Race theory, 19, 35
Marxism, 37, 130
Marx, Karl, 186
Marzotta, Orlando, 5
Maymyo Hospital, 214
MCA (Malaysian Chinese Association), 226
McFadzean, 187
MCP (Malayan Communist Party), 155, 171, 176–79, 183, 187, 189, 226
MDU (Malayan Democratic Union), 151, 185
Menon, K.P., 172
Menon, M.C.P., 179
Menon, Y.K., 170–72
Menon, Y.S., 170
MGLU (Malayan General Labour Union), 176
MIC (Malayan/Malaysian Indian Congress), 30, 66, 102, 138, 222, 225–26
  Constitution, 150
  John A. Thivy, and, 148–49, 151–57
  Indians for, 150

Malayan Union, response to, 151–56
Military College, 81
Minami Kikan, 125
Mingaladon Hospital, 208
minority groups, equal rights for, 133–35
M.N. Othman, 138
MNP (Malay Nationalist Party), 140–41, 143–44, 185, 227
monarchical nationalism, 131
monarchy
  absolute, 55–56
  constitutional, 56
Mother Goddess, 201
Mountbatten, Lord Louis, 9, 83
MPAJA (Malayan People's Anti-Japanese Army), 177–78
MPAJU (Malayan People's Anti-Japanese Union), 177
Mukherjee, Girija, 112
multi-racial politics, 185
Muslim-Buddhist riots, 52
Muslim League, 21, 77, 101
Muslim separatism, 148
Mustapha Hussain, 65, 85, 138–39, 141, 145
Mutaguchi, Renya, 74
Myanmar, *see* Burma

N

Nagasaki, 49, 145, 177, 215
Nahappan, Athi, 222
Nahappan, Janaki Athi, *see* Davar, Janaki

Narayanan, P.P., 179, 188
Narula, Isher Singh, 58
Nath, Dina, 137
Nath, Janaki, 201
Nathan, R.H., 170–71
Nathan, S. R., 31, 45
National Bank of Azad Hind, 47, 75, 110
National Council of Women's Organization, *see* NCWO
National Education, 175
National Emergency, *see* Emergency
national identity, 185, 190
National Planning Commission, 25
National Revolutionary Army, 71
National Revolutionary Party, 50
National Trade Union Congress, *see* NTUC
nationalism, 21, 25, 29, 56, 119, 123, 131, 134, 140, 148, 155, 168, 175, 177, 182, 184, 190
nationalist journalism, 138
Nazi Germany, 67
Nazism, 6
NCWO (National Council of Women's Organization), 223, 227
Negri Sembilan Indian Labour Union, 179
Nehru Brigade, 120
Nehru, Jawaharlal, 11, 77–78, 80, 83–84, 96–97, 123, 130, 148–49, 222

Nehru, Motilal, 13, 168
"Nehru Report", 14
Nehruvian secularism, 21
"Netaji", Subhas Chandra Bose
    as, 6, 18, 78, 110, 124, 136
"Netaji Week", 48, 110
New Order, 70
    see also "Pan-Asianism" and
        "Pan-Asian nationalism"
Nippon Army, 65
No. 1 Guerilla Regiment, 46
No. 4 Guerilla Regiment, 94
No. 2 Infantry Regiment, 94
non-cooperation movement,
    see Civil Disobedience
    movement
NTUC (National Trade Union
    Congress), 190

O

Onn bin Ja'afar, 146, 156
"Operation Coldstore", 186
Operation U, 74, 76
Ottama, U, 116
Ownership and Control in the
    Malayan Economy, book, 185

P

Palanisamy, Muthammal, 195
"Pan-Asianism", 69
"Pan-Asian nationalism", 40, 70, 75
Pandit, Vijay Lakshmi, 42, 86
Panglong Agreement, 135
Panglong Conference, 134

PAP (People's Action Party), 184
Partai Rakyat, 145
passive resistance, 13–14
    see also non-cooperation
    movement and Civil
    Disobedience movement
PBF (Patriotic Burmese Forces), 128
Pearl Harbour, attack on, 67
peasant rebellion, 52, 123
Penang Radio Station, 141
People's Action Party, *see* PAP
People's Revolutionary Party, *see*
    PRP
People's Volunteer Organisation,
    see PVO
Perak Indian Labour Association, 179
Persianized Hindustani, 96
Perumal, Meenachi, 217
Phan Boi Chau, 68
Phibul Songkhram, 56–58
"planned economy", 131
Ponnusamy, Anjalai, 217, 219
Prabhabati, 201
Presidency College, 4, 112
Presidency Jail, 32
Pritam, Amrita, 84
Provincial Government in
    Southeast Asia, 26
Provisional Government of Azad
    Hind [Free India], 44–46, 72,
    75–76, 95, 103, 108, 119,
    121, 149, 206, 213, 224
Provisional Government of Free
    India, 8, 42

PRP (People's Revolutionary Party), 125
Punjab Regiment, 171
Puri, Swami Satyananda, 57
Purna Swaraj, 15–16
Putera (Pusat Tenaga Rakyat), 147, 151
Puthucheary, James J., 27–28, 37, 183–87
PVO (People's Volunteer Organisation), 128–29

Q
Quit India, movement, 17, 41, 77, 84, 106

R
racial unity, 97–102
Raffles College of Singapore, 185
Raghavan, N., 100, 147, 149, 170–72
Rahman, Habibur, 18, 94, 101
Rajawade, Rani Lakshmi Bai, 25
Ramakrishna Mission, 8, 17, 33
Rance, Hubert, 129
Rangoon Radio, 120
Rani Laxmibai of Jhansi, 109
Rani of Jhansi Regiment, 8, 24, 28, 45, 48–49, 73, 98, 102, 104, 197, 200, 202–07, 218–19, 224–25, 228–30
  composition, 206
  fatalities, 207
  homecoming, 215–17
  Southeast Asia experience, 207–15
Rao, Peshwa Baji, 109
realpolitik, 6
Red Dragon bookshop, 130
Red Fort, 26, 30, 46, 48, 94, 114
  trial and aftermath, 76–85
red revolution, 177
Reformed Government of the Republic of China, 71
Rei, Dilbagh, 142
religious unity, 97–102
Reuters, 105
"revolutionary suspect", 4
RIAF (Royal Indian Air Force), 79–80, 82, 184
RIN (Royal Indian Navy), 79
"Roman Alphabet for India, A", article, 96
Roman Hindustani, 97
Rowlatt Act, 34
Roundtable Conference, 16
Roy, Dilip K., 10
"Rubber Boom", 60
Russel, Wilfred, 81
Russo-Japanese War, 40, 67–69, 71

S
SACSEA, 83, 85
Sahgal, Lakshmi, 96, 112, 204–05, 208–10, 214–15, 218–20, 225, 228
Sahgal, Prem Kumar, 26, 28, 48, 76–77, 94

Sakinah Junid, 227
Saklatvala, N.B., 168
Salt *Satyagraha*, 15–16
salt tax laws, 105
Samy, A.M., 180–81, 192
Sandhu, K.S., 60
Saw, U, 129
Saya San, rebellion, 52, 117, 121
Schenkl, Emilie, 3, 197–98
Scottish Church College, 112
SEAC (South East Asia Command), 9, 83, 178
Second World War *see* World War II
Secrets of Crew House, 107
secularism, 20–21, 132–33
Selangor Estate Workers' Trade Union, 182
Selangor Indian Association, 148
Sen, Amartya, 41
Sen, Prafulla Kumar, 55, 57
Sepoy Mutiny, 35
Shamsiah Fakeh, 227
Shaukat Ali Malik, 47
Shumei, Okawa, 69
Shwedagon Pagoda, 122, 134
Simon Commission, 14–16
Simon, John, 14
Singapore, 8
  crown colony, as, 146
  Indian community in, 62–63
  Subhas Chandra Bose in, 8, 10, 44, 111
Singapore Factory and Shop Workers' Union, 183

Singapore Harbour Board, 176
Singapore Municipality, 176
Singapore Special Branch, 185–86
Singh, Baba Amar, 57, 173
Singh, Banta, 76
Singh, Bishen, 107
Singh, Giani Pritam, 44, 57–58
Singh, Gulzara, 47, 184
Singh, Mohan, 39, 44–45, 58, 99–100
Singh, Sardar Budh, 155
Singh, Zora, 137
Sinha, S.K., 83–84
Sinn Fein movement, 10, 130
  see also Irish independence struggle
Sinyetha Party, 126
Siraj-ud-dawla, Nawab, 101, 159
SITC (Sultan Idris Training College), 138
Sivaram, M., 100, 105, 110, 173
Slim, William, 48
Smith, Dorman, 128–29, 137
SOE (Special Operations Executive), 176
socialism, 130–31, 143, 170, 175, 186
"socialist India", 126
Somasundaram, V.J., 147
Sook Ching, 177
Southeast Asia
  Subhas Chandra Bose in, 43–49, 65
  under Japanese regime, 40

South East Asia Command, *see* SEAC
Southern Army, 73–74
Special Operations Executive, *see* SOE
Springing Tiger, emblem, 6, 33
Stenson, Michael, 187
Stowell, Ellery C., 67
Straits Times Group, 144
Suara Rakyat, newspaper, 143
Subhas Brigade, 46–47
"Subhas Lobby", 109
Sugiyama, Army Chief, 73
Sukarno, 83–84, 139, 141, 142
Sultan Idris Training College, *see* SITC
Sun Yat-sen, 40, 68, 71, 130
Sunday Times, 112
Swami, N. G., 31
Swaraj, 5, 168
Swarajist Party, 13
Syonan Sinbun, 27, 49, 54
Syonan Times, 43

T

Tagore, Gurudev Rabrindanath, 17, 55, 68, 72, 95, 99, 183
Taiwan, *see* Formosa
Takahashi, Major, 115
Tamil Nesan, newspaper, 170
Tamil-speaking diaspora, 26, 45, 60
Tan Cheng-lock, 226
Tantabin incident, 129
Tata Iron and Steel Company, *see* TISCO
TBCL (Thai Bharat Cultural Lodge), 57–59, 88
Tenshin, Okakura, 68
Terauchi, Count, 73
Thailand
  Indians in, 57, 88
  Subhas Chandra Bose in, 55–59
Thakin Nu, 130, 132, 135
Thakins, 51, 54, 116–18, 121, 123
Thakin Thein Pe, 130
Thangaiah, R.K., 171
Thaver, G.V., 148
Thevar, M. Satyavati, 212, 225, 228
Thimayya brothers, 76
"Thirty Comrades", 122, 125
Thivy, John Aloysius, 66, 102, 147, 175, 188, 204, 222
  MIC, and, 148–49, 151–57, 225
thodar pedai (labourer's militia), 180–83
Thomas, Shenton, 64
Tiger of Mysore, The, 33
Tilak, Bal Gangadhar, 2, 136
Tipu Sultan, 33, 109
TISCO (Tata Iron and Steel Company), 168
Tojo, Hideki, 7, 33, 43, 46, 70, 73, 75–76
Tope, Tantia, 109
"Total Mobilization for Total War", slogan, 8, 102, 104, 107, 109, 204

Toye, Hugh, 76
trade unionists, "Big Six", 184
Tunku Abdul Rahman, 156
Turkey, Subhas Chandra Bose in, 96
Tyabji, S.A.S., 137

U

UMNO (United Malay National Organisation), 66, 145–47, 151, 153–54, 226, 230
Union Jack, 79, 180
University Officers' Training Corps, 20
UPAM (United Planters' Association of Malaya), 182–83
Urchs, Dr O., 6

V

"Vande Mataram", national anthem, 98
Viet Minh, nationalist group, 83
Visva Bharati University, 55, 213
Vivekananda, Swami, 4, 9, 12, 18, 198, 200
Volunteer Corps, 20, 129

W

Wan Waithayakon, Prince, 59
Wang Jing Wei, 71
War College, 73
War Office, 20
"War of the Springing Tiger, The", 11
Wartime Falsehoods, 107
Washington Conference, 68
Wavell, Lord, 83, 106
We Burmans Association, *see* DAA
Werth, Alexander, 6
"White Paper", 127–28
Wichitwathakan, 56
Wisara, U, 116
women, Subhas Chandra Bose and, 197–99, 225
Women's Federation, 226
women's rights, 23–25
Women Teachers' Union, 223
World War I, 60, 67, 167
World War II, 9, 16, 66, 81, 145

Y

Yamamoto, Colonel, 32
Yellappa, Attavar, 204–05
Yosuke, Matsuoka, 69
Young India, publication, 14, 22, 34, 175
YWCA (Young Women's Christian Association), 223–24, 227

Z

Zafar, Bahadur Shah, 101, 109
Zamindar of Ziawadi, 208

ABOUT THE AUTHOR

Nilanjana Sengupta is a Visiting Research Fellow at the Institute of Southeast Asian Studies (ISEAS), Singapore and has been a journalist and freelance feature writer with eminent Indian dailies like *Hindustan Times*, *Midday* and *DNA*. Her research interests cover feminist awakening in Southeast Asia, cultural exchanges between Asian nations and the Indian subcontinent and questions of integration, identity and hybridity of borrowed cultures.

www.ingramcontent.com/pod-product-compliance
Lightning Source LLC
Chambersburg PA
CBHW030107010526
44116CB00005B/128